How to Behave Badly in Renaissance Britain

Ruth Goodman

Michael O'Mara Books Limited

This paperback edition first published in 2020
First published in Great Britain in 2018 by
Michael O'Mara Books Limited
9 Lion Yard
Tremadoc Road
London SW4 7NQ

A CIP catalogue record for this book is available from the British Library.

Papers used by Michael O'Mara Books Limited are natural, recyclable
products made from wood grown in sustainable forests. The manufacturing
processes conform to the environmental regulations of the country of origin.

ISBN: 978-1-78929-266-4 in paperback print format
ISBN: 978-1-78243-852-6 in ebook format

1 2 3 4 5 6 7 8 9 10

www.mombooks.com

Cover design by Estuary English
Jacket image reproduced by kind permission of the Raymond J. Lord
Collection of Historical Combat Treatises
Typeset by Ed Pickford
Author photo © Mark Goodman

Printed and bound by CPI Group (UK) Ltd, Croydon, CR0 4YY

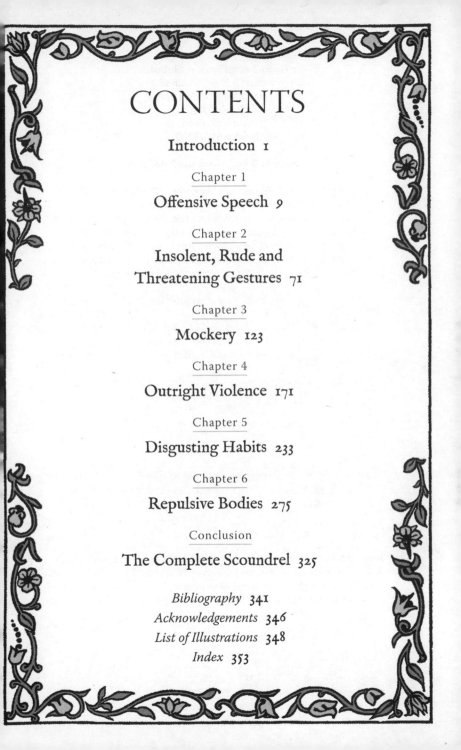

CONTENTS

PRAISE FOR *HOW TO BE A TUDOR*

'This book is packed with delicious kernels of
knowledge . . . all served up by the most delightfully
eccentric author I've ever encountered.'
The Times

'Always entertaining, and her narrative is often
lifted by the fact that she has taken the trouble to
experience many of the alien aspects of Tudor life.'
Observer

'Goodman's latest foray into immersive history is a revelation . . .
It's the next best thing to being there.'
New York Times Book Review

'A deeply researched and endlessly fascinating account
of what it was like to live as a Tudor. The narrative is rich
in period detail and based upon a thorough review of the
contemporary sources, but what makes it unique is the fact
that Goodman has put it all into practice – sleeping, eating,
washing and dressing like a Tudor. [It] is one of very few
books which can justifiably claim to bring every aspect
of this enduringly popular period dazzlingly to life.'
Tracy Borman

'[Goodman's] enthusiasm is exhilarating and contagious.'
Kate Tuttle, *Boston Globe*

'Riveting. This is a real "people's history" that takes us straight
into the sensate feelings of ordinary life – the feel, touch,
smells and labour of people living five centuries ago, giving an
earth͏   Tudors.'

PRAISE FOR *HOW TO BE A VICTORIAN*

'I absolutely love this book. Exuberant, absorbing.'

A. N. Wilson, *Mail on Sunday*

'Ruth – a woman who possesses so much elbow grease that she could probably can the overflow to sell on the side.'

Independent

'Written with such passion that one cannot help but be carried along . . . Will fascinate and inform anyone who is in any way interested in Victorian ways of life.'

Ian Mortimer

'Makes you feel as if you could pass as a native.'

New Yorker

'If the past is a foreign country because they do things differently there, we're lucky to have such a knowledgeable cicerone as Ruth Goodman.'

Wall Street Journal

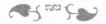

INTRODUCTION

Welcome to a century of bad behaviour. Forget the tales of the great and the good: this is a history of flawed and imperfect people. People whose misdemeanours lead us deeper into their world, as they show us the way that they carved out a life for themselves and reveal some of the thoughts and feelings that made them tick.

For behind the much vaunted gloss of ruffs and shimmering silks, the deeply committed religious reformers, the political visionaries and the great literary figures of the years between 1550 and 1660 lurks the rest of humanity and human experience in all its grubby glory and tarnished glister. Sixteenth- and seventeenth-century England was a place of vitality, experimentation, expanding horizons and lots of small-minded, petty, badly mannered, irritating and irreverent oiks, guls, gallants and harridans. And I love them all.

Every age and every social stratum has its bad eggs, those who break the rules and rub everyone up the wrong way. People who behave like square pegs in round holes abound in history just as much as in contemporary life. There are people who genuinely don't understand the social conventions of their day, who struggle to follow the subtleties and unwritten rules that govern daily life, and then there are those who deliberately and knowingly flout all codes of conduct. Sometimes the 'flouters' act alone as rebellious individuals, ploughing their own furrow, like Mary Frith who smoked, drank, swaggered and wore men's breeches in public on a regular basis, both shocking and intriguing her fellow citizens. Sometimes people join together in their rule breaking as an act of defiance and seek to forge their own separate group identity, like the idle, arrogant youths of the Damned Crew who drank, fought and bullied their way around the capital, or the 'holier than thou' hotter sort of Protestants, who irritated their neighbours secure in their own sense of superiority. Some navigate their way around and between the rules for their own ends, and others are tossed into transgression by circumstances. The subversion of normal rules can have many causes and many motivations. But the rules are the rules.

Societies in all times and all places are governed by intricate, overlapping codes of conduct. Some of these rules are both open and explicit in the manner of legal pronouncements or formal regulations; others stem from religious beliefs and understandings that can have a more nebulous edge, sliding into the realms of unexplained taboo. Still more grow from allegedly factual interpretations of the world around us that designate certain behaviours right and 'natural' and others perverted and strange. Some have long lost their rationale entirely but persist as part of widely held traditions, rules that demand obedience because 'we have always done it like that'. Many are implied or understood rather than formally spelt out, learnt from the reactions of family, neighbours, colleagues, enemies and friends. They cover every form of social interaction, from hanging out the washing in a communal yard to drinking with mates in the alehouse. The most socially aware and adept individuals can take all these interwoven, and occasionally conflicting, rules and turn them into a seamless performance of confidence and belonging – at least some of the time. For historically, just as now, many people struggled to pull it off, to behave perfectly at every encounter and in every situation.

I have a sneaking sympathy for all of them: for the blithely clueless bumbling through the disapproving looks; the acutely embarrassed who would conform if only they knew how; the deliberately curmudgeonly who define themselves by their resistance; the makers of new rules who seek to change the world; the calculating social climbers who pick and choose when to be good and when to be bad; the furiously angry who have gone beyond all care and restraint; the comedians poking fun; and the downright mischievous who just can't resist giving the world a little stir.

This is a book for, and about, all of them. It is an exploration of the written and unwritten rules of Tudor and Stuart England, and how people went about breaking them. It is not a history of criminal behaviour as such, although some of the activities in this book will edge into the legally dubious; rather it is a study of all the niggling, antisocial, irritating ways that people used to kick against prevailing social mores. And because the offence and the meaning is all contained within the specific details of these behaviours, you will find, too, within these pages, step-by-step instructions that lay out exactly how to be that annoying and irritating person. We shall rehearse the various ways in which you could embarrass your parents, mock a sober clergyman, disgust your dinner guests and put down your enemies. There are instructions for fighting in various styles so that you can hold your own against the city watch, or at least intimidate the uninitiated into letting you have your way. There are crib sheets of verbal insults outlining the vocabulary but also providing you with a key so that you can extemporize upon certain themes and customize your linguistic attacks to suit the occasion. You will find pointers about sartorial inelegance in several forms that could cause terrible worry to stuffy parents, and also diagrams of rude gestures to assist you in performing them with accuracy for maximum impact. It is a sort of basic toolkit for navigating your way around the edges of society and sliding between the gaps.

And why this particular hundred years? Well, that is very personal. I always have trouble articulating exactly why it is this bit of English history that so captures my attention, heart and soul. But it does, and I can't help but hope that it captures yours, too. I love the combination of the exotically different mingled with the almost familiar, the way you can trace ideas, words, attitudes and habits that at first glance seem so alien as they gently shift into the background of modern life. So much of the twenty-first-century way of life can be illuminated by an understanding of this era. Our current brand of religion and non-religion was shaped at this time. Both the emergence of new forms of worship, the hammering out of new creeds and religious practices and the beginnings of a deep and almost visceral distrust of fundamentalism and overly enthusiastic spiritualism can be found here. Secularism, as well as Quakers and Baptists of various denominations, emerged from these years.

Our form of democracy, too, was first argued about and fought over at this time. Ideas about votes for all men (alas, not women) get their first hearing in the 1640s. Representation and taxation become deeply entwined as a principle and the monarchy is forced to take several large steps back from power. The impact of these struggles and arguments upon the global stage is profound and ongoing.

No one can seriously dismiss the impact of linguistic evolution at this time, either, as it emerged on the streets, the stages and the printed page, brimming with vigour and creativity, to be carried outwards by trade and colonization far from Britain's shores.

Nor were any of these great ferments purely the preserve of the wealthy and elite members of society. People from the humblest of backgrounds found ways to make their voices heard upon the great matters of the day. The poor, elderly widow at the very bottom of the social heap could be engaged in the most profound of spiritual speculation and navigate her way to services and debates of her choosing. Those who propounded the most radical of political ideas hailed in large part from the workshops rather than the manor houses. The period's greatest poets and dramatists were drawn from a variety of backgrounds and often had patchy and incomplete formal educations.

Despite its powerfully hierarchical and misogynistic social structure, this was an era with a surprising degree of room for manoeuvre. There were gaps through which the brave, determined and lucky could find opportunities for independent thought and action. It is an era, too, that holds more than its fair share of shocks, violence and dramatic moments. The medicine was terrifying and the diseases and epidemics that such poorly equipped physicians were attempting to treat were among the most virulent and unpleasant of all time. Threats of invasion proved to be mere precursors to the military pain of civil war that tore up and down the country, and there are few historical moments more dramatic than the beheading of a king.

All these are good arguments for highlighting these years, but for me there is also a more intimate fascination with people's motivations at this critical moment in history. I want to know why our forebears did things in particular ways. How did it all hold together as a world view? I want to know what was going on inside people's heads; I want to know what they cared about, how they understood their world. I would love to find out which things gladdened their hearts and which things annoyed and irritated them. I am drawn again and again by a desire to understand the human experience of this rapidly developing culture.

Bad behaviour can be so much more illuminating than the world of the respectable conformist, for it is those who push against the boundaries of cultural etiquette who most accurately define where the lines are drawn. It is easy to dismiss, for example, the role of bowing in the smooth running of society until you encounter the few who refused to make the gesture. Their stubborn denial of this seemingly trivial courtesy provoked outrage, anger and violence, the vehemence of which give us a sure-fire indication that bows were far from frivolous trifles. Indeed, these instances of transgression show how bowing occupied a central role in peacekeeping and social cooperation.

Within the community of those who did bow to convention we find many subtler ways of offending, ways of poking fun or subverting the central message of the bow proper. Those who were too perfunctory in their performance and those who extended and elaborated the gesture help us to see the range of meaning, from respect to contempt, wrapped up within this commonplace interaction. Bad bowing speaks volumes about personal tensions within society, about interactions between different social groups and where the dividing lines lie.

Armed with an understanding of the differing forms of badly executed bows it becomes possible to unpick aspects of Tudor and Stuart life that went unvoiced. When Queen Elizabeth left the French ambassador deep in a bow for fifteen minutes before giving him the sign that permitted him to rise, she was signalling her political displeasure, her determination to stand against the international pressure France was attempting to exert. The ambassador, in holding that bow for those agonizing fifteen minutes, chose to bear that displeasure with the dignity and pride befitting his and his nation's position. It was high political drama, without a spoken word. This is just one example of the communicative power of the convention; bowing can also express an adherence to tradition, a preference for fleeting fashion, or an expression of political affinity or dissent. All of these meanings could well have escaped our notice if it had not been for those who flouted conventions by using foreign or inappropriate forms, who sneered and jibed about the Frenchified effeminacy or rustical leadenness of other people's bows, who performed their curtsies sloppily or with a sneer.

If bowing is perhaps an unexpected form of communication, vulnerable to subversion, it is just one among many of a whole realm of badly behaved interactions that open up a window into the past. Other forms of body language, from rude gestures to mimicry, nose-blowing to hat choices, join together with verbal faux pas and deliberate insults in telling us something about what people thought and felt. Social interactions are made up of these many small things and their multifarious tiny nuances. When people behave with perfect manners, in full accord with all the social rules, much of the performance is taken for granted and is commented on only in the most general terms. But bad behaviour receives much more attention and much more detailed discussion and analysis. Anger, disgust, revulsion and deep disquiet are expressed over and over again by people wishing that others were better behaved. Irritation and annoyance spur people into print where harmony and quiet would not.

Luckily for us there was no golden age when everyone lived in peace and harmony, no time when manners were perfect. Speech has never been free of profanity and clothing has always been sexually provocative. In following the antics of rustic drunks in the alehouses, aristocratic hoodlums in the taverns and investigating the insults hurled in the streets we gain a rounder, fuller picture of just what made the British Renaissance world so special.

Chapter 1

OFFENSIVE SPEECH

Anyone who has ever tried to learn a new language knows that it is the rude words that somehow stick in the memory, even when one is struggling to remember the basics of ordering coffee and cake at a café. Renaissance Britain was an English speaking nation, but the language has since undergone just enough subtle change to slow and befuddle our modern understanding. If we want to get under the skin of Tudor and Stuart minds we are going to have to take a little time to 'tune in' and decode many linguistic quirks and shifts. So let's begin with the easy bit – the rude words.

'A turd in your teeth'

What a delightful way to begin! This was a phrase that was screeched in the street and intended to shock and disgust. How could you not be repelled if someone spat that in your face? And it is a phrase that lends itself to a loud, angry, spitting sort of delivery. This is offensive speech in its rawest, earthiest, most aggressive and public form. We could, of course, have started with something much more recognizable and far less real.

Many people are familiar with the witty and inventive language of insult and repartee found in Shakespeare and other Renaissance writers. Dip into *Henry IV Part 1*, for example, and there you will find Falstaff in just one single scene calling his friend Bardolph 'a perpetual triumph, an everlasting bonfire light' because of the redness of his nose, riffing on the theme for about ten minutes. He goes on to berate his hostess, saying that 'There's no more faith in thee than in a stewed prune' and likens her to an otter that counts as neither fish nor flesh, then he calls the Prince 'a Jack, a sneak-cup' behind his back and a 'lion-whelp' to his face. In between he delivers expletives like ''Sblood' and 'God-a-mercy!' But there is something essentially comical and unthreatening about all this. It is just bluster and only the more po-faced and religiously sensitive of audiences, both period and modern, would truly take offence.

Poking fun at someone's appearance is not exactly kind, but when the raillery is original, varied and linguistically clever, much of the sting is taken out. Indeed, the name-calling can become nothing but a game. '[T]his sanguine coward, this bed-presser, this horse back-breaker, this huge hill of flesh,' exclaims Prince Henry earlier in the play, laughing at Falstaff's large girth only to be insulted in turn for his own relative skinniness: 'Away, you starveling, you elf skin, you dried neat's tongue, bull's pizzle, you stockfish. – O for breath to utter what is like thee! – you tailors yard, you sheath, you bow-case, you vile standing-tuck.' These comparisons are made more cutting by their reference not just to being long and thin but hollow and empty, extending the conflict out from the initial criticism of bodily form into the realm of character. Yet there is little real anger here; the characters are clearly enjoying the competitive nature of the exchange and we the audience are called upon to applaud the sharpness of wit. Such exchanges made Falstaff one of Shakespeare's most popular characters. Leonard Digges, in his preface to the second edition of Shakespeare's works published in 1640, claimed that when plays by other authors have 'scarce defrayd the Seacole fire, And doore-keepers; but let Falstaff come, Hal, Poins and the rest, you shall scarce have room.' Other plays might run at a loss with barely enough audience to pay for upkeep and admission staff but a play with Falstaff and his witty banter packed the house night after night.

'A turd in your teeth' is a rather different matter. For a start it's not from a play or any other consciously literary source but is a report of real speech, hurled in anger in the street. There is no carefully thought-out subtext and no personalization. This is a standard stock phrase used by many people in many situations and recorded in court cases about disputes between people as diverse as a fishwife and her neighbour, and a moneyer and the pastor of Stepney. It's short, easy to remember in a moment of deep frustration and it is a disgusting image along the lines of today's phrase 'eat shit'. It is not meant to be clever or witty and it can be aimed at anyone who annoys you. If you truly intended to behave badly in Renaissance Britain, this was the sort of language that you needed; forget the flowery language of literature (unless you intend to launch into print yourself), and concentrate instead upon the stuff that hurts, that gets under the skin and turns people's faces bright red.

If you got tired of 'a turd in your teeth' then you could vary it a little with the ever popular 'kiss my arse'. 'Kiss my arse' can, however, require a little caution as it does leave an opening for a sharp reply such as that in the following exchange. Mary Goates and Alice Flavell were arguing in the London street outside their respective houses when Mary

Fishwives were notorious for the volume and caustic content of their speech.

went for 'kiss my arse'; quick as a flash, Alice retorted: 'Nay, I will leave that for John Carre' – implying not only that Mary had an illicit lover, but that he was a subservient and perverted one, and Mary was a low-value whore. Few people, however, had the presence of mind to manage such a come-back in the heat of the moment. (I'd like to make it clear that this is not the relatively polite modern US usage of 'kiss my ass' that refers to buttock kissing, but rather to the British 'arse' or 'arsehole'.)

'Kiss my arse' remained an effective insult in most situations and was particularly useful against those who set themselves up as moral superiors. It was the sort of thing you could say if someone tried to tell you off about your level of drinking or the noise you were making in the street. It was a phrase that epitomized good old-fashioned insolent defiance. If you felt the need to expand upon the admittedly rather concise 'kiss my arse', you could add 'I care not a fart for you', which, again rather neatly, told the busybodies and overly righteous that you did not accept their reproofs.

Defying authority like this was, of course, not supposed to happen. According to preachers and philosophers alike, everyone was to know their place and behave gravely and soberly with due deference to those located above them in a divinely ordered world hierarchy. Men above women, adults above children, masters over servants, those able to financially support themselves over their dependents, the titled in strict rank order holding sway over the commoner, with God and his ministers holding authority over all. Each person occupied a particular niche within this structure, one that could change over time as they grew from child to adult and moved from the single into the married life. Marriage increased the honour of one's standing, while old age and infirmity often brought about a decline. A person's place was constantly redefined and reinforced by those around them, reminding them of their duties towards their 'betters'.

It was the element of divine organization that gave this idea its overwhelming power and authority. It wasn't just luck and circumstance that meant some were born rich and some were born poor, or that you happened to be male or female. God himself had chosen both the structure of society and who would fill each role within it. No social division of our own age and in the Western world carries anything like this weight and psychological importance. When one woman screams 'a turd in your teeth' to her neighbour, a social equal, it is of course offensive; but for John Pye – our moneyer – to say such a thing to a man of the cloth, an ordained minister of God, was a much more serious and socially disruptive act. Thank goodness he didn't use the term 'kiss my arse', with its deep sense of disrespect. Insubordination threatened the divine plan; it was a direct challenge to the whole of society, not just the individual. While Mary Goates and Alice Flavell's altercation resulted in a case brought by the one against the other for defamation of character in the church courts, John Pye's words were passed on up the chain by the churchwardens to the Bishop of London's Commissary. The women's grievances were primarily a private affair concerned with their local reputation, but the same words hurled across a social boundary required a much more concerted community response.

Bad language such as 'kiss my arse' was fundamentally a deviation from the rules about social harmony, order and respect. Disrupting the peace by voicing discord or attempting to undermine authority was one of the main thrusts that rendered speech offensive. A shouting match in the street unsettled everyone within earshot. There was a danger that such hostility was magnified and spread by this linguistic behaviour, severing ties within the community, prolonging and deepening personal feuds, damaging the daily cooperation that many people relied upon for survival. In some ways the actual words used were irrelevant, the offence was in the situation. 'A turd in your teeth' aimed at an authority figure was not necessarily an attack upon that individual, but upon the authority that he represented.

Up Close and Personal

Many of the recorded incidents of insult were, however, entirely personal and individually targeted. Pointing out the deviancy of others formed the second main prong of verbal shenanigans and most common when the insult was focused upon an individual. As we move forwards through a list of all the hurtful and upsetting things that you could shout at people in the street, we will encounter again and again accusations that the victim is failing to live up to expectations in some way. Much of the efficacy of the insult is derived from taunting a person with inappropriate, antisocial behaviour. You may be behaving badly by your disruptive name-calling, but it is nothing in comparison to the alleged bad behaviour of your victim.

Most foul words were strongly gendered: there were things you said only to women and things you said only to men. Only a man, for example, could be called a 'knave'. Don't be fooled, however, into thinking that this is a mild insult to be shrugged off just because it has largely gone out of use. It was once a perfectly respectable title for someone of lowly birth, but the meanings of words change and even as the Tudor dynasty took the throne the emphasis was shifting. A 'knave' became someone not just lowly in birth but uncultured and unmannered. The anonymously authored *The Babees Book* of 1475, aimed at teaching manners to high-born boys, described larking about at inappropriate moments as 'Knavis tacches' (knavish tricks) but, just a few years later, a 'knave' came to mean a man whose morals were in question as well as his manners. For most of Henry VIII's reign the word was a relatively polite, descriptive one for someone both crude and rather deceitful. By the close of Elizabeth I's reign, however, a 'knave' was the scum beneath your feet, someone not fit to be in the company of decent people and most emphatically not a word that one could use in a book aimed at children. The word had changed from a simple signifier of social status into an insult, and an insult, moreover, that increasingly stung.

Part of the power of 'knave' lay in its ability to attack the social status of a man. Titles were deeply important to the self-respect of Renaissance men. Those born to noble or gentle families were genuinely perceived as being 'better' than common people. Medical men even held that their bodies were subtly different, having 'finer' digestive processes that demanded a different diet from the common man. No labourer could be expected to derive nourishment from the delicate meats served at a nobleman's table (they would burn away to nothing in his hot strong stomach), just as no nobleman could survive upon the coarse bread of the labourer (where it would sit cold and hard in his more gently heated belly). Denying or denigrating a man's title cut to the core of his being. Within social brackets, each man journeyed through life hoping to be afforded a series of graded respect titles as he moved from child to adult to patriarch, with increased responsibilities and social standing along the way. Even the humblest man hoped to be accorded the title of 'Goodman' once he was married, rather than be known purely by his given name. A large proportion of the adult male population also felt themselves entitled to the epithet 'Master' as they employed servants or apprentices. The word 'knave' at the latter end of the sixteenth century, however, downgraded even simple Goodman Carter who made his living labouring for neighbouring farmers. At this point in time it made him appear sub-adult, irresponsible and untrustworthy. Social respect was a prize that came with appropriate titles; the wrong title was hurtful and degrading.

As we all know, a single, one-syllable word is rarely completely satisfying when used in anger – you need just a little bit more. As a result, 'knave' was often used in conjunction with some other term. While 'knave' attacked social standing, most of the additional words associated with it undermined a man's self-image as an upstanding pillar of the community. You might shout 'filthy knave', 'lying knave', 'canting knave' (one that holds forth loudly on subjects he knows nothing about) or, one of my favourites, 'polled knave' ('polled' meaning castrated). All of these words were digs at the popular image of man as the embodiment of familial power and authority. A man who could not keep himself clean, uphold the truth, guard his tongue and father children was failing in his duties as head of the household. Along with the word 'knave', these terms downgraded him from a respectable adult with a stable position in his community to the much lower status of a feckless and footloose youth. John Barker combined several versions when he blew his top in 1602. In response to 'some speeches' by the vicar, the Reverend Foster, John 'in angry, brawling, quarrelling and chiding manner' called him 'a knave, a rascal knave, a scurvy rascal knave', while several of the neighbours tried to step in and calm things down. Such words could often spill over into violence.

'Varlet' was a less popular insult. It stemmed from a similar source, a word for someone of lowly origins, but it never had quite the same bite as 'knave', carrying fewer overtones of dishonesty. 'Sirra' and 'saucy fellow' were likewise milder in tone than 'knave', while 'Jack' stood somewhere in the mid-range of derogatory terms along with 'rogue'. All implied worthlessness but each had a subtly different hue. 'Sirra' was slavish and servile, 'saucy fellow' was insolent and mouthy, and 'Jack' was more thuggish, while a 'rogue' was distinctly criminal in his behaviour.

Combinations and compounds once again added to the effect. Calling someone 'Jacksauce' conjured up images of a worthless, loud-mouthed bully full of meaningless but unpleasant bluster, and the oft-used 'jackanapes' linked 'Jack' with an ape to produce an insult that derided someone as subhuman, a mere mockery of human form with no self-control. 'Wastrel' was a much simpler concept that had the advantage of cutting to the chase, describing a good-for-nothing waste of space.

Stupidity provided another rich seam of potential for insult. A man could be a 'fool', a 'gul', a 'clowne', a 'blockhouse', a 'loggerhead', a 'ninny-hammer' or an 'ass'. It was 'fool' that held the most vitriol. Similarly to 'knave', this word sounds mild to modern ears, but don't be lulled into a false sense of security: 'fool' was no mealy mouthed cop-out. Its present mildness probably stems, like that of 'knave', from overuse gradually eroding its power to shock.

Within my own lifetime I have seen many words lose their edge as far as offence goes. The word 'tart', for example, was distinctly more uncomfortable in the 1970s, and one barely encountered 'fuck' at all. Now we live in a world in which to be a 'tart' is almost a good thing and the f-word is everywhere and frankly not all that shocking any more. Words are slippery things.

The word 'knave' was probably at its most offensive in the 1590s, but it still packed a punch in the 1620s and '30s before gradually starting to slide out of use from the 1650s onwards. The word 'fool' had a slightly longer period of virulence and was still provoking full-scale fist fights in the 1650s. It got under a man's skin because it undermined his masculinity. Women were supposed to be foolish, to need the guidance and restraining hand of fathers and husbands; men were supposed to be calmer, more level-headed and much more intellectually capable. God's natural order, it was believed, put men in charge. He had created their very bodies with this in mind, giving them more blood, in the balance of the four humours, in comparison to women's phlegm-dominated bodies. Such divinely influenced physical differences were supposed to provide men with more mental fortitude as well as physical vigour. A boy might be foolish in his youth as he learnt the ways of the world – and indeed the medical consensus of the day held that as a child he had not yet acquired his full quota of blood – but as he grew and matured, wisdom and common sense were expected to develop. To call a man a 'fool' was to say that he was not a proper man; it questioned his ability to rule his household and made him appear effeminate.

The professional fools at court were not thought of nor treated as fully adult men. For example, while the uniforms provided for them were lavish and expensive (the costs are listed in the Royal Wardrobe accounts), the colours, shape and cut of them were deliberately reminiscent of children's clothing. They frequently wore long coats like schoolboys, and leading reins were sometimes attached at the shoulders, just like those on toddlers' clothes. They also often carried staffs covered with bells and ribbons, rather like a baby's rattle. If you wanted to make the most of the insult 'fool', you could emphasize this infantile aspect of its meaning by adding the words 'babbling' or 'prattling', words that evoke infantile pre-speech.

A 'prating fool' was something slightly different, describing boastful, self-serving, inaccurate and often rather dull speech, and was a perfect phrase to attack someone who set themselves up as a moral authority, telling you how to live your life. Those of puritanical religious leanings were perfect targets for a cry of 'prating fool'.

'Blockhead', 'loggerhead' and 'ninny-hammer' were a bit flowery for everyday use. They were more the sort of thing that you might say about someone when you were pulling their character apart in conversation with your friends down at the alehouse, rather than something you would shout at them in the street. The same applies to 'gul', a term that meant someone was gullible, naive and credulous. But 'clown' and 'ass' were excellent shouting terms.

The phrase 'you are an ass' turns up in multiple court cases as well as on the stage, most famously in *A Midsummer Night's Dream* when Bottom is magically turned into one. My personal favourite 'you-are-an-ass' scene appears in *Much Ado About Nothing* when Dogberry, the local constable who clearly is something of a fool and has been making a ridiculous mess of the proceedings, takes umbrage at the phrase and wants to sue: 'O that he were here to write me down as ass! But, masters, remember, that I am an ass; though it be not written down, yet forget not that I am an ass.' Dogberry is all the more indignant because at the time the slur was made he was acting as a local official, a position of some minor authority that he felt accorded him a measure of respect even when dealing with someone of higher social station than himself. After all, the conduct books of the day were quite explicit on this point: 'They who are in dignity, or in office have precedence in all places' (*Youth's Behaviour*, translated by Francis Hawkins in 1646); for someone not born to the privileges and automatic respect of gentle birth the honour of even a minor position was one to really hold on to. As genuine court cases show, 'you are an ass' was an actionable term. Dogberry's sense of outrage was one that will have resonated with many men in the audience just as they simultaneously laughed at him for his incompetence and officious pretensions.

Having established that your enemies were worthless (knaves) and stupid (fools), you could then get a little more specific in your accusations. 'Thief' and 'liar' were unsurprisingly popular epithets. These words once again centred upon a man's social credit, his trustworthiness and reliability, but instead of being general catch-all attacks, they narrowed the focus to more specific failings. Along with terms such as 'drunkard' and 'braggart', they are a bit more personal, a little more tailored to the individual, and perhaps this more detailed approach could convince listeners, rightly or wrongly, of the accuracy of your analysis. 'Thief' and 'liar' were the strongest words within this group. Those nearer the bottom of the social heap were more susceptible to accusations of thievery. It was generally accepted that those with the fewest financial resources were most likely to turn to theft. But it was also this group who had most to lose from such a label, for it was the poorest in society who were most reliant upon the assistance and goodwill of their neighbours. If you were called a thief, you could find yourself refused alms in your hour of need and be turned away by potential employers.

The term 'liar' had a higher social reach. Call a merchant a thief and he could brush it off with relative ease: what need did he have of outright thievery? But call him a liar and all of his business dealings became suspect. Convince the community that a man's words could not be trusted and soon that man's finances would be in ruins. For gentlemen the label 'liar' was the very worst of all words, the one that was almost guaranteed to spark a duel. Honesty was fundamental to every claim of authority based on natural 'worth'. The leaders of society had more need of apparent honesty than any other group. Women might be sly-tongued and deceitful with very little harm done, and paupers too would cause very little upset when they embroidered the truth. But gentlemen, who might be called upon to administer the law, hold public office, serve as ministers of the Church or lead men into battle, set very great store upon the unchallenged truthfulness of their word.

'Stinkard' was a particularly fine word for highlighting someone's lack of personal hygiene. You could also accuse someone of being covered in lice. Again, the word 'lousy' has ameliorated over the years, shifting from a literal description to a gentler and more generic implication. But if your audience are accustomed to taking the word at face value (as an Elizabethan audience was) then 'lousy' is a real irritant – all the more so if you make it clear that you mean pubic lice rather than just body lice in general. Humphrey Richardson cannot have enjoyed being called a 'lousy rogue, nitty britch knave, and scurvy nitty britch knave' in 1610.

Insults aimed at women were almost always about sex. There was little point in accusing a woman of being worthless; women were, of course, worth very little to start with. Yes, you could add to an insult by calling a woman 'beggarly' or 'tinkerly' (like a travelling tinker of no fixed abode and little financial worth), but by themselves, accusations of worthlessness really didn't have the same impact on women as they did on men. Women's social position was ideally one of subservience to men at all stages of life. A good woman was one who had fully internalized this belief, who embraced humility and obedience. Even when she held authority over children and servants she was always supposed to hold on to the concept of submission to higher authority. 'The man must be taken for God's immediate officer in the house, and as it were the king in the family; the woman must account herself his deputy, an officer substituted to him, not as an equal, but as subordinate' (*A Bride Bush* by William Whately, 1619). A woman was expected to bear talk about her lowly place with patience, acceptance and forbearance. Pride was a sin that was especially abhorred in the female sex. There was equally little to be gained from accusations of stupidity, foolishness being one of the defining qualities of womanhood to Renaissance eyes. So while any woman might have been pleased to be called a wise and sober wife, she was only too used to being called a weak and foolish woman.

If you wanted to hurt a woman's feelings, you cast aspersions about her sex life. In particular, you accused her of prostitution; the number of words in common usage to delineate a commercial sex worker was quite extraordinary. Most popular was the simple 'whore', a word that continues to be screeched outside nightclubs to this day, and it does carry well across an urban space. You might not quite catch the rest of the diatribe but the word 'whore' is generally very discernible over considerable distances. It was a heinous word that could have dire consequences for the victim of the insult. Easy to say and hard to actively disprove, it attacked a woman at the very heart of her self-respect and social standing.

Chastity was the ultimate source of social and personal status for the female sex. Honour was everything for both men and women, but that honour and the way in which you attacked it was fundamentally different. For women, honour was always about sex. A woman could be a convicted thief and yet still be termed 'an honest woman' as long as she took no extramarital lovers. Every scrap of advice to women hammered this message home, be it in conduct books, sermons or popular ballads. Men, too, were constantly reminded of the importance of female chastity. Unchaste female relatives reflected very badly upon them, with their honour almost as much at stake as the woman's. No failing in a woman was as grievous as promiscuity; nothing else provoked the same disgust.

Promiscuity was also seen as a gateway activity. When women sinned in other ways it was generally assumed that illicit sex was at the bottom of it all. Murder your husband or children and everyone began looking around for lovers as an explanation. To call a woman a 'whore' was to cast everything about her life in doubt. No one respected a whore: friends and neighbours would shun her company, husbands and fathers had the right to cast an unchaste woman out of the home. Its very power, however, could mitigate against it. When you openly accused a woman of whoredom you faced a very real possibility of prosecution for defamation, as well as a public backlash. The church courts were kept busy with such cases as women and their menfolk chose to spend good money on publicly and legally refuting the claims, demanding public penance and apologies from those who spoke the word.

Nonetheless, in the heat of the moment it was a fantastic way to injure your enemy; it was a word that few could ignore or brush off altogether. There were also many alternatives and variations to choose from. 'Harlot' and 'quean' were common variants on 'whore' and meant almost exactly the same thing, and the choice between them may have been more down to local dialect than any other consideration. They all covered general sexual misbehaviour in women and were not exclusively reserved for sex-for-cash encounters. Adulterous affairs were generally described in these terms. 'Quean' may have been the more common or plebeian word of the three as it rarely turns up in any context outside of reported speech. When preachers or magistrates write about the subject they generally use 'harlot' and, less often, 'whore'. But 'quean' is very common among the reports of words shouted in the street.

A 'gill', 'drab' or 'trull', however, was an out and out prostitute. A 'jade' was technically a cheap horse for hire, but it is easy to see how this could also be applied to the language of insult, particularly as 'jades' were ridden. 'Punk' was also a term for a prostitute and seems to have implied, in addition, that they were the sort of prostitute who stole their client's purse. It was, moreover, a word that switched sex, as by the 1660s it was beginning to be applied to male prostitutes. Over the centuries, 'punk' has been positively promiscuous in its multiple meanings. Slightly lighter terms included 'slut', 'strumpet', 'flap', 'draggletail', 'waggletail', 'flirt' and 'bitch'. They tended to cover a more casual attitude to prostitution, the occasional rather than the habitual accepter of cash or favours for sex.

Picking just the right variation for the situation gave weight to the word. The most hurtful insults held just a hint of believability, which is one of the reasons why the more catch-all 'whore' had more currency than the more specific 'trull'. Call a seemingly respectable housewife a 'trull' and few would believe it, giving her and her husband little difficulty in shrugging it off, but call her a 'whore' and a worm of suspicion could linger. No one could keep up a veneer of respectability if they were regularly receiving paying clients – the comings and goings would be just too obvious – but an occasional inappropriate moment with a particular friend was easier to hide and thus harder to refute. 'Strumpet' and 'waggletail' were less likely to provoke calls for proof than 'whore', for although they implied sex for cash, they could also mean a more general willingness to accept favours. A 'waggletail' was more guilty of touting for socially inappropriate male attention than necessarily receiving it. If someone challenged your shouts of 'strumpet', you didn't have to think of a likely candidate for the male partner.

If you felt like developing your theme with an additional word or two, there were three main topics to choose from: personal hygiene, sexually transmitted diseases and bestial behaviours. 'Lousy' could just as easily be applied to a woman as to a man, with the added benefit that 'lousy whore' pretty much says pubic lice all by itself without any need for reference to articles of clothing.

Plain old 'dirty' turns up now and again but 'filthy' was generally preferred for the purpose of insulting someone. Again one suspects that the preference for 'filthy' has much to do with the way the word feels in the mouth. If you rehearse to yourself the two phrases 'dirty whore' and 'filthy whore', I think you will agree that 'filthy' has the edge. It is just a much more satisfying thing to say. The rector of Rowth in Yorkshire went for a roundly fulsome 'scurvy scabbed lousy filthy whore' when he chose to insult Anne Griffith.

'Slut' and 'sluttish' could also be used in this context as an alternative to 'slovenly'. The word 'slut', then as now, could either mean one of loose sexual morals or one who didn't keep up with the housework. You could technically accuse someone of being a 'slutty slut' using the word in both forms.

Sexually transmitted diseases offered fertile ground for particularly vicious language. There was no effective cure for any of these diseases and the prognosis for those infected was dire, with years of foul symptoms, often including madness and leading ultimately to death. Medical knowledge of the era had not separated out the various infections, but tended to lump them all together under the title 'pox', describing the presence of pustules, a particularly confusing name since it also covered smallpox and chickenpox.

Certain symptoms, however, held popular currency as sure-fire signifiers of venereal contagion. The presence of rashes, blisters and pustules around the genitals was unsurprisingly one sign (a condition often described as being 'burnt') and the loss of pubic hair was another. No one in Renaissance Britain would have chosen to have a Hollywood wax; to be hairless down under was to be riddled with disease. Lush pubic hair was a guarantee of sexual cleanliness and health.

Reference to these two main signifiers of STDs formed the primary language of insult. A 'pocky whore' and a 'burnt-arsed whore' were both crude and to the point. 'She has no thatch on her house' was slightly more circumspect but amounted to the same thing. Where 'whore' alone would do for a woman who had had an extramarital dalliance, a 'burnt-arsed whore' conjured images of a much more inveterate offender, one whose lovers were particularly unsavoury and one who spread death and despair. Faith Wilson of Bury St Edmunds had a particularly nasty turn of phrase: 'Pull up your muffler higher and hide your pocky face, and go home and scrape your mangy arse' were her words in 1619.

Likening women to various animals allowed for great creativity of insult once you moved beyond 'bitch' and 'salted bitch'. 'Bitch', of course, is still in currency, but generally is used in a modern context to describe vindictive behaviour rather than doglike traits. In the sixteenth and seventeenth centuries all animals were understood to be very separate and very much lesser than human beings. God had given souls only to people and, it was thought, had created all the animals for particular purposes, subordinate to humans and available for their use. Comparing people to animals was far more demeaning than we now would view it. Being a bitch or indeed an ape, as we saw with 'jackanapes', stripped a person of their dignity, their rights and privileges as a human being in relation not just to other people but also to God.

A 'salted bitch' was a bitch in heat, doubly insulting as a phrase for a woman, as it spoke of a panting, sexually aroused creature running through the streets with no self-control or self-respect. Unrestrained sexual appetite formed the subtext of many of the beastly insults. 'She had more bulls following her than her cows had' was one cruel comment that extemporized upon this theme, and there were plenty of options when referring to cocks as well as bulls. 'Dung-bellied drunken sow' was an unusual animalistic insult in that it lacked any overt sexual reference, but its imagery of a fat, inebriated pig wallowing in its own filth was hardly a flattering one.

Sex could also play a role when insulting men, but from a rather different angle. One didn't insult a man by reference to *his* promiscuity but rather his wife's. A man was not supposed to be a philanderer – good men were just as chaste as good women – but nonetheless a man's reputation suffered far less damage from accusations of extramarital sex than a woman's. The language of insult is noticeably lacking in words to describe male sexual incontinence. But there are words for men whose wives stray, the most notable being 'cuckold' and 'wittol'. A 'cuckold' was weak and sexually inadequate, a pale imitation of a real man. His wife strayed because he couldn't sexually satisfy her and he had failed to exercise proper masculine authority over her. Anyone who called a woman a 'whore' was automatically branding her husband a 'cuckold' whether they used the word or not. It worked the other way around, too, of course; 'thy husband's a cuckold' was just another 'whore' variant.

Popular literature, whether ballad or play, loved a cuckold; he was a stock character who always got a laugh, or at least a snigger. No one likes to be a laughing stock and some men could be very touchy indeed about the merest hint of cuckoldry. A really good way to wind up such a man was to mention cuckoos in conversation or imitate their call. The similarity of the two words, coupled with the cuckoo's habit of laying its eggs in other birds' nests, was highly suggestive but still allowed plausible deniability – particularly useful if the fellow in question was bigger than you.

If you were feeling a little bolder, you would refer to horns. Quite why a pair of horns on the head was a recognized

The foolish and emasculated husband whose wife looks elsewhere for sexual satisfaction. He was the butt of many jokes, and invariably pictured with a pair of horns.

symbol of cuckoldry I am not sure, but it most assuredly was, and had been for centuries. The exact shape and style of horns could vary, although it was always a pair and they usually curved slightly; most frequently, in the many, many surviving images, they resembled the horns of a goat. Images of the devil also featured goat-like horns, but the devil had cloven hooves rather than human feet, and it is the feet that are always mentioned as the devil's signature attribute – the horns get much less press. A man with horns was a cuckold, not a devil, and rather like Pinocchio's nose, the size of the horns reflected the scale of the offence: 'Alas poore cuckold thy horns are soe great thou cannst not come into the doore,' sneered Edith Andrewes in 1640. In images, the horns could be drawn or painted on, and on stage actors could don a special headpiece, a feature seen more in the early period and in less formal drama where stock characters and stereotypes carried the action. It is also no coincidence that traditional fool outfits included horned hats. In real life, tricking someone into wearing a pair of horns was an excellent joke and could easily be achieved by slipping a couple of sticks or feathers onto a hat.

While a 'cuckold' could be unwitting, merely duped by his wife, a 'wittol' was fully aware of what was going on, perhaps even being involved as her pimp. Technically, it was the more insulting term, implying an even weaker character; one who even when he discovers the truth is unable to do anything about it and is sucked into a position of aiding and abetting his wife in her attack upon his manhood. He has become the servant when he should be the master. The world of the 'wittol' could be expanded upon with 'whoremonger',

Worse than a cuckold was the wittol, a man who knowingly connived with his wife in her infidelity.

'whoremaster' and 'bawd', which all described acting as a pimp on a wider scale involving other women instead of or as well as your wife. Nevertheless, 'cuckold' was the more versatile insult, more likely to strike the mark as it could magnify fears and insecurities whether there was any truth in it or not. By its very definition you either knew you were a 'wittol' or knew that you were not, but 'cuckold', well, that was a matter of trust.

Related to a woman's sex if not actually to her sexual behaviour was a body of insults about female speech. It was a culturally commonplace assumption that women talked far too much. Men's talk was generally characterized as serious, important and relevant, while women's speech was frequently portrayed as idle, petty and excessive. Women were 'tattlers', their tongues 'wagged' to little purpose, or worse, they were 'scolds' whose constant nagging made their husbands' lives a misery and unsettled the peace of the neighbourhood with their harsh remarks. It was a subject area that could prove useful if you wished to insult a woman who might be widely seen as too old to be convincingly accused of extramarital sex. Anything that alluded to a particularly large mouth, such as 'frog mouthed', 'flounder face' or 'long jawed', brought to mind an unattractive image of a face that had been stretched by verbal overuse and incidentally tapped into the imagery of old and 'overused' vaginas. Such insults were not quite as immediate as the 'whore'-based ones but they still carried a taint of lewdness.

There was one other significant focus for insults primarily aimed at women: the word 'witch'. Now, our modern popular culture would have you believe that everyone in sixteenth- and seventeenth-century Britain ran around

Words were seen as a particularly female failing, and the sight of women gossiping like this was one to provoke a great deal of male concern and disapproval.

accusing their female neighbours of witchcraft, but it was not in fact a popular choice for using aloud in a public place. When historian Laura Gowing analysed the language of insult found in the consistory courts of London, she discovered that between 1572 and 1594 only 4 per cent of all the cases brought before the court included a shout of 'witch' in any form, while between 1606 and 1640 the figure had dropped to fewer than 1 per cent of cases. Scroll through the courts of any other area of the country and the same light scattering appears.

'Witch' was a word that people would demand legal redress for, but not one that many people needed to counteract. When it did get an airing it was often as part of a longer string of insults – 'thou art a witch and a bitch' or 'blackmouthed witch and whore' – used more as an intensifier to the main thrust of the argument rather than the core subject matter. The court cases also highlight the fact that when randomly shouted in anger, such an accusation could result in the accuser being convicted of slander and the accused walking away triumphant. Joan Ded needed such an outcome after one of her neighbours had called her a 'witch'. Clearly, the words touched a chord with other townsfolk as two of the local bakers in Devizes banned her from their shops. This put her in a difficult and dangerous position, with the possibility of things escalating. So she turned to the local magistrates and asked them to hear the charge, in effect bringing a prosecution against herself, in order to gain an opportunity to publicly and officially clear her name. Unfortunately, we don't know if her neighbour suffered any punishment for the alleged slander, but Joan is not among the list of those ever convicted of witchcraft.

Me and My Big Mouth

So how often did insulting the neighbours land a person in trouble? Just how likely were such words as 'whore' or 'knave' to result in a prosecution? Was it a rare thing to hear this sort of language in the streets, or did the soundscape of Renaissance Britain ring with obscenities? In truth, we just don't know. Laura Gowing found 2,224 defamation cases that were brought to court in and around London between 1572 and 1640. In a city with around 100,000 inhabitants this represents a steady trickle of around 30–40 a year. Her researches among the records of Chichester over much the same period show a similar pattern. But this probably only represents a very small proportion of the whole. Court cases cost money – between £1 and £10 at a time – and when a day labourer earned just 8d a day, this was much more than many people could afford. Furthermore, it was the injured party who had to stump up the cash. So if your victim was poor there was little they could do: you could insult them with impunity, at least as far as the law was concerned. Bringing the matter to court also required time, determination and connections, at least locally. Witnesses had to be gathered and persuaded to testify and procedures could be rather long-winded and confusing. Nor would everyone wish to further air the matter in public. We must therefore assume that the court cases reflect just the tip of the iceberg. Even the better-off could choose to outwardly dismiss your words, especially if you were a woman.

According to the more earthy literature of the day, such as the ballad 'The Schole House of Women' published by Edward Gosynhyll in 1541 on the nature of the female sex,

> *Malyce is so roteth in theyr harte,*
> *That seldom a man, may of them here,*
> *One good worde, in a hole yere.*

Elite voices such as the Puritan minister John Brinsley in 1645 were broadly in accord. He preached that women were 'naturally more prone to be deceived and misled'. Weak-minded women, full of error and prone to petty malice, were surely not to be taken too seriously. For a man in particular, brushing off a woman's angry words could often be not just the cheaper option, but a relatively easy one, which allowed him to laugh misogynistically with fellow men about the pettiness and untrustworthiness of women in general. The courts shared such scepticism about women's words; while male witnesses, defendants and plaintiffs were challenged about their financial independence (and thus likelihood to be open to bribery and intimidation), women were questioned about their ability to understand oaths, about their truthfulness and sexual 'honesty'.

Then, of course, there must have been many slightly lesser

grades of insult that were not quite serious enough to go to court over. Paradoxically, it is sometimes through court cases that we hear of attempts to get this balance right: offensive enough to hurt, but avoiding particular actionable words and phrases. 'I am a better woman than Mrs Dugress. I never showed my arse in an alehouse, nor pawned my muff for drink' was one such attempt ('muff' being slang for vagina). Sadly for this foul-mouthed parishioner the ruse failed; she might have managed to avoid using 'whore' by employing a euphemism, but the description was just too graphic.

If your words did land you in court, it was still not the end of the world. Around three quarters of cases didn't go the full distance, with most being settled privately. Often the whole purpose of bringing a case would have been to force such a settlement, whereby the slanderer made some form of public retraction and apology. If the case did reach a full conclusion and formal conviction, the punishments meted out centred once again upon apology with the possible addition of public shaming rituals. Slanderers could be made to appear at church in front of the whole parish wearing a white sheet so that everyone could point, tut or laugh at them; they could be required to make very particular apologies, sometimes reading out or repeating words that were written out by the court, and they might additionally have to pay compensation to those they had slandered as well as perhaps being required to pay the court's costs.

But if most people got away with insulting the neighbours either due to their poverty, willingness to turn a blind eye or the strategic use of an apology, there was still a danger in overindulging. Clearly anyone who made a real habit of shouting 'whore' or 'knave' in the street eventually found that their words began to lose impact. If this was the twelfth woman that you had accused of being a 'stinking quean' then very few of your fellow companions were likely to lend much credence to your words and your victims were more likely to receive sympathy and support than the distrust and ostracism that you might have hoped for. You may well have found that the vicar retrieved his *Book of Homilies* (largely written by Thomas Cranmer and first issued to parishes in 1547) and treated the congregation to a lesson on the value of verbal restraint. 'He that hath an evil tongue, troubleth all the town where he dwelleth, and sometime the whole country. And a railing tongue is as a pestilence so full of contagiousness, that Saint Paul willeth Christian men to forbear the company of such.'

If you persisted long enough in hurling public insults, you could graduate from simple defamation cases heard by church courts up to the criminally defined offence of 'scolding', which could be tried in the manorial, borough and ecclesiastical courts.

Mind you, if you were a man you stood much less chance of being prosecuted as a scold, or even of being called one. Scolding was seen very much as a female sin associated with loose, out of control, unreasonable, weak, phlegm-dominated minds. The manorial court records of Acomb in Yorkshire, for example, reveal two men, Robert Spayce and George Gill, in trouble for 'scolding in court' in 1584, but there are more than a dozen women prosecuted as 'common scolds' or for particular incidents of scolding at various times in the same records. If you look at a wider selection of court records, the imbalance between the sexes is even more pronounced. It could well be that Robert Spayce and George Gill only attracted the 'scolding' label because their outburst actually happened in the serious context of a courtroom.

At the mild and rarely prosecuted end of the scale, a scold was a woman who disrupted harmonious family life, pushing against the natural authority of her husband with constant nagging. It was a recurrent theme in popular ballads played in large part for comic effect. One published in 1615 began:

> *A wedded wife there was,*
> *I wis of yeres but yung,*
> *But if you thinke she wanted wit,*
> *Ile sweare she lackte no tongue.*

Another, of 1586, described it as endemic: 'But scolding is an exercise that married men doe know.'

There are plenty more variations. It might not have been quite as shameful as being cuckolded, but allowing your wife to get away with such insubordinate behaviour smacked of masculine weakness. The victim of scolding within the home was a risible figure, a legitimate butt of jokes. Accusing a man of being 'hen pecked' and calling his wife a 'scold' constituted just the sort of insult that got under the wire, leaving no recourse to law as it was simply not sufficiently severe and made no reference to actual sexual immorality. It still had the power to upset people, though.

But scolding as an offence was not confined to the home. A woman who scolded her husband might also be tempted to try out such verbal exercises upon her neighbours.

The protagonist in our first ballad, for example, is portrayed as making an enormous public fuss over the most trivial of disputes.

> *A neighbours maid had taken halfe,*
> *Her dish-clout from the hedge;*
> *For which great trespasse done,*
> *This wrong for to requite,*
> *She scolded very handsomely,*
> *Two daies and one whole night.*

This is a plainly ridiculous and exaggerated scenario. No one really screams and shouts for two days over the loss of half a dishcloth that has been put out on the hedge to dry. But putting the comic exaggeration to one side, repeated flares of temper outside the confines of the home could be what earned a woman the title of 'common scold'.

The majority of convictions for scolding resulted in fines, generally fairly small ones of a shilling or two, but repeat offenders could, and occasionally did, have to face the ducking stool, or in Scotland and the north of England, the scold's bridle. Some communities were much keener on this form of punishment than others. The parish of Henley in Arden where Shakespeare's mother grew up, for example, had a working ducking (or cucking) stool that was used a number of times in the 1620s and '30s. But not every parish had one. Several cases where a woman had been sentenced to a dip turned into a bit of a farce when makeshift arrangements had to be made or a stool that had gone unused for thirty or forty years proved to be too rotten to use. The oddness of the punishment has given it rather more prominence in the popular imagination than its actual historical use can support. Nonetheless, it was probably wise for the potential user of invective to avoid Henley in Arden, Gillingham in Dorset or the city of Nottingham.

To sum up then, the effective use of insult when out in public required a good knowledge of your victim's habits, gender and local reputation. A powerful insult held just enough truth to be taken seriously, for the hurt to linger. It was best to condense everything into a few really pointed attacks in order to maximize the impact and avoid anyone turning on you and accusing you of being a scold. It was best to pick on the poorest, who couldn't afford to take you to court. There was not much point spending ages devising something long-winded, literary and witty; stick with the nice simple formula of a single main word, such as 'jade' or 'wastrel', and then add to and modify it with the usual compounds. A great long string of invective worked well, as not only was it easy to remember and satisfying to shout good and loud, but it was also easy for your audience to catch the main thrust of your argument.

You may be rather pleased to know that popular culture, if not the formal pronouncements of preachers and philosophers, sometimes had a sneaking respect for the hurler of insult – even the female ones. In 1630, 'A Pleasant new Ballad, How the Devill, though subtle, was gul'd by a Scold' appeared, featuring a husband who attempts to deliver his scolding wife to the devil, but she is more than equal to the challenge:

'Here take her!' quoth the Devill,
'to keep her here be bold;
For hell will not be troubled,
with such an earthly scold.

She returns from hell, triumphant and undeterred, to scold another day.

It's the Way That You Say It

There was nothing quite like a regional accent for raising a laugh in London – something that dramatist Richard Brome made repeated use of in his plays, writing out the lines phonetically so that everyone could read the joke in the published version just like they heard it in performance. 'All that e'er he had o'me, was but a kiss. But I mun tell yee; I wished it a thoosande, thoosande till him,' his title character in *The Northern Lass* declares, before adding 'and what did he then do, trow you, but tuke ne thus by th'haund, and thus he

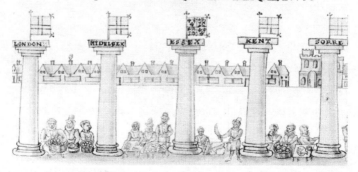

London was awash with a variety of regional accents as people moved in and out of the capital.

kust me.' Oh, the hilarity! Any regional accent would do, just so long as it sounded strange to the ears of those in the city. Even somewhere as close as Finsbury Hundred in Middlesex, which hugged the walls of the City of London on its northern and eastern edges and included places like Islington and Clerkenwell, had its speech parodied in Ben Jonson's *A Tale of a Tub*.

The West Country was one of the most popular targets:

> *Ruddle, ruddle, nebour Tan,*
> *Whare ich a late a benn a.*
> *Why ich a benn to Plymouth man,*
> *The lik wah neuer zeene a.*
> *Zutch streates, zutch men, zutch hougeous zeas,*
> *Zutch guns wth things ther tumbling.*
> *Thy zul wth me woudst blest to zee,*
> *Zutch bomination rumbling.*

So runs a ditty written out by William Stoude for his own amusement, making fun of both the accent and the supposed awe of a simple country man upon visiting the port of Plymouth. (It is relatively easy to work out if you just say it aloud, but just in case you are struggling, it roughly translates as: 'Well, well, neighbour Tan, guess where I have just been, I have been to Plymouth, the like of which you have never seen, such streets, such men, such huge seas, such guns with things tumbling out, Your soul like mine would be blessed to see, such abominable rumbling.')

The writers of popular cheap ballads were just as keen as gentlemen and playwrights to tap into this vein of humour.

The best of them make a fairly convincing job of reproducing genuine accents but others plump for a sort of generic 'local yokel' style that seems to have been adequate for raising a superior smirk among their city customers. The prejudiced idea that country dwellers were intellectually challenged in comparison to sassy urbanites was firmly in place by this time, and language was an ideal expression of that perceived inferiority. As far as Londoners were concerned, a regional accent was a sign of stupidity. It is perfectly possible that people from Devon had their own jokes about London speech that may have been just as condescending, but if so they did not get written down and were never circulated around the country at fairs and in pedlars' packs as the London ballads were. The more literate and mobile members of communities up and down the country were soon made aware that their traditional forms of speech were somehow 'lesser'.

Utilizing the 'wrong' regional accent was a rich source of irritation, not just because people found themselves being laughed at but also because of the simple difficulties of not being able to make yourself understood. English was 'so dyuerse in yt selfe' that 'some contre can skante be vnderstondid in some other contre' moaned one writer in 1530. People travelling across the country frequently griped about the thick accents and the use of utterly strange words. As the historian Adam Fox points out in his work on oral culture, the vocabularies were hugely varied as well as the pronunciations and accents. The simple word 'I' in London was 'Ich' in Devon, 'Each' in Gloucestershire and 'Ay' in Yorkshire, for example. Richard Verstegan pointed out in 1605 that where a Londoner would say, 'I would eat more cheese yf I had it,' the northern man (he didn't specify quite where in the north) said, 'Ay sud eat mare cheese gin ay hadet,' while his generic fellow from the west might say, 'Chud eat more cheese an chad it.'

John Smyth from Gloucestershire left us a particularly full record of one quite small but distinct region when he self-consciously, and rather proudly, recorded the local language and pronunciations of Berkeley Hundred in 1639. It gives a good feel for just how impenetrable many of the local accents really were. He explained how a native of the region, when asked where he had been born, would answer: 'Where shu'd y bee y bore, but at Berkeley hurns, and there, begis, each was y bore'; or in a shorter version: 'Each was geboren at Berkerley hurns.' Our author was particularly keen to highlight the use of 'y' as a word that was inserted into sentences to make them flow in a way that sounded right to locals.

John Smyth was an educated man who noted proudly that several of the words he found in Chaucer and other ancient writers turned up in local usage despite being no longer present in contemporary London speech. I am struck by the addition of 'ge' at the start of a word and 'en' at the end to indicate the past tense as in 'geboren', something redolent of German grammar; John Smyth would have seen this as the legacy of old Saxon speech. He also noted the frequent swapping of 'v' and 'f' such as 'fenison for venison' and 'vethers for feathers' and a similar propensity to swap 'c' and 'g' when compared to London usage. The two-letter combination 'th' was often pronounced in the middle of words more like a 'd', as in 'moder and fader' instead of 'mother and father'. He goes on to list hundreds of local words and particular usages such as the phrase 'thick and thuck' where we would say 'this and that'. Put all of this together and have a go at working out the following simple sentence: 'Each ha'nnot wel y din'd, ga'as zo'm of thuck bread.' Any luck? And after I gave you all those clues, too!

Moving around the country could be challenging as you traversed one speech community after another. But, on the other hand, if you wanted to behave badly, just think how you could use the confusion to your advantage. Language like this could be used to shut other people out, to bamboozle strangers and generally get your own back on London types who thought themselves better than everyone else (Londoners are still occasionally guilty of this today – ask any northerner).

There was actually one type of talk that was consciously designed to confuse outsiders: that of thieves and conmen. This was not an accent but a collection of slang words and specialized vocabulary that helped those who were up to mischief to disguise their activities. It is recorded as being in use all over the south of England from Devon to Suffolk and especially in London. To 'nyp a bong' was to cut a purse (purses were generally suspended from belts so to steal one it was necessary to cut the ties) and to 'fylche some dudes' was to steal clothes. This second phrase, incidentally, is still in use, though rarely as an entire phrase – in Essex and among the long-established East End inhabitants of London, to 'filch' is still to steal and 'duds' are still clothes.

There were words for different sums of money and for likely rendezvous locations. According to a pamphlet published in 1552 about cheating at games of chance, there were also terms for the tools of the trade including fourteen different types of loaded dice with names such as 'light graviers', 'brystelles' and 'cater trees'. If the tools had names, so too did the various 'trades': there were 'priggers of prancers' who stole horses and 'Abraham men' who pretended to be mad and begged in the street, while the people using loaded dice were 'coney catchers'. If you wanted to be part of the underworld of thieves and chancers, you needed to know the 'cant'. It clearly carried a sort of glamour. Playwrights were enthusiastic borrowers of thieves' cant; from Shakespeare down we find characters like Autolycus in *The Winter's Tale* and Simpcox in *Henry VI* acting out the same scams and using the canting language that also appeared in various warnings to citizens. Pamphlets about the subject sold very well, going through multiple editions; something that provided a living for both Robert Greene and Thomas Dekker (both playwrights) at financially difficult moments. Naturally, this dissemination of information through the wider population impacted upon the practical advantages of a secret thieves' language, especially as several of the people who published the information were magistrates ostensibly intending to aid their fellow elite legal practitioners in prosecuting the criminal element. But there were always plenty of fresh-faced youths up from the country who had yet to penetrate the talk.

Amazingly, there is still something recognizable in every one of our vernacular examples so far. The modern regional accents of Britain still contain traces of these speech patterns, although they have generally been eroded over time to something much closer to the London 'norm'. Perhaps even more amazing is the fact that you can also still hear such tones, structures and vocabulary in several different areas in the US, where regional speech patterns travelled with different groups of settlers, each still discernibly distinct to the modern ear. A particularly amusing side effect of this is the word 'like' as a sort of punctuation. There is a strong fashion for this usage throughout Britain, which arrived about fifteen years ago when it felt as if everyone under the age of twenty-five needed to include 'like' with a slight rising inflection in every single sentence they uttered. To most people in Britain this sounded like an American import sponsored by a string of TV shows, but in truth it was simply a repatriation of an ancient Devonian habit that had left these shores centuries before, heading out from Plymouth with band after band of 'founding fathers'. It had almost, but not completely, died out in its native county and of course was utterly unfamiliar to those from other parts of Britain when it burst back on the scene.

Written English was much more uniform. When William Caxton first set up business in London in 1475 and prepared to print his very first book in the English language, he and his workforce arranged the letters in the manner that they felt most at home with. There was no agreed spelling, no formal codes of any sort to guide their hands; they simply made it as intelligible as they could, informed mostly by Latin writings and phonetically rendering their own speech into a written form. Naturally, it was a London form of English that they used since that was where they and the majority of their customers were based. Print would henceforth project London words and London pronunciations out across the country, bringing those with a large exposure to books to recognize and expect a certain form of English.

Political power was also beginning to be more exclusively framed in a London accent with a London vocabulary. As the Tudor dynasty took the throne, government was becoming increasingly focused upon the capital. Elizabeth was the last monarch to haul the entire court from place to place as she went on 'progress', but she travelled shorter distances and less often than any of her forebears. Aristocrats continued to split their time between court and their own estates, but they were spending much larger parts of their lives in the metropolis. The London accent became synonymous with the court itself. In teaching tracts we start to find this one form of English being held up as the model that anyone with pretensions to social station should follow. The long history of accent as a signifier of social class had begun.

When Sir Hugh Rhodes wrote his book of manners for children in 1577 he already felt the need to explain in the introduction:

> *Corrupt in speech be sure I am,*
> *My breezes from longes to know,*
> *And born and bred in devonshyre to,*
> *As playne my tearmes do show.*

Despite being a titled member of the elite he was clearly self-conscious about his West Country accent, aware that many people might sneer at him for it. A good strong regional accent used in elite company could already raise eyebrows and those brows were just going to get higher as the seventeenth century began. It also gave those with 'good' accents and impeccable breeding a great opportunity to enjoy poking fun at country people, and as we have seen many of them did so with gusto.

But the 'right' accent quickly became more than just the one used in the London region. In *Youth's Behaviour*, first published in 1646, young men are advised to speak English 'as men of qualitie of the Town speak it, not like the mean sort'. We are hearing here of a posh accent that may well have begun as one inspired by a London accent but is now distinct from that spoken by the actual city folk. According to the various sets of advice to gentlemen and their sons, elite speech was neither 'vulgar' nor 'rustic', 'harsh' nor 'flat', distinctions that are all hard to pin down and could have offered little guidance to those who had never heard the relevant voices. The one thing that the books could help with, however, was tempo. Without exception guides to polite conversation across several centuries advised their readers not to be 'hasty' in their speech. Speaking too fast, or 'gabbling', was indicative of the lower social classes and several writers even termed it 'brutish'.

The 'flatness' that the same writers advised against seems to have derived from a different pronunciation of vowel sounds. If you look at the spellings used in documents written by London churchwardens – pretty much the lowest status of official office holder who had to keep written records – there are significant and consistent differences from the spellings chosen by the more educated and wealthier elite and from printed material. Where formal literature wrote 'coffen' or 'coffin' and 'bond', these local records generally write 'caffen' and 'band', changing the short 'o' sound into a short 'a'. Other letters underwent similar changes with 'Jenuarie' and

'Perresh' replacing 'January' and 'Parish', 'rile' for 'rail' and 'shutt' for 'shout'.

Henry Machyn was a substantial Londoner, a wealthy member of the Merchant Taylors' guild, but in his diary he tends to move his 'h' away from some words and attach it to others so that 'holes' is written as 'olles', and 'oaths' translates into 'hoythes'. He also had a tendency to use an 'f' instead of a 'th' if it came at the beginning of a word or with a 'd' if it was in the middle so that 'other' became 'odur'. These shifts are very familiar to anyone who has ever heard a modern cockney in full flow. This is not to say that the accents haven't changed over time, but rather to point out that there is some measure of continuity.

Meanwhile, the upper classes sneered: 'a craftes man or carter, or other of inferiour sort, though he be inhabitant or bred in the best towne or citie in this realme … doe abuse good speeches by strange accents or ill shaped soundes, and false orthography', wrote George Puttenham in 1570. The lower classes it seems could neither speak nor spell properly, and they tended to write phonetically, shunning the generally accepted forms adopted by the upper classes. But since there was no formal spelling as such (Shakespeare famously spelt his own name in at least five different ways) the upper classes were generally also spelling phonetically, but their writings were based upon the phonetic rendition of upper-class speech coupled with forms that they were familiar with from printed works. Not so great a difference after all, despite the rhetoric.

If you wanted to make the gentry cringe, there were a couple of other verbal faux pas you could employ, which were not so much to do with accent but more something that could be termed speech hygiene. Both stammering and mumbling were frowned upon. Sir Hugh Rhodes, in a preamble aimed at parents, began his book of manners by demanding that all incidents of stammering were to be rebuked. Other authors were a little more forgiving, advising those afflicted in this way to try to remain silent and speak only when absolutely necessary if they could not curb the problem. Mumbling, however, found no excuse in any of these texts. Erasmus laid down the rule that those of gentle birth should 'take hede ye in speaking he doe not precipitate his purpose, to breake it in hys tonge, to murmer between his teeth, but to accustome hymselfe to pronounce every woorde distinctly, clerelye, and from point to point'. The same passage appears word for word in almost every manners book published in England for the next 150 years. Mumbling was distinctly associated with those of lower social class; the gentleman spoke clearly, precisely, smoothly and at a steady pace, ideally using an accent derived from that of London and printed matter; his voice was 'sweet', calm, not too loud but not so quiet that people struggled to hear him. It was intended to be a voice of authority, a voice that laid down the law and expected obedience.

If, however, you were a humble waterman plying your trade by rowing people across the River Thames, rather like a waterborne taxi driver, and you addressed your clients in this upper-class voice … oh dear, oh dear, oh dear! Behaviour appropriate to your station in life was already an essential ingredient for social approval. Being too posh was just as bad, if not worse, than not being posh enough. The clergyman and poet Clement Ellis presented an archetypical 'gallant' (a term laden with disapproval and implying someone who pretended to hold a greater social station than he really did) who put on a totally inappropriate voice: 'all Affected and Apish' he would 'interlard an affected discourse with many impertinent parenthesis'. Elite speech was for the elite; humbler folk should stick to their own ways.

Affected and Apish

Accent was not, of course, the only way in which your speech could be used to give your hearers conniptions. The way that you used language, even supposedly polite or posh language, could be stretched, modified, adulterated and generally played with. With strongly held opinions about how language should sound already in place, there were plenty of directions you could take.

If you did want to venture into the realms of affected and apish speech, you could not go wrong with including as many foreign phrases as possible. Endless Latin epigrams were ideal, from *Quod tibi fieri non vis, alteri ne feceris* (do as you would be done by) to *Frangenti fidem, fides frangatur eidem* (to him that breaks his trust, let trust be broken). You didn't even need to actually know any Latin to do so; collections

Flatterall

The flatterall a uery Court knaue is
That prayseth great owes: when they doe *mi*
he hath less honestie. then vsefull witt.
and may be excusd because he liues by it

The flatterer: Flowery phrases and elaborate respectful formulae could easily tip over into empty flattery.

of such epigrams with their English translations were widely available in print as, for example, in *Youth's Behaviour* in 1661, which is where I found these two.

Latin was all very well, but if you could mix in other languages, all the better. A touch of ancient Greek was excellent, hinting in a rather heavy-handed manner at an extensive education; a spot of French or Italian was very annoyingly cultured, alluding to diplomatic contacts; and then a few scattered words of Dutch thrown in implied that you had extensive mercantile qualifications as well. All mixed up together into an almost completely unintelligible polyglot, it ensured that members of your audience were both confused and irritated. Half of your audience would feel as if their noses had been rubbed into the sad fact of their own scant education, while the other half would be appalled by your ignorance of the true meaning of your own speech. All would be faintly disgusted by your boasting.

The second part of affected and apish speech centred upon the overuse of titles and long obsequious flatteries. As our period progressed from the early Tudor into the Stuart era, forms of polite address were becoming more elaborate and formal. The use of these new formulae was one way to differentiate between social classes. Keeping up with this change, ensuring that one presented oneself as cultured, educated and an up-to-date member of the elite, could be a source of worry. The manners books reflected this evolution and this nervousness, changing their emphasis over time from dealing with the details of dining rituals to discussions about polite conversation and letter writing.

Early instruction upon how to address people was relatively simple, utilizing a couple of simple principles that could be applied in all cases and comprised a small number of respectable but fairly all-encompassing stock phrases. In the 1520s, Erasmus instructed children to address all scholars and tutors as 'honoured masters', every clergyman as 'reverend father'; all men whose title you were unsure of could be addressed as 'sir' and all women as 'dame'. If you knew the correct title then it was polite to use that within your speech to them once or twice in every conversation, not just when you first met. Ideally, you worked it in as a sort of polite punctuation along the lines of 'and then I said to him, your Worship, that the cat is up the tree ...'

Good manners required the avoidance of anything that would offend or inconvenience anyone around you. You shouldn't interrupt other people or hog the limelight, be rude or insulting, boastful or overly inquisitive, but instead cultivate a little humility. It was more about a respectful attitude than any particular formulae. Essentially, the ceremonial aspect of gentlemanly talk was short and to the point. Such simplicity, however, was already under pressure as new ideas came in from the Continent, principally from

Giovanni Della Casa's *Il Galateo*, published in Venice in 1558, and Baldassare Castiglione's *Il Cortegiano*, which was translated into English as *The Courtier* in 1561. Both advocated a much more elaborate and deferential method of addressing social superiors. Knowledge of this new Italian manner brought a significant social cachet and marked out its practitioners as cultured and educated sophisticates. But an imperfect understanding that led one to use the wrong forms or to add far too much flummery was 'affected'.

By 1586, polite conversation in English texts included a plethora of rather empty self-effacing courteous phrases that padded out the discourse. 'I am very glad that my poore reasons have taken good effect ... for I acknowledge you of much more wisdom and judgement then I am, Doth it please you to command mee any further service?' asked one character in *The English Courtier and the Country-gentleman*. 'You will never leave your Ceremonies (maister Vallentine) I know you are more wiser, and more expert then I am: but your naturall curtesy and modesty, doth move you to yield more respect then is due unto mee. I thanke you for it'.

The dedications to illustrious patrons that writers of period literature felt necessary at the very beginnings of their works follow a similar trajectory. These dedications sought to secure the favour of important persons and to lend a touch of glamour and legitimacy to the author's musings in the eyes of his readership. They were essays in courtesy and courtly speech – or at least they aspired to be such exemplars. At the start of the sixteenth century they generally consisted of a couple of hundred words, but as time went on more elaborate and long-winded examples become increasingly prevalent, sometimes stretching into tens of pages. To a modern reader they can be pretty tough-going, saying very little at great length. By way of example, this is a sample letter suggested as a model in 1656 for a gentlemen to write to a potential tutor for his son (someone technically of lower social station than himself):

> *Worthy sir, My long observations, and the fame from many others of your virtuous deportment in the world, and especially of that kind integrity, found in you, in that position which you spend your time, hath easi overcome my reason, and confirmed my judgement, that you are the fittest of all other to whom I, as an indulgent Father, commit the tuition of this my little Sonne, of whose instructions in the ways of virtue, now in his tender years, I am, as nature binds me, no lesse provident of, then of his vyands, wice I do certainly know, that without the one the other will but softer a lump of rudenesse, producing nothing but the sad effects of our originall depravation.*

Have you lost the will to live yet? Oh, and that's just the first sentence. There are another three pages along the same lines. And yet by this point in the period this did not count as overly ceremonious; indeed, the main body of the same publication advises *against* too much ceremony and verbiage, warning readers not to be 'boring' or at another point 'be not tedious'. I can only leave you to imagine what an 'affected and apish' man sounded like if that letter merely counted as polite.

In total contrast to the obsequious gent was the person who was overfond of 'thee' and 'thou'. Just as German has 'Sie' and 'du', English used to have two forms of the word 'you', one for formal and polite situations or when addressing someone of higher social status to yourself and another for personal and intimate use or when addressing people of a lower social station. 'You' and 'yours' were the formal versions, while 'thee', 'thou', 'thy' and 'thine' were reserved for the more intimate usage. If you look back at all those insults that were shouted in the streets, you will notice an almost total absence of 'you' and 'yours'. That 'th' was in itself part of the insult, signifying the inferiority of the person you were attacking. In polite conversation people were urged to err on the more formal side, in line with the preference for elaborate deferential introductions and extensive use of titles. Over time this pressure towards greater courtesy was to push 'thou' and 'thee' out of the language entirely. In the meantime they became increasingly potent as put-downs.

When the religious group who came to be known as Quakers decided that everyone was equal in the eyes of God (a radical and potentially subversive idea at the time because it both argued for gentlemen to be treated the same as everyone else and included the belief that no one was singled out as a special messenger of God's words, and thus there could be no ministers or clergy of any sort) they made a deliberate choice to use only the 'thee' and 'thou' forms of address. It sat well with their overall philosophy of religious brotherhood and sisterhood but it provoked enormous hostility in the daily business of life. This wasn't just a group who behaved differently at worship, who set themselves worryingly apart on a Sunday; this was a set of people who were rude and disrespectful to everyone in every aspect of ordinary interaction. Many people who may have been willing to allow a little religious leeway to respectable members of the community had their feathers ruffled by the daily lack of respect intrinsic in all those repetitions of 'thou'. As we all know, the biggest differences between people can be easier to handle with sympathy and respect than the little niggles that somehow seem to erode all our good intentions and forbearance.

Acquiring the perfect gentlemanly style of speech, according to the author Richard Brathwaite in 1630, could be achieved through repeated exposure to good models. He gave a recommended reading list of authors and their works that epitomized good English, including Sir Thomas More's *Life of Richard III* and *Arcadia* by Sir Philip Sidney. Most of the authors were strongly grounded in Latin grammar and style. Practical and contemporary speech models were to be sought out by listening to renowned ministers delivering sermons, speeches in Parliament and wandering along to listen to cases in the Star Chamber. Again, these role models had strong classical roots. The more your words sounded like you had just translated them out of Latin the better.

Bad role models were also available: William Shakespeare was one of them. Admittedly, he wasn't the very worst example, but taking your words from the playhouse was very bad form. Butchers quoted *Hamlet*, not gentlemen. Cheap, accessible entertainment was what the theatre offered and no matter how clever or beautiful the language was, it remained tainted with popularity. And who, after all, was this upstart from provincial Stratford? A half-educated son of a tradesman who betrayed his origins with the bits of Warwickshire dialect that crept into his work! You couldn't expect good English style from someone like that.

Clement Ellis's badly behaved gallant in 1660 took much of his inspiration from 'Don Quixot or some Romance more in fashion', used lots of 'new-coyn'd' words – another black mark against Shakespeare here, as he was the most prolific coiner of new words of them all – and invested in every new 'Baudy piece of Drollery' that was for sale. A comprehensive knowledge of something like

The Damēe

Damēes a rouring knawe that weares good.
If his credit serue his prayer are his oathes,
Hees stout where sure he cannot be out braud
And sweares by God, but hardly will be saiid

Swearing by God or damnation was sure to upset plenty of people.

Shakespeare's *King Lear*, after all, was indicative of multiple afternoons spent at the playhouse idly enjoying oneself in the company of common citizens, right next door to bear baiting and brothels.

Good speech could be further eroded by frequently calling upon the name of God for emphasis. 'I swear by God's Blood this is good beer' was the sort of phrase that the devout and gentlemanly found distasteful. And with such talk we are back again to Falstaff with his cries of ''Sblood' (by God's Blood), 'zounds' (by God's Wounds) and 'God-a-mercy' (God have mercy upon my soul). When period commentators moan about swearing this is what they mean. To our modern ears, swearing means peppering your speech with rude words whose meanings are generally of a sexual nature. Expletives, like the 'turd in your teeth' that we began this chapter with, are the closest Renaissance equivalents of the modern habit of telling people to 'eff off' and as we have seen there was certainly no shortage of sexually explicit words that you could press into offensive action. The period understanding of swearing, however, really meant 'to swear by …'. It was also described as 'taking the Lord's name in vain'. Foul language was foul language but swearing was something different, a separate evil that need not involve any actively rude words at all. A few of these swearing phrases have made it through to the modern age such as the familiar 'oh, for God's sake' and 'oh my God'. 'By all that is holy' is used less often in modern life but does pop up now and again, and anyone with an Irish heritage will be familiar with 'b'Jesus'. 'O, for the love of God' is an exasperated version and 'bloody hell' serves well for expressing shock. So common are such usages that many of us who use them have all but forgotten their religious foundations.

Loud and brash, such swearing was very widely condemned but seems to have been equally widely popular among men – and it does appear, in the main, to have been a particularly masculine habit. Most of the popular preachers whose sermons made it into print included long sections upon the sinfulness of the habit and its wide dissemination through the ranks of young men. They decry the way in which swearing was used to bolster a swaggering, martial persona. It is also mentioned repeatedly in the early seventeenth century as something adopted by a few badly behaved women who were aping men's behaviour. Indeed, it seems to have been a signature habit for this small group of fashionably naughty young women along with daring hairstyles and pipe smoking. Religious people hated the use of all oaths that called upon divine sanction, as they felt that using the sacred name of God in such contexts was disrespectful, perhaps even blasphemous. Many of those who indulged in it largely did so, of course, in order to see the looks of shocked outrage – shock that made the words seem all the more daring and exciting.

Oh Curses

Another form of verbal transgression was the curse. '& never since that tyme, that the woman could have any pease growe in her ground or any other Corne would growe in the same place.' From that moment onwards the ground was barren, nothing would grow for this land had been cursed. Not poisoned or strewn with salt, but cursed with words. Such stories might seem to us just like fairy tales, but this was a deadly serious business. Margaret Harkett had been interrupted and challenged as she helped herself to some of her neighbour's pea harvest. She protested that she had gleaning rights (traditional permission to take any of the crop that was spilled or dropped on the ground during harvesting). Her neighbour felt that rather more than just gleanings were being taken and told her that she could have those that were in her apron but not the basketful as well. In her humiliation Margaret lashed out and 'did flynge the pease downe on the ground, saiynge "if you make so much a doo for a fewe pease, take them all, the next yere I will have enough of my owne, and you shal have fewe enough". So she cursed the same ground and stamped on it & went her ways.' Several years later when community relationships had become rather poisonous and suspicions were at an all time high, her words were remembered. In 1585, the resulting trial was reported in a pamphlet entitled 'The Severall Factes of Witchcraft' and Margaret Harkett was hanged as a witch. Cursing did not inevitably lead to witchcraft trials – there are many more cases that appear in the records that are entirely unrelated to such trials – but it was one of those behaviours that could be interpreted in this dangerous manner.

One of the best-known contemporary writers on the subject of witchcraft, William Perkins, whose *Discourse of the Damned Art of Witchcraft* was published in 1608, summed up the popular belief that 'witches are wont to practise their mischievous fact by cursing and banning'. Many people did curse but 'if after cursing there followeth death, or at least some mischeif' he believed that actual witchcraft had been proved. A significant number of the witchcraft trials that we have records of include an incidence of cursing.

The pamphlet 'A Detection of Damnable Driftes', written by Edward White in 1579, outlines four cases tried in Essex, each one centred upon curses. Elizabeth Frauncis of Hatfield 'cursed Poole's wife, and bade a mischief to light upon her' when Mistress Poole refused to give her some yeast. Elleine Smithe of Maldon, the pamphlet claimed, had a row with her stepfather and 'in great rage saied unto hym, that it had been better for hym, he had never fallen out with her, and so it came to pass'. It was alleged that he could keep no food down from that moment onwards and eventually starved to death. The long list of complaints against Mother Staunton included one that alleged she had gone away 'murmering' after she had been denied yeast and a child of the house had immediately sickened. The fourth of the cases involved Ales Nokes of Lamberd who sought revenge on her daughter's behalf for some stolen gloves and also cursed a woman whom she believed was having an affair with her husband: 'thou hast a Nurse childe but thou shalte not kepe it long'.

The child died. Three of these four women were executed as witches, although Mother Staunton escaped with her life as no one was believed to have actually died due to her actions. Such prosecutions indicate just how real people believed curses to be. Words had the power to kill, to maim and cause a huge range of different forms of damage.

Despite the enormity of the risk, people were still tempted to curse, generally because they believed it would work. If you wanted to do it properly, you cursed people to their faces or you staged a very public performance so that word got back to them loud and clear. The more justified your grievance, the more force your curse was seen to carry, so it was good to state the reasons for your anger in a clear and concise manner. It was also a good idea to drop to your knees as you began the curse and to raise your arms as if calling down authority from on high.

There were several well-recognized general formulae that you could employ. Praying to God for vengeance was powerful and well in line with semi-official theological thought. In 1598, John Smith of Herefordshire went to the churchyard at Yarpole, about the most public spot in the parish, knelt down and began loudly naming his enemy and 'praying unto God a heavy vengeance and a heavy plague might light upon him and all his cattle'. Helen Hiley opted for the face-to-face method rather than the public place, but used much the same formulation of curse. She knelt in front of John Wood and said 'a vengeance of God light upon thee Wood'. She was less interested in his cattle but cursed 'all thy children, and I shall truly pray this praier for the[e] so long as I live'. Both found themselves being officially complained about but there was no hint of a witchcraft accusation in either case. If the cause was just, many people felt that this was an entirely legitimate response, and that God's providence would fall upon those who had sinned, particularly if they had sinned against the weak and helpless. Such attitudes were expressed even in published sermons. William Whately in *The Poore Man's Advocate* of 1637 held that those who did not help the poor could expect that 'God will punish … with execution of the curses denounced against them'. In most instances you could get away with this more prayerful form of cursing. Margery Bluck, for example, 'prayed to God, that an evil end might come to her [neighbour]' but Margery was never accused of witchcraft and nor was Catherine Mason who 'prayed to God' that Robert Davies should lose his 'house, children and all that he had' to fire.

Curses that called upon God for retribution were one form; those that called upon the devil were another, perhaps more frightening, construct. God's punishment was to be feared by those who deserved it, by those riddled with guilt, but the devil need have no such restraint or discrimination. Even your most petty bouts of malice could do harm if you called upon Satan to do your bidding. Such curses lent power to the powerless.

How much trouble you called down upon your enemies was of course up to you, but there was a distinction drawn in many people's minds between material loss, maiming and death. To curse someone's cow was to potentially cause them serious damage, but it was nothing like as serious as making a child sick with your words. And verbal murder was different again. Where people held firmly to the belief that words caused physical injury, they sometimes responded in much the same way that they would respond to other criminal cases of property damage, bodily harm or murder. As we saw with Mother Staunton, where there was perceived to be damage and injury but no murder the sentence was lighter. Many of those who were moved to curse made similar evaluations and distinctions. Naturally, the more severe curses were more likely to attract official attention, and thus were more likely to be written out in detail. The plethora of more general complaints found in local records for people 'cursing and scolding' where no further details are given may well represent a mass of curses limited to property damage.

We now have a great variety of rules to break in our quest for bad linguistic behaviour. Cursing could frighten people, swearing offended their religious sensibilities and insults angered them. The 'wrong' accent could bemuse and mystify or make someone into a laughing stock. In the backstreets and taverns of London lurked a constantly shifting host of socially inappropriate speakers who failed to meet the high standards of gentlemanly speech, but still shunned the conventions of plain humble voices. They set themselves apart with a pretended superiority over the common Londoner, dropping in endless Latin epigrams and smatterings of European languages. By adding in long-winded and overly obsequious phrases they could annoy both high and low, seeming to sneer at the lack of fashion among the humble while cheapening the manners of the elite with their ham-fisted attempts to ape true sophistication. Others affronted people with overfamiliarity, employing 'thee' and 'thine' when hearers hoped for 'you' and 'yours'. Women, and men too, scolded in streets the length and breadth of the country with a rich repertoire of invective at all times of both day and night. Tongues wagged and listeners winced.

Chapter 2

INSOLENT, RUDE AND THREATENING GESTURES

Words alone can only take you so far. There is also a world of hurt that can be inflicted by gesture. It is useful in noisy, crowded places where words would go unheard, or over distances that blur the pronunciation of your well-chosen sentiments. It can be used during periods when silence is mandatory or when words could get you into deep trouble. Gesture can also form a commentary to someone else's speech, mocking them to their face or behind their back, for the amusement of onlookers. Failure to make socially approved or supportive gestures at the appropriate moments can be disconcerting or downright hostile, and overplaying them can be deeply embarrassing.

Just as we needed to know how to select the most offensive words in order to employ them effectively, so too do we need a repertoire of gestures in order to make our meaning truly sting.

Bowing and Scraping

Cheerfully misinforming his audience, Thomas Dekker advised, 'Being arrived in the roome, salute not any but those of your acquaintance: walke up and downe by the rest as scornfully and as carelessly as a Gentleman-usher.' There was no surer way of upsetting people from all walks of life than to mishandle the traditional gestures of respect. Such disrespect could and did lead to violence in Tudor and Stuart England, a time and place where 'honour' was taken very seriously. All social encounters began with a carefully selected combination of approved postures and movements before anyone had the chance to open their mouths. Words then either magnified or undermined the meanings of these non-verbal communications. It was possible to patronize, insult, demean, embarrass, satirize, deflate, dismiss and sneer while speaking the politest of phrases, or, of course, to soften foul words into banter or even affection. Body language provided the context and set the scene. It was a complicated and subtle business that provided endless opportunities for self-expression, social manipulation and personal commentary.

Thomas Dekker knew a thing or two about just what you could get away with in the big city. His *Guls Hornbook*, published in 1609, outlines many of the bad habits possessed by upstarts, posers and ne'er-do-wells, who occupied a precarious world of pretension and financial penury. Inspired by a Latin satirical poem called 'Grobianus' (1549), by the German author Friedrich Dedekind, he addresses a foolish lout, or gul, supposedly giving him tips on sophisticated conduct, but instead driving him towards further ridicule. 'Observe no man, doff not cap to that Gentleman to day at dinner, to whom, not two nights since, you were beholden for a supper,' he advises, and when you spy a man of some social standing, 'salute him not by his name of Sir such a one, or so, but call him Ned or Jack'.

Thomas Dekker's true audience, of course, was the Londoner who could recognize elements of these boorish behaviours in those around them, particularly in those who had come up from the country with money in their purses. It was these pamphlet-buying locals who were best placed to enjoy the joke. After all, casual insolence and a lack of manners were exactly the behaviours that marked out naive, cash-rich young men, drawing the attention of crooks and con men. Guls could be gulled – they were gullible. The more they strutted and dealt out arrogant insult to all around, the more those in the know smiled and hungrily licked their lips.

The correct forms of address acknowledged the social and personal positions of both parties and established a mutual respect appropriate to that relationship. That may sound simple, even perfunctory, but it wasn't. As you approached someone it was necessary to almost instantaneously make a series of judgements about the nature of the relationship between you. At the simplest level you needed to know your relative social status: were they above or below you and by how much of a margin? If you knew who they were, this might not be too difficult, but if it was a stranger, you would have to make a snap decision based on their clothes, the company they were keeping, or the location. This status judgement then had to be modified by an appreciation of their age and gender in relation to your own. Male was clearly above female and older people demanded more respect than the young, although some people chose to show more respect than strictly necessary to women, particularly upper-class women, a form of behaviour that advertised their own knowledge and adoption of new, fashionable Italian-style courtesy.

Then it was time to move on to more subjective judgements about how much respect they commanded among other people within that particular environment. A merchant among merchants might, for example, be valued for his financial muscle, but among a group of religious enthusiasts the same man with the same character traits could be derided as an overenthusiastic worshipper of Mammon. In purely formal situations between mere acquaintances, that set of competing judgements – status, gender, age and personal social standing – could be enough, but different rules applied at the various levels of personal intimacy and in more or less informal situations, adding further dimensions to the puzzle. Family members clearly required very different responses than strangers, while friends or guests called for others. One set of behaviours was necessary in public and another set in private. The permutations were endless.

Whatever solution you came up with in that split second would then have to be translated into actual movements, which required familiarity with all the options and for you to be well practised at performing them. Nor did any of this remain static; fashions and social conventions were constantly on the move as elite groups sought to mark themselves out from the common herd and the young kicked back against the behaviours and habits of older generations. That which had been polite in your twenties became clod-hopping, common and embarrassing in your thirties, and the elegant gestures that you mastered in your thirties were considered faintly ridiculous and stuffy just another decade later. The opportunities for error were enormous and thus also fertile ground for those who sought to deliberately disrespect.

The first and most obvious expression of disrespect was simply to omit all acknowledgement of someone, to ignore them, to fail to respond, as Thomas Dekker advised his 'guls'. Even if you avoided the attention of the pickpockets and tricksters, this was rather more serious in the sixteenth and seventeenth centuries than it is in the twenty-first. A simple lack of population pressure explains some of the difference. Most of us in the modern era live in an urban environment, in settlements far too large for us to know all of our neighbours personally. Ignoring the vast majority of passers-by is the way we cope with what would otherwise be a social overload; this was not the case for most people of the Tudor and Stuart ages. Only in London, and perhaps Bristol and Norwich, were there enough people for real anonymity. Vague familiarity was a much more likely experience for those walking through the streets. Moreover, in this less populated world, there was statistically a much higher chance that the person you walked past one day would be the person you were doing some form of business with on another. Completely blanking someone thus stood out far more harshly, not just to the person who was passed over, but to everyone else around.

Therein lay one of the main problems with this tactic: to refuse to acknowledge someone, to fail to offer courtesy when courtesy was due, was to expose yourself to criticism. There was a danger that in your lack of everyday deference you hurt your social standing more than you hurt that of the other person's. Gentlemanly behaviour was one of the main signifiers of gentlemanly status. The more you behaved like a gentleman, the more people considered you to *be* a gentleman. By failing to behave in a courteous manner you marked yourself out as lesser, coarser, baser. Paradoxically, refusing to perform respect gestures did not so much act as a snub to your enemy as much as it degraded you in the eyes of the world. The opposite strategy could be very much more effective; if you made a point of performing rather more fully the appropriate gestures, you could wrong-foot your opponent, making them look like an ill-mannered oaf while you maintained the smug high ground.

So what exactly were these gestures and how did it work? How precisely could you successfully offend? The earliest comprehensive written instructions are those of Erasmus in 1532, contained in his manual for children (well, upper-class boys), which was translated from the Latin into English as *The Civility of Childehood*. Much of the advice that he gives is echoed by images in manuscripts and printed works, which capture idealized snapshots of particular poses. He begins by pointing out that practices varied across Europe. As a well-travelled man he will have seen this for himself: 'Some doe

An upright spine and a bend in both knees, one well in front of the other, were the defining characteristics of the Henrician English bow. This is not the full, knee to the floor version, but a more usual genuflexion, denoting friendship or near social status.

bowe the knees together, and som holde them righte up: and other somewhat crooked.' He describes the fashionable bow in England as one that keeps the body perfectly upright, bending first the right and then the left knee. It is not all that helpful as a description but luckily there are images in other sources that depict the legs with one in front of the other, not side by side. The toes point forwards and the knees are in a half bend. If you hold your weight over the back leg then there is an appreciable feeling that the back, weight-bearing knee bends before the front one does. Images also indicate that the left leg was generally in front and the right behind, as Erasmus suggests, and there is no forward lean as yet; this is more of a half kneel with a vertical spine. To perform the manoeuvre in an elegant fashion, it helps to regulate the distance between the feet according to how deeply you intend to bend the knees.

If you begin with your feet side by side, a couple of inches apart with the toes pointing forwards, and then step your left foot directly forwards so that your left heel is now about two inches diagonally forward and to the side of the toes of your right foot, you will be in the perfect position for a small everyday sort of bow, in which both heels remain flat on the floor. A deep bow that lifts the right heel requires the left heel to be about twelve inches in front of the toes of the right foot, and a full bow, where the right knee touches the floor, needs something closer to eighteen inches of clearance.

As bows go, this style has the advantage of flexibility; the degree and speed of the knee bend can be easily varied according to the situation. It is also easy to perform in any of the outfits that a man might have been wearing in 1532 – even full armour.

Having practised the movements and made your social judgements, you were in a position to twist the entire performance to your will. If, for example, you happened upon some social equal whom you disliked heartily in a public and formal space, such as the courtyard at one of the Inns of Court where the lawyers had their chambers, you might employ the slow, sarcastic version. To achieve this you could come to a complete halt, pause for a second to heighten the impact and draw attention to your actions, and then sink artificially slowly into a deep bend letting your right heel rise off the floor but not touching the knee quite to the ground – leaving about six inches of air – and hold it for a second too long before rising. The slow speed throughout the bow could be seen as a surfeit of respect but the pauses both before and at the depth of the bow would highlight your mocking intent.

Such a bow said, 'I am not the one lacking in good manners and breeding.' The length of those pauses could communicate the degree of contempt in which you held your adversary.

If, however, you were in a hurry and willing to risk under-bowing, perhaps in a crowded space where your perfunctory gesture could be interpreted either as a personal slight or as a result of the crush, the bow could be executed on the move, requiring nothing more than a slight dip of bended knee in the middle of a step forwards, barely interrupting your stride as you surged on past.

Only in the most formal of situations was it necessary to complete a full bend where the left knee came to rest on the ground. You might feel the need to do this when begging for a favour from a superior (this is where getting down on one knee to propose marriage comes from), trying to worm your way out of some form of trouble, or attending a church service. But if you ever wished to add a little insolence to the performance, you could simply lean forwards and put your left elbow or forearm on your left knee. The addition of the arm and the lean forward was traditionally seen as the posture adopted in the Bible by the soldier who mocked Jesus: 'I salute thee King of the Jews.' In the pre-Reformation world this moment of mockery was regularly depicted on church walls and in other religious imagery. It was a familiar visual sneer that everyone would have understood immediately.

All of this, however, was just part of the picture. We now have to discuss what you did with your arms, head and hat while you were bending your knees. In the 1530s, hats were generally flat and every man wore one most of the time. Removing your hat was a gesture of respect because

Bowing on the move could look just like this dance move, but with the hat removed first.

it was also a gesture of inferiority and subordination. The bareheaded were humble and exposed. Not one of the period advice manuals tells a man, or boy, to wear his hat; it was simply assumed behaviour. While he might need to be reminded to carry a handkerchief, a hat was unforgettable and taken utterly for granted. He wore it from the moment he had finished combing his hair in the morning until he went to bed at night – when he probably wore a nightcap instead. Removing your hat was thus a very meaningful thing to do. The timings were important and so was the manner in which you did it.

If taking your hat off was an expression of deference then keeping it on was one of superiority. Social superiors had no need to remove their hats when acknowledging underlings, and adults were under no obligation to do so in the presence of children. But just as refusing to bow could reflect badly upon the refuser, so too could failure to remove a hat. It was generally best to err on the side of caution if you wanted to hold on to your own reputation.

One way of working this convention to your advantage, however, was a careful use of timings. Hesitate a little as you approach, as if unsure whether a person merits your attention or not, and then at the very last moment remove your hat in an ostentatious manner. This way you neatly demonstrate confidence in your superior position while graciously allowing that person a measure of respect that they don't really deserve. It leaves them with nowhere to go since they can't object to your insolence after you have so openly and obviously removed your hat.

You could also offer a casual insult by allowing your hat to drift slightly in your hand, revealing the underside. Even with today's daily showering and shampooing regimes, the inside of a regularly worn hat becomes greasy, sweaty and sometimes covered in dandruff. A Tudor hat had similar and likely more intense problems. It was a matter of common decency when removing a hat to keep the inside out of sight. Erasmus advised boys to hold the hat in the left hand close to the body or to use both hands neatly at their navels with the two thumbs tucked into their belts. Both positions stopped the hat from flapping about and revealing the inner surfaces. For those not wishing to be humble and respectful, displaying the underside of your hat was a usefully ambiguous gambit; it demonstrated a lack of concern about the viewer's feelings but could always be passed off as unintentional.

If you were less concerned about appearing to be a gentleman, you could risk a more blatant set of hat-based behaviours: tossing it about from hand to hand, waving it around in the air and casting it casually onto tables, or tucking it under your arm ('a rude thing', according to our friend Erasmus). Such loose abandon with your hat spoke of mockery. Yes, you had gone through the social convention of removing your hat, but you had done so outside the spirit of the thing; you had paid lip service only to the idea of deference.

If you knew that your enemy was an educated and sensitive person, you could even disconcert them by using the wrong hand to remove or hold your hat with. Did you notice that Erasmus told boys to hold their hats with both hands or with the left hand, specifically leaving the right hand free to accompany speech with gesture? Medical theory of the day made a strong distinction between the right and left sides of the body, maintaining that fresh, pure blood from the heart made its way first to the right side of the body; thus, strength, vigour and honesty were all linked with the right hand. It was a subtle point but many people would have felt rather uneasy about someone who removed their hat in a show of respect and then held it in their right hand as they spoke, emphasizing words with their left.

Women had much less to work with. Long skirts obscured leg positions and nothing was removed from a woman's head. The subtleties of timings and the depth of the knee bend, however, worked in just the same way for women as they did for men. Without any hat removal to worry about, a woman's arms were supposed to be quiet and still – definitely no skirt plucking, which is a very modern habit largely put forward by Disney – and so instead the focus shifts to a woman's eyes. Ideally, as a woman bent her knees and sank downwards, her body and head remained erect but her eyes were focused upon the ground in front of her. To maintain eye contact with the person opposite throughout the whole curtsey was an act of real hostility and defiance. To flick the eyes up when in the ebb of the bob could be cheeky, flirty and mischievous. It certainly wasn't modest, as several writers pointed out.

Maybe all of this sounds rather upper class to you – and of course it was – but a lot of it trickled down to even the lowest levels of society. Ploughmen and dairy maids were not expected to perform the courtesies with any great degree of elegance and polish, and touching the knees to the ground was not looked for in muddy, outdoor situations, but the essential core of the movements and their meanings remained the same across all boundaries. A hired ploughboy dragged his hat off his head and bent his knees when he spoke to the yeoman farmer who employed him and expected a blow to the head if he failed to do so, and the dairymaid made sure that she bent her knees and lowered her eyes when she bade her mistress good morning.

The lower down the hierarchy you were, the rougher and more approximate your bows could be, in part because you had to enact them so frequently. If everyone is your superior, your hat barely gets a chance to keep the rain off, and half your life might seem to consist of an eyes-down semi-crouch. A certain leeway had to be allowed to those at the bottom of the heap or little would have got done.

Indeed, elegant and punctilious bows and hat flourishes performed by ordinary working people were generally interpreted as subversive behaviours overturning the natural order. Elegance in someone dressed in second-hand russet and frieze appeared ridiculous to Tudor eyes and rather disturbing. 'Artificers, and other persons of low conditions, ought not to trouble themselves to use many ceremonies,' declared Francis Hawkins, the translator of *Youth's Behaviour*. Notice how he does not say that people need not trouble themselves but uses the phrase 'ought not'. Successfully aping your betters undermined their authority and broke down class barriers – something that the upper classes were not at all keen on. Anyone overcome by a desire to be an insolent and uppity member of the lower classes should take note: a prettily executed curtsey could be just the thing to get up the nose of an overweening master.

Another way that you could disconcert those around you was to be more up to date and cosmopolitan than your fellows. As the Reformation arrived, the half kneel that Erasmus had characterized as English was being replaced by French fashions. 'The Frenche men do bowe onely the right knee with a certayne swete turning and moving of the body,' explained Erasmus. But perhaps we should turn to an actual Frenchman for advice and clarification here. Jehan Tabourot was a provincial churchman, a Catholic canon who served as right-hand man to the Bishop of Langres. He had learnt to dance in Poitiers in the 1540s when he was a student, and as he approached his twilight years published a manual upon the subject, under the pseudonym Thoinot Arbeau, in 1589. His description of the French bow is not all that extensive but in an innovative move he included in his book not only music notation but

RÉVÉRENCE

Thoinot Arbeau's depiction of the French bow, a style that was sometimes termed 'to make a leg'.

a few useful images: '… keep the left foot firmly upon the ground and bending the right knee take the point of the toe behind the left foot, removing your bonnet or hat the while and bowing to your damsel and the company as you see in the picture.' And thank goodness for that picture! The man stands with his weight upon the back, right foot, the knee bent. His left foot is pointed out in front of him resting on the floor, the knee straight and both feet slightly turned outwards rather than pointing straight ahead. His hat is in his left hand and is held against his thigh concealing the inside from view. His body is tilted very slightly forwards from the hip joint and twists just a smidgen to his right towards the 'damsel'. 'After the reverence is completed straighten your body and replace your bonnet, then bring your right foot forward and place it beside the left,' his instructions conclude. It is clearly the same bow that Erasmus was describing so many years before. However, it is both more elegant than the earlier style of bow and a little trickier to perform well.

Just imagine how provincial and backward you could make some alderman of Coventry feel if you, a cloth merchant of the same town, could pull off one of the new French-style bows when next you bumped into him in the street. You might well have been able to hold the advantage for a considerable time as there are a whole host of ways in which this new fashion could go wrong, making the unpractised look like buffoons. Many people took their time before publicly adopting the new mode, creating a two-tier bowing landscape for many years with courtiers, the young and the well travelled 'making a leg' while the older and stodgier members of society still 'bent the knee'.

The most common difficulty that people have when they first try the French style is remembering to keep their body weight over the back leg. The older half kneel had allowed weight to be carried almost equally by both legs, particularly when executing the quick fly-by version, but if you try that with the French bow you tend to look like a chicken pecking the ground. The small turn out is also critical. If you try to perform this bow with your toes pointing resolutely forward you will find that your balance is compromised. Too much bend and twist and you look like you are trying to do a bad impersonation of a hunchbacked Richard III.

Once again, as I am sure you noticed from the picture, women have much less to play with. Both her feet are firmly on the ground next to each other and her curtsey still consists of a two-knee bend with a straight back; no 'swete turning and moving' of the body here. The only update is in the toes pointing a little outwards rather than straight forward.

Even as Arbeau's book was published, however, English gestures of respect were coming under the influence of the Italians. Their version of the bow was once again a dual knee bend, but one that incorporated both a forward lean and turned-out toes. Fabritio Caroso, writing in 1600, takes us through the most common Italian ballroom bow, performed to four beats of the music: 'In the first beat raise your left foot slightly. In the second beat draw it back. In the third gracefully bend your knees a little. In the fourth beat return your left toes to your right arch, gracefully raising your body.'

In this tradition, the woman gets slightly more to do and runs rather more risk of looking ridiculous. She too draws the left foot back, although only a very short distance, keeping the foot flat on the floor. She then inclines her body forward a little before bending both knees and finishes by gracefully returning to an upright position. 'Be careful not to adopt the habit of some who first draw their bodies back while bending deeply, and then thrust their bodies forward (a movement so unseemly that were I to say what it resembles, everyone would die laughing). Still others bend so very straight down and then rise, that they truly resemble a hen about to lay an egg.' To humiliate a lady, one need only cluck a little at the opportune moment.

Among the top end of society the formalities of greeting had become dominated by the teachings of dancing masters. In Erasmus's day the forms had been fairly simple and well known. Error, ridicule and rudeness had rested more fully in misinterpreting the social situation, rather than the actual performance of the actions, but a century later the technicalities of the movements had become more precise, more socially divisive and distinctive. By 1586, Robert Jones, in his book *The English Courtier and Country-gentleman*, was already arguing that it was impossible for even the elite to keep up to date with their bows if they didn't visit the court. When his country gentleman tries to make a case for good manners among those who have been 'brought up in service' in a country house (the traditional method of educating elite young men by placing them as senior servants in a grand household) and 'know what reverence or countenance to use towards all sortes of men', he is shot down as being like an unskilled workman who throws together a basic coat rather than a tailor who sculpts an elegant garment.

Quite what those intricacies of correct court respect

gestures were by 1623 come to us from the pen of François de Lauze, a Frenchman in London hoping to win favour from George Villiers, the man who was about to become the Duke of Buckingham. Villiers was the King's favourite, a man of almost unlimited influence at court, partly educated in France and acknowledged across Europe as an excellent dancer and model of courtly behaviour. De Lauze was a dancing master who had worked in Paris before coming to London in hope of the patronage of, and possibly employment by, George Villiers. His fellow dancing master Barthélémy de Montagut had achieved just that and looked set for life. However, things did not go quite as planned. De Lauze showed an early draft of his writings to Montagut, who promptly took a copy to a printer and published it in his own name. Poor de Lauze managed to get an extended and revised version into print three years later with a stinging introduction accusing Montagut of plagiarism, but it was Montagut who went on to become dancing master first to Queen Henrietta Maria and then to Charles I, while de Lauze eventually returned to Paris where he secured a minor position for some years at the French court.

The dance instructions within de Lauze's work (including the plagiarized version under Montagut's name) are extremely hard to follow, but his etiquette notes are wonderful. What we get is a sort of hybrid between the French and Italian models, with six different bows for use in different circumstances, instructions for women, some up-to-date advice on hat management, general advice on deportment and practical tips upon projecting the fashionable style into your movements. It soon becomes apparent that it would take rigorous training to be able to successfully pull off courtly behaviour in the years leading up to the Civil War. De Lauze begins by recommending that these skills be learnt in childhood, for they are much harder to attain as an adult. The point being that this was, of course, excellent for maintaining a visible public difference between those born to privilege, who had the time and money to learn, and those who were self-made and spent their formative years working. However rich a merchant became, he was always going to struggle to look like a bona fide gentleman. Which, frankly, was the whole point of the exercise. Making such extraordinarily complex movements look effortless and natural emphasized your long familiarity with this mode of movement, a mode that even demanded that you re-learn how to walk: 'For whatever gentility he would have naturally, he would be unable to do this of himself with the required exactness, whether for the movement of the eyes, the carriage of the leg, or the gravity of his steps, which should be made in a straight line, without bending the knee, the toes turned well outwards.'

I suggest at this point that you put this book down and have a go at walking without bending your knees. Don't worry too much at this stage about eyes and toes, just try the straight-legged walk. How did you get on? It helps if you have had some ballet training, or at least watched a lot of male ballet dancers moving across the stage during some of the more classical repertoire. Ballet, after all, developed directly out of French court dance of the mid-seventeenth century, so there is a significant crossover in some of its basics.

Another aid here is the study of classical statuary. The new fashion had been directly inspired by the discovery and discussion of new-found examples of classical Greek and Roman sculptures and new translations of Latin texts mentioning posture and beauty. The key element was that which the Italian commentators referred to as '*contrapposto*', the slight twist in the torso that projects forward one hip and the opposite shoulder (think of Michelangelo's *David*). The body weight is borne by the back foot allowing the front knee to bend lightly and gracefully. Further elegance is added by permitting a small amount of sag or slouch, which pushes out the supporting hip to one side and encourages the other hip to drop. The overall impression is of a controlled asymmetry, of a body held in active tension, flowing through natural movement. This S-curve posture is very familiar to us, we have grown up surrounded by images of classical statuary and countless copies of it, from catwalk models to Hollywood glamour poses, but in the sixteenth century it carried the 'shock of the new' or perhaps more accurately the shock of the 'rediscovered ancient'. Knowledge of these 'finds' were very much confined to a select few. 'Correct' classically inspired posture was a very visible badge of rarefied cultural capital. Only those with access to the latest Renaissance learning and examples of classical art or copies thereof could learn first hand. Everyone else had to hope that their teacher knew what he was doing and could successfully guide them from classical pose to classical pose through the medium of a straight-legged walk.

It also helps if you are wearing a heeled shoe, about an inch high. Begin by thinking tall thoughts, drawing yourself up very erect, keep your weight forward onto your toes, don't allow yourself to slump back onto your heels (except when standing), and begin by circling the moving leg around to the front. When you first start walking with straight legs the circling will probably be quite pronounced and it will feel very strange and slow. With practice the amount of circle will gradually decrease and the walk will speed up and flow better, but be warned it really does take a very long time before this walk becomes second nature and appears effortless. A busy merchant didn't stand a chance.

Having mastered the walk, you could enter the room and approach someone. The hat was the next thing to require attention. It was important that it was removed with the right hand, which, as we noted before, equated with the more honourable side of the body, but was then swapped over to the left hand and held 'negligently – not on the thigh as was formerly the custom, but in front of the busk of the pour point'. 'The busk of the pour point' meant just below your belly button, so in this instance we are actually returning to the 1530s English format. With the hat safely off, you raised your eyes towards those you intended to salute.

And once again we have an opportunity for inserting an element of disrespect. If you bowed to one individual you looked straight at them, if it was several people at once you moved your gaze between them, ideally catching each eye in turn with, as de Lauze tells us, 'a smiling countenance'. It's very easy in such a group bow, however, to leave someone out. Moreover, you can do it without anyone else in the room being aware of your omission. A lovely little personal dig.

Next you had to choose the correct bow: a simple general one for use among equals, a more formal one for social superiors, a bow for when you were on the move, or one of three different forms for use in ballrooms associated with particular dances. You might, of course, be called upon to perform several of these different types within a few minutes of each other in the same room as the social mix changed.

The simplest and least formal required gently sliding one foot from behind, past the supporting foot, bending both knees as they came close together, 'the toes well turned out', rising again and walking on. It was, in fact, very close to the old half-kneel style bow on the move, but with turned-out toes and a new emphasis upon gentleness and smoothness – a sort of English/French cross.

The more formal bow, as described by de Lauze, smacked of Italian manners.

> *The right leg, well stretched, must slide before the left, and at the same time, in bending the knees, not forwards but outwards to each side, bend the waist also. Thus without lowering the head except the body, the right arm being well extended, lower all equally, as much or as little as the quality of whomsoever one wishes to salute obliges. And without stopping on this action, in rising, one must kiss the right hand, then carrying it back to its place, separate the left foot at once to the side and slide right behind, where it will be disengaged gently in bending just a little, and thereupon stop to converse.*

Rising out of the bow was just as important and nuanced as the bow itself. The 'disengaged' leg allowed one to adopt the correct and elegant posture for conversation or onward movement (mimicking the statuary). Your body weight rested entirely upon the other leg, the disengaged was held loosely, knee slightly bent and toes just resting upon the ground tucked behind the supporting foot in a seemingly casual manner. Again, such apparently careless naturalness takes considerable practice to pull off convincingly.

Then we're back to the hat again. If you are speaking to a superior then the hat must remain off (at least to begin with) but at some point you will have to re-cover. To 'cover' was to put on a hat, to 're-cover' was to put your hat back on. It is indicative of the antiquity and ubiquity of the gesture that the word came to mean any sort of return to a normal state: that it became possible to 'recover' from illness or mishap rather than to simply return to a hatted state. When two social equals met and bowed to each other, recovering was supposed to happen automatically and simultaneously. Delaying or jumping the gun could give the knife a further little twist if you were deliberately trying to annoy; both actions, if done in the right way, could imply that you didn't think much of the other person. Delaying your recovery worked particularly well when preceded by an exaggerated bow, part of a sarcastic display of your own superior breeding and manners. Jumping the gun could be employed where you wished your bow to seem insincere, a mere social nicety conveying no true respect.

Wherever there was social disparity, the superior person was supposed to give permission for the inferior to recover: 'It is ill said, Sir, be covered, or put on your hat, to one of more eminence than thy self' (*Youth's Behaviour*). Likewise, you could leave a subordinate hanging, waiting for permission to recover that never came. This was a tactic that Queen Elizabeth is recorded as using upon one memorable occasion when she left the French ambassador in a deep bow for a full quarter of an hour – which must have been quite excruciating, akin to one of the stress positions used in torture. Even monarchs, it seems, were tempted into bad behaviour upon occasion.

Permission to rise and recover was often given verbally but could also be given by a hand gesture. The hand had to be held low down so that the person with lowered head and eyes could see it while in the depth of their bow or curtsey and consisted of a small upward beckoning movement. A good deal of play could be made by refusing to recover in a display of courteous humility – a sort of 'I am not worthy' exclamation. Generally, a short pause was considered to epitomize the very height of refined manners, but keeping it up for too long clearly grated on some people's nerves. Manners writers, for instance, were keen to encourage a limit to the number of refusals; 'and therefore one ought to be covered after the first, or the most part after the second time', remarked the author of *Youth's Behaviour*. When invited to recover from a bow it was polite to refuse at the first request, but to refuse the second or third request began to put everyone in a difficult situation. The exchange became embarrassing and awkward and drew plenty of attention – marvellous!

All Kissy Kissy

You might also have noticed the kissing of hands being mentioned as one of many courtly gestures of the time. This was understood by both the Italians and the English to be an addition inspired by the Spanish, although it had pan-European antecedents within Catholicism. The English had become accustomed to the gesture in the first half of the sixteenth century through influxes of Spanish courtiers accompanying Katherine of Aragon and later her daughter's husband, Philip of Spain. In the Elizabethan period, it made another appearance through the third-hand lens of French dancing masters who had been influenced by Italian manners. Italian practice had in its turn been heavily influenced by Spanish custom through the royal court in the Kingdom of Naples, ruled at that period by Spain.

According to James Bulwer (a divine who sought through his book *Chirologia* to help preachers communicate effectively by employing hand gestures in their sermons), by 1644 kissing a hand had become the single gesture 'most frequent in the formalities of civill conversation' and took a number of forms. To kiss the back of someone else's hand was a mark of loyalty, respect and humility, and was particularly used by social inferiors to those of great worldly position and prestige. You doffed your hat, stepped forwards in an elegant bow and picked up their hand, bent your body over it and planted your lips squarely on the centre of the back of their hand. If the person was especially prestigious, or a woman, you might well forego touching the hand with your lips, simply hovering a fraction over the hand in a move that implied you didn't feel worthy to actually touch their hand with your lips. Rather trickily, the gesture of offering your hand to be kissed had, by the 1640s, come to be seen in England as rather arrogant, a mark of overweening pride. This, alas, had the potential to either leave a hand half-offered hanging in the air, or be responsible for the ungainly business of a determined petitioner making a grab for a hand that had not, in fact, been offered. As a result, court etiquette across the Continent laid down strict rules about whose hand and in what circumstances this sort of hand kissing was supposed to occur, attempting through codification to reduce the potential embarrassment.

Kissing the hand of a lady. Notice how she offers a softly falling hand, both elegant and negligent.

Then there was the question of gloves on or gloves off. The high-born kept them on in order to distance themselves physically from the supplicant, giving weight and significance to taking the glove off before offering the hand, which was taken as a mark of special favour.

This hand has been kissed and is being offered towards the recipient of the gesture.

Another form occurred where the higher ranked individual did not offer a hand, gloved or naked, but instead the person of lower rank kissed the back of his own hand and then gestured, with the kissed back of the hand, towards the object of his devotions. This was by far the most common form in England. The difference between looking like an elegant gentleman and appearing a ham-fisted clown lay in the shape of the hand and the smoothness of the movement. Once again, the key here is to think like a ballet dancer. Hold your hand in an open soft curve with the middle finger just very slightly bending inwards more than the index finger.

Avoid anything that looks bent or stiff or twisted. When you bring your hand to your lips make sure that you don't jerk it; move, if anything, with slightly exaggerated slowness. As you raise the hand the palm will be facing your body, but as it approaches the lips turn at the elbow gently so that the palm is facing downwards when you actually touch your lips to the back of the hand. Don't aim for the centre of the hand but, rather, lightly graze the knuckle of your index finger with your lips, turning the palm back towards yourself as you complete the kiss. This kissed section of hand is now offered straight towards the object of your courtesy, the palm of the hand still facing you in a large, slow, sweeping gesture.

There were a huge number of ways to embarrass yourself, or the person you were saluting with a kiss. Awkward jerky performances could make you look like a country clown but were nothing in comparison to muffing the timings. Choosing to offer your hand, naked or gloved, or not at all, thrusting your hand at someone who has made no attempt to reach for it yet, or alternatively being late in offering your hand were all possibilities if you were the kissee. If you were the kisser, you might make a grab too early or leave it a fraction too late or fail to coordinate the bow movements with the hand kissing. Wet slobbery kisses could easily offend and disgust, but elaborate air kissing could seem disdainful. Even when you employed your own hand the gesture could be mistimed or inappropriate or just plain clumsy.

Hand kissing was not restricted to court or even to elite venues, but could be seen up and down the country out in the streets, between courting couples and good friends of many social classes. 'To bring the hand to our mouth and having kissed it, to throw it from us, is their expression who would present their service, love and respect to any that are distant from them. A gesture that I have often observed to have been used by many at publique shews, to their friends, when their standings have been remote,' observed James Bulwer of a more general outdoor version of the kissed hand.

However, there was more to kissing than hands. Erasmus never mentioned it in his book of manners, confining himself to the norms of formal public behaviour, but in a letter to a friend way back in 1499 he records the English practice with enthusiasm:

> *there is a fashion which cannot be commended enough. Wherever you go, you are received on all hands with kisses; when you take leave, you are dismissed with kisses. If you go back, your salutes are returned to you. When a visit is paid, the first act of hospitality is a kiss, and when guests depart, the same entertainment is repeated; whenever a meeting takes place, there is kissing in abundance; in fact whatever way you turn, you are never without it.*

This, however, was not courtly behaviour and woe betide you if you launched into kissing your lord and master uninvited. You could cause havoc with such overfamiliarity, if you were willing to suffer the consequences.

Kissing was acceptable, and indeed compulsory, in more private, equal and personal interactions. Samuel Kiechel was a merchant from the city of Ulm in Swabia, Germany, who visited England in 1585 and remarked in his journal, 'when a foreigner, or an inhabitant, goes to a citizen's house as a guest, and having entered therin, he is received by the master of the house, the lady, or the daughter, and by them welcomed – as it is termed in their language – he has even a right to take them by the arm and to kiss them, which is the custom of the country, and if anyone does not do so, it is regarded and imputed as ignorance and ill breeding on his part'. Now, reading this, and in light of more modern manners, you might think that he, and Erasmus before him, was referring to hand kissing, or perhaps air kissing. A female character in John Marston's 1605 play *The Dutch Courtesan*, however, makes the nature of the kiss quite plain as part of her complaint: 'Boddy a beautie! Tis one of the most unpleasing injurious customs to ladys; any fellow that has but one nose on his face, and standing collar, and skirts also lined with taffety sarcenet, must salute us on the lipps'. Her complaint continues with moaning about the uncomfortableness of stubble and beards. You don't see any of this in the costume dramas, do you!

While foreign observers were particularly struck by mixed-sex kissing, same-sex kissing may have been just as important and as prevalent. War was to make the male kissing habit just that little bit more visible and public.

In August 1642, long-standing political tensions broke out into open warfare when Charles I raised the Royal Standard at Nottingham, intending to use military force to put down what he saw as a rebellion by Parliament. The ensuing years of bloodshed, civil war and the execution of the King swept aside the influence of the court upon personal behaviour, at least for some people, for a generation. Surely, you might think, Oliver Cromwell and all those Puritans didn't go in for kissing and well-stretched right legs.

Like so many civil wars before and since, and despite the huge numbers of ordinary people who lost their lives, the English Civil War was essentially a struggle for power between two sections of the elite. In a horrendously oversimplified sense, the lines were drawn between those members of the elite who identified with the court and its courtiers and those who identified themselves with the traditions of the country gentleman. I am sorry to reduce such a complicated, important and bitter struggle down to such caricatures, but for the purposes of understanding what happened to good and bad manners it can be broadly helpful. The court faction quickly attracted the epithet 'Cavaliers', a name that was intended as a bitter denunciation, focusing not on their politics but upon the cultural affinities of the King's supporters. 'Cavalier' was the French term for gentleman and it encapsulated the hostility that many people felt towards courtiers trained by French dancing masters in French courtesies in a court with a French-born (and Catholic) Queen.

Look, for example, at a political pamphlet printed in London (stronghold of the Parliamentarian cause) in 1643, following the defeat of the King's forces at Edgehill, entitled 'The Welch-Mans Complements'. Pre-war, the popular stereotype of the Welshman – at least as far as Londoners were concerned – was bound up with leeks, toasted cheese and poverty. This piece of political triumphalism was ostensibly about a Welsh gentleman returning to his sweetheart after running away from the battlefield. The Welsh had in the main sided with the King so the partisan nature of the

Courtly hand kissing.

image is clear. The words make considerable reference to cheese toasting and parody a Welsh accent, but rather than poverty we are treated to an image of a very well-dressed gentleman executing a courtly posture, the very one, in fact, that is described by de Lauze when a gentlemen bowing to a lady rises from the bend, disengages his right foot behind and begins to speak. It even appears that he has kissed his hand. Manners and political affiliation are here portrayed as synonymous. The high-fashion behaviours of court in the 1620s and '30s were now viewed as partisan. A court bow was increasingly understood by many in this newly divided land to symbolize sympathy with foreigners, Catholicism and royal tyranny.

Meanwhile, this opposing group found themselves

being dubbed 'Roundheads' in a sneer derived from their conspicuous lack of fashionable hairstyles. At least as far back as the 1580s, as we have seen, those with court etiquette training had been sneering at those without such experience, and country gents as well as prosperous townsmen had felt wrong-footed and embarrassed by their own lack of sophistication. It all seems very petty in the context of war, but we human beings can be petty. Years of feeling slighted, ridiculed and shut out do colour our judgements of even the most important issues of the day. Few of us are totally dispassionate when we weigh up the advantages or disadvantages of a major political decision. Facts, figures and logic are seen through a tinted lens of personal relationships and feelings. And the 'Cavaliers' had been hurting the feelings of the 'Roundheads' for quite some time. Let me emphasize once again that I am not claiming that the Civil War was just caused by a collective fit of pique. I am pointing to a cultural divide and suggesting that it broadly aligned with the political and religious fault lines running through society and may have played a part in bolstering them.

If, then, you were a gentleman who sided with Parliament in this conflict, how should you greet a fellow officer? Some Frenchified court bow would have seemed most inappropriate, but that did not mean that you were willing to throw away all expressions of respect and courtesy. The need for such gestures had been instilled in you from childhood. Nor would you wish to abandon something that lent you gentlemanly status in the eyes of those around you. Maintaining social distance between the gentleman officer and his common men, could, if anything, be more of a concern for the Parliamentarian than for one of the King's party. Parliamentary gentlemen, busy overturning one form of the ancient social order, could be very anxious indeed not to let too many cats out of the bag in case they woke up one day to find themselves suddenly at the bottom of the social heap. At the end of the Civil War, when soldiers and Levellers were discussing the future state of Parliament over in Putney, fears that social privilege might be overturned completely seemed very pertinent. How many gentlemen would have been comfortable with the idea of every man over the age of twenty-one having the vote, I wonder? The maintenance of social distance and order cut close to the bone. Outward forms were not something to be neglected. But which outward forms?

Or maybe you were a London apprentice who had joined up to fight against the King and his courtiers; you were in your early twenties and Parliament was winning; you had heard the speeches of Lilburne and everything seemed possible. How much should you abase yourself in front of one of your officers? As much as before the war? And who was he anyway? Some minor gent you had never heard of? Were all men equal in the eyes of God? It was all very difficult and there were no nice, simple pre-agreed rules, manners books or dancing masters to help. People were casting about for respectful forms of address that felt traditional and English, that were sufficiently honourable and not tainted with foreign insincerity.

One of the forms open to them was the kiss on the lips. As we have seen from the account of Samuel Kiechel, the kiss was an uncontroversial traditional greeting gesture between equals in non-formal or semi-formal situations. It also carried memories of the old religious 'kiss of peace', a gesture used as part of formal Church-brokered reconciliations. Unlike many other older religious gestures, such as making the sign of the cross, the kiss of peace somehow moved fairly comfortably across from Catholic into Protestant practice. There is, by way of illustration of this usage, a fabulous wall painting within Knightsland farmhouse near South Mimms in Hertfordshire depicting the return of the prodigal son painted around 1600. This is conventionally Protestant imagery and describes the reconciliation of father and son with an embrace and a kiss on the lips. Greeting one's equals with an embrace and a kiss therefore felt to many contemporaries like an honest and heartfelt form of respect,

Prodigal son: A full kiss on the lips between father and son. It echoes the old 'kiss of peace' and conveyed messages of reconciliation, welcome and hospitality.

unsullied by artifice and affectation.

For those with strong puritanical religious feelings it could be particularly attractive, emphasizing brotherly love and common endeavour under God. Meanwhile, war increases the need for peace, so it should be no surprise that a gesture of respect that encompasses all of these meanings should find fresh currency in military circles. At least one of the political pamphlets of the day, for example, carries an image of two military leaders standing at the front of their respective forces, dressed in armour, bareheaded, embracing and kissing each other. The pamphlet is all about a newly brokered alliance. We have no idea whether those two particular leaders did embrace and kiss upon that particular occasion but the imagery was chosen because of its easily understandable symbolism. This was exactly the behaviour that people expected to see from two godly and honourable leaders.

At the most radical edge of society, a number of small religious groups were also employing the greeting kiss with noticeable enthusiasm. In 1657, George Fox (widely seen as the founder of the religious group that came to be called Quakers) wrote, 'The Custome, and Manners, and Fashions of the World, which are practised among the people of the World, are vain; when they meet with one another, they will say how do you Sir, d'off the Hat, scrape a Leg, make a Courtesie. I am glad to see you well, your servant, your servant my Lord, (or Sir) or Mistresse, and when they are past them, with the same Tongue wish evil to them, speak evil of them, wish hurt to them.' Turning their backs upon all forms of hypocrisy and untruthfulness, as they saw it, became one of the central tenets of the Quaker faith and that meant that empty ceremonial gestures had to go. It was to prove a difficult business.

A number of problems arose, some of which were pointed out by Francis Higginson, a Puritan preacher, in 1653. He complained that when a Quaker met someone out in the street, he or she would simply walk on by, 'as though they were beasts rather than men, not affording a salutation, or re saluting though themselves saluted'. It was extremely disconcerting behaviour to everyone else. He went on to say that without the usual respect gestures and words, 'their departures and going aside to ease themselves are almost indistinguishable'. An odd turn of phrase perhaps, but it highlights just how deeply courtesy rituals were embedded within the daily rhythm of life. People encountering this lack of bowing and hat honour for the first time frequently assumed that the Quakers were mentally ill or incapacitated. In 1652, George Fox found himself by turns stared at and ignored as the bemused judge he was trying to speak to turned to the man he was with and asked whether George 'was mazed or fond'.

Bemusement often gave way to real anger and even violence as people interpreted the hatted and unbent posture as a major personal affront. In 1663, Benjamin Furly suggested a solution to his fellow Quakers to some of the issues this decision of conscience raised, declaring that 'giving the hand, falling on the neck, embracing, kissing' were all 'demonstrations of true honour' and could be substituted without compromising Quaker principles.

Friendly and Honest

Worries about the insincerity of the courtly respect gestures were nothing new and many people of varied religious and political outlooks expressed them, but unlike almost everyone else the Quakers were willing to abandon bows, hat doffing and curtsies entirely. Even other radical Puritan groups looked on in fascinated disgust, not so much at the kissing, which was perfectly acceptable among friends and relations, but at the lack of bows and hat doffing, which, together with the disrespectful use of 'thee' and 'thou', seemed even to them aggressively confrontational. If you had been under the impression that the offence offered by inadequate or inappropriate respect gestures was really rather minor or petty, please let the violence, beatings and imprisonment meted out to bow-refusing Quakers set you right.

For the less radical there were a number of ways in which you could round off the courtly edges of your bows. The Dutch provided a useful model here; they were well known internationally for the bluntness of their manners, and themselves sometimes boasted of this trait as one indicative of a people who were less beholden to great princes and aristocrats. When, for example, the Dutch translation of Antoine de Courtin's manners book, showcasing the very latest rules of etiquette at the French court, was published in 1672 it omitted several of the extra little flourishes for formal bows that were in the French original. Their ideal person worthy of respect was more often the prosperous merchant or senior townsman than the courtier. They were also frequent visitors to English shores and political and religious allies. Many military men had learnt their trade on the Continent alongside the Dutch so this was a familiar code of conduct among the second sons of gentlemen and merchant families alike. Naturally, they followed pan-European fashions in the main, doffing hats and executing bows, but it appears to have been in a toned down, simpler format and this chimed very well with what many Englishmen were looking for in troubled times.

One form that turns up quite often in period imagery is the completely straight-legged bow with the weight on the front foot. It can appear to be little more than a step forwards and lean, leaving the right foot trailing behind. Indeed, it can often only be identified in images because the person is bareheaded with their hat in their hand. Woodcuts produced in England, and paintings from the Netherlands, show this posture from the late Elizabethan period as a variant on the general bowing theme. It doesn't make an appearance in either manners books or dance manuals until late in the seventeenth century but it was clearly in use well before that. It is just possible – and this is mainly a guess – that this was a more merchant-class, townsman's bow to begin with. It may also have risen to prominence as a solution to the riding boots issue.

From the end of the sixteenth century onwards, boots for use on horseback were rather generously sized. Heavy and practical around the foot, ankle and calf, they had a tendency to balloon out fashionably around the knee, incorporating a large tuck or turn down. In the worst of weather, and while actually riding, they could be pulled up to protect the thighs, but when you dismounted this top section was folded down and sat large, stiff and wide at or just above knee height. Executing a court-style bow with double knee bends in such boots was a challenge. The straight-legged forward step and lean was much easier to manage, and during the hostilities, gentlemen in command of troops and accustomed to long hours in the saddle probably became very familiar with this simple form of bow.

Handshakes were another option. In 1607, a Scotsman living in Oxford published a manners book praising the 'good olde Scottish shaking of the two right hands together at meeting with an uncovered head'. It was, he felt, a much better and more honest gesture than all that French bowing. It certainly continued to be part of the greeting repertoire available in less formal situations and among equals in an English

Although more popular in Scotland, in England the handshake was mostly used for the settling of business and of quarrels, until its brief adoption by the more punctilious of godly souls as an alternative to bowing.

as well as a Scottish context. 'To shake the given hand is an expression usuall in friendship, peacefull love, benevolence, salutation, entertainment, bidding welcome, reconciliation, congratulation, giving thanks, valediction and well bidding,' said the same James Bulwer who told us about public hand kissing. I am sure you also noted that Benjamin Furly included it in his advice to fellow Quakers, and in the same year (1663) the English translator of Della Casa's book of manners, *Il Galateo*, inserted an extra line or two about the manners current in England, including the information that it was common to 'embrace one another in token of union and friendship, and shake hands to intimate a league and contract'.

With so many options to choose from and so many political and religious connotations to negotiate, the Civil War period and the interregnum that followed was one in which you could probably annoy, insult, disconcert, wrong-foot and outright insult someone somewhere no matter what you did or did not do. And since it was a time of violence and uncertainty you could provoke some really vehement responses in the process. Respect gestures had become a minefield.

The ceremonies of greeting that had long been employed to express respect and promote social harmony could now be used to highlight deep political and religious divides, to communicate contempt for a person's ideas and affiliations, as well as simple personal dislike. Offering a blunter or sloppier style of bow in return to someone who took care to be gentlemanly and precise could be a slur against their political position or the exact flavour of their Protestantism. Equally, a punctilious execution of a formal movement could do the same.

It wasn't just a simple matter of behaving badly to those whose allegiances fell on the other side of the martial boundary, either; you could express your distrust of and disrespect towards many of your own camp, too. Those who were judged to be lacking in enthusiasm for a particular cause might find themselves ostracized in this way. Nor was there any lack of opportunity for more general mischief. The greatest opportunities lay with the Parliamentary side where there was more experimentation with different forms – exploiting the widespread procedural uncertainty could be great fun. If you held back a moment, it was possible to see which greeting form someone was beginning to launch into, and then with fervour and exaggerated movements you simply initiated one of the alternatives, preferably one that didn't gel at all. As they stepped forwards with an outstretched hand you crushed them into an embrace and kissed them on the lips, for example. Or seeing them head for a clinch you employed your hat in a suitable flourish that put feathers up their nose.

The return of the King (well, his son Charles II) in 1660 saw an about-turn in this attitude, ushering in French ways in a French accent with added Frenchness. The royal family and all their closest supporters had spent their years of exile in Paris and become deeply imbued with French court etiquette and behaviour. The English gentlefolk waiting back home were aware that they would have to adapt if they were to ingratiate themselves with the right people in this new political climate. Blunter Dutch and Puritan manners were pushed aside. Hats were larger than ever and so were the feathers in them; bows were accompanied by more flourishes and were employed with greater frequency, while handshakes and kissing faded back out of view for the time being.

Manners, power and insult are intricately linked. Bows, curtseys, handshakes and kisses were all visual physical manifestations of the power relationships within society. Individuals regularly declared their social standing within each and every social group and encounter day in and day out. Greetings, moreover, provided ways of marking out in-crowds and outsiders. Quakers, for example, derived as much of their sense of identity from such rituals as did groups of young fashion-conscious courtiers. The draw for mischief-makers is clear: the more it matters, the more impact your misbehaviour has. While the subversions were often subtle, they could really hit their mark.

Giving the Finger

Beyond the gestures of respect, whether mishandled, over-laboured or deliberately ignored, there was a whole world of other gestures whose entire purpose was insult. A few are still familiar to us, others have disappeared entirely, and still more have meanings that have oscillated over time.

Firstly, we must bid adieu to the two fingers formed into a V and used in an upward jerk; it just didn't exist as a recognized gesture this early. There is a popular myth that it developed around the time of the Battle of Agincourt when Welsh and English archers defiantly displayed their bow-pulling fingers to the French. But, sadly, it's only a myth. Evidence of the gesture before 1900 is severely lacking, and after that it seems to have been confined to the working class in northern England until around 1930 and does not become an everyday expression in the rest of the Isles until the 1970s. (It still hasn't crossed the Atlantic to the USA, where the gesture is likely to be interpreted as a sign of peace!) But do not despair: there were plenty of other rude gestures of equal potency, both homegrown and foreign.

Paradoxically, you may be more familiar with sixteenth-century continental rudeness than the British period versions. This is all the fault of William Shakespeare, who seems to have had a good working knowledge of just what annoyed a foreign aristocrat. In *Romeo and Juliet*, which is set in Italy, he has a character who declares that he will 'bite [his] thumb at you', and in *Henry V* Pistol refers to the gesture known as 'the fig of Spain'. The first of these obviously required a little explanation to his largely English audience, as Sampson says, 'Nay, as they dare. I will bite my thumb at them, which is a disgrace to them, if they bear it,' carefully pointing out to those who had never come across it that this was a gesture that attacked the victim's honour, and that letting it pass unchallenged would mark them as cowards. Within the play the ruse is successful in starting a street fight. This was excellent ethnographic knowledge upon the playwright's part, but also rather handily got around any censorship and offence issues. Here was a rude gesture, rude enough to provoke a fight, that Shakespeare could use upon the public stage without upsetting anyone except a few foreign diplomats and traders.

In modern Sicily you can still see a form of this gesture in use. An upright thumb held so that the pad points outwards is tucked behind the top front teeth and then flicked forwards out of the mouth towards the intended insultee. I have also seen a version in action on the outskirts of Venice – although I don't know if it was a native Venetian performing it – where the pad of the thumb was placed horizontally between the top and bottom teeth in a bite and then flicked out, rotating as it went so that the bitten pad was thrust forwards.

The 'fig of Spain' gesture warranted no explanation in the text of the play; this was a much better-known action as far as the London public were concerned. But whereas the thumb biting was expected to be enacted upon the stage, the 'fig of Spain' gesture is only spoken of and did not need to be physically performed to move the plot onwards (once again avoiding offence).

Known across Europe, but particularly common in both Spain and Italy, the gesture appears to have been popular as far back as ancient Rome and was then associated with fertility. In both Renaissance countries the words for fig and vulva were very similar (*fico* and *fica* in Italian, for example) and the name of the gesture had clearly become *mano fico* in a polite, euphemistic move. In English it was generally translated as 'fig of Spain', although it more literally means 'fig hand'. The hand is held in a fist with the thumb tucked inside protruding between the index and middle finger. Again, this one is still current in both Spain and Italy. It had also crossed over into English use, if only among the plebs, and perhaps only in the port cities where Spanish and Italian sailors were present to spread the habit.

So, biting your thumb would probably not have been all that

The fig of Spain, sufficient to provoke an Italian to a duel.

effective within these shores. A person needs to understand a particular movement in a deep and visceral manner if it is to create a genuine feeling of hurt and insult. Both parties must share a mutual interpretation of the movements for such a symbolic attack to take effect. When, for example, an Iraqi journalist threw a shoe at US President George W. Bush in 2008, the thrower meant it as a deep personal insult; in Iraq it is regarded as an expression of disgust and contempt. But if you look at the footage of the incident, it is clear that Bush experienced it simply as a random projectile; concerning from a security point of view, but of minor significance in and of itself. He missed the insult entirely. Rude gestures are deeply imbedded in cultural context, so de-contextualized they are empty and easily dismissed. Foreign Shakespearean gestures, therefore, were wet and wimpy things.

We do, however, have one English gesture that is recorded as actually provoking duels. It was known as a 'filip', and James Bulwer reports that Francis Bacon had a lot of trouble because of it when he was Attorney General during the reign of James I. Apparently, a number of rather persistent gentlemen petitioned him to have it made illegal. The law, they argued, granted redress to people whose honour and reputation were damaged by words, both written (libel) and

The filip, quite likely to provoke an Englishman to challenge you to a duel.

spoken (slander), so why not provide protection for those whose social standing was attacked by gestures? The 'filip' was causing great offence, damage to reputations and was inciting daily violence, particularly among the top echelons of society. Duels might well be illegal, they argued, but they were not going to stop until men had some recourse to justice for such insults, other than the sword.

The filip was a gesture of contempt: it demonstrated your assertion that the other person was worthless, useless, a bag of hot air with no substance and no true honour. With a filip you dismissed a person, their opinions and social pretensions. You performed it by bending your elbow and bringing your hand up to shoulder height. The palm was to face outwards and then you bent your middle finger and caught it upon the pad of your thumb, held for a moment and flicked it straight. When James Bulwer described this gesture in his *Chirologia* of 1644 he made it clear that it could be both a small 'triffling punishment' and 'a slur of disgrace if used to a man'. It all depended on how you wanted to take it, but it may also have depended upon how it was delivered.

This opens us up to the argument about how much we can infer from modern behaviours. The modern use of the V sign in Britain, or the single middle finger jerked aloft that is used on both sides of the Atlantic (more so in America, where Italian influence is stronger), can be carried out in a number of ways that communicate rather different emotions and meanings. A slow smooth raise of the fingers that wag a little back and forth at the end of the action, accompanied by a grin, can be cheeky and might even be used as an acknowledgement of a joke; a swift jerk upwards with a very sharp and defined stop, often accompanied by a stiff face, is extremely aggressive – a warning that we are but a breath away from violence. Could we perhaps assign a similar range for the filip? Would the same general variations in performance produce a similar gradation of meaning? A smooth, slow, languid delivery aimed in someone's general direction being a milder, more sardonic treatment, while a swift, forceful jerk and flick right in someone's face carried all the intimidation and insult needed to start a fight? Is this where a culturally learnt movement (of which we have definitive written evidence) joins with innate natural body language (which is a matter of surmise)? You might need a time machine to find out. If the Doctor ever does give me a lift in the TARDIS, it is one of the things on my list to check out. I promise to report back should it ever happen.

Clicking or snapping your fingers at someone was a milder version of the filip, more often applied to worthless things than people, but useful nonetheless for those lighter moments of derision and social put-down.

Not so much of an outright insult, but more an expression of your anger and passion, was thigh slapping. No one outside of pantomime slaps their thigh in Britain any more and the gesture now seems quite ridiculous; all the more so since even within pantomime the only character who indulges in the practice is an attractive young woman dressed up as a boy. But when the theatrical form was crystallizing at the end of the nineteenth century, thigh slapping still represented a sort of traditional physical shorthand for virile young men of adventure. In the seventeenth century it was the 'practise and conversation of common life ... so deeply imprinted in the manners of men, that you shall in vain persuade a man angry and enraged with grief to contain his hand from his passion'. It was a form of physical emphasis giving weight to your words, making them more aggressive and forceful, just as a modern V sign adds to the 'eff off' phrase.

Fist shaking was also used in much the same way. But while a shaken fist was something that an angry woman could get away with (particularly a non-elite woman), thigh slapping was the sole preserve of men. A woman wishing to add physical support to the enmity of her words used an entirely different gesture – one that few men would employ. Women made both hands into fists and planted them firmly upon their hips, palms facing backwards and elbows pointed out to the side. The finished position was slightly less emphatic than the movement into the posture, so timing was key. It was only at the very height of the invective that you brought your fists up and round, making the action large and firm with a strongly defined stop as fists reached hips. There was also a second version that only utilized one fist, leaving the other hand free for finger wagging. But more often the most effective deployment involved a two-fisted beginning, with one hand, generally the right hand, being later released from the hips and brought forwards into the finger wagging position. It is a much more familiar gesture to us today than the male version, for although both have largely passed out of daily usage, the female version has lingered longest; indeed, it still hangs on among more traditional citizens of African and Caribbean British heritage.

Both sexes employed the right fist beaten repeatedly against the palm of the left hand in a loud clapping motion to drive home a good insult – the more mocking the better. You use the little finger side of the fist against the palm, and if you keep the fist quite loose you can produce a reasonably loud sound in the process. Our old friend James Bulwer thought that it was a gesture particularly redolent of Billingsgate fish market,

which points quite firmly to its raucous feminine use. Fishwives who bought wholesale at the docks and then hawked their wares around the streets of London were notorious for their loud voices, quarrelsome ways and bawdy jokes.

Finger wagging was a more feminine gesture of reproof.

Accusations of stupidity were communicated by a hand mimicking the waggling of asses' ears held next to the head. Rather like the 'bunny ears' that were such a common mocking gesture of the 1970s and '80s, you could make the gesture next to your own head or stretch across and form them next to the head of your target.

The sign of the cuckold. It could be employed openly to someone's face, or sneakily behind their backs for the enjoyment of onlookers.

It is possible that the twentieth-century 'bunny ears' were a descendant of the earlier 'asses' ears' gesture, although the finger positions are different. While 'bunny ears' consisted in my own youth of the index and middle finger being held aloft with the thumb holding the other two fingers down, the palm facing forwards (unlike the V sign) and the two upright fingers bent over and waggled, the sixteenth- and seventeenth-century 'asses' ears' used the index finger and the little finger (known at the time as the ear finger) with the middle two held down and the thumb held hard up against the temples at the side of the head. One small change in your performance of this gesture, however, and you entered different territory, one containing a world more hurt. Hold those two fingers stiff and still without the waggle and this was the gesture signifying a cuckold.

Gestures were wonderful as accompaniment to words, rounding out the insult and attracting attention in noisy crowded spaces, just as Robert and Thomas Talbott did at the alehouse in Upwey, Dorset, in 1625, when they kept up a display of 'beating their breeches' while calling for the local constable to 'come and kiss their tayles'. But gestures were also useful when used in stealth mode behind people's backs. They could play to the larger audience, provoking titters and guffaws at the expense of the intended victim, or give you the last word as you made your escape. Another added advantage was that lack of legal redress we mentioned earlier. Calling someone a cuckold verbally could provoke a case for slander, but following them around making the gesture for all to see was perfectly legal, and if they tried to thump you for it, why, that was assault!

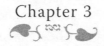

Chapter 3

MOCKERY

Anything that is held to be superior, right, true and proper lends itself to mockery. The higher a person or idea is raised to, the further it can fall and the more satisfaction available to the one who does the mocking. It is dangerous, of course, to ridicule the powerful and culturally dominant so a high degree of sensitivity is required to judge how far you can go.

The Ministry of Silly Walks

Take up a large wooden spoon and thrust it into your girdle on the left-hand side. Rest your left hand upon it with your elbow jutted out to the side at the sharpest possible angle, throw your weight as far back as you can, swing your right arm in an exaggerated manner and walk with your feet six inches apart. Yes, you too can mock a soldier, raise a laugh from your friends and a blush from the martially minded – especially if you are a member of the female sex, and thus less likely to be skewered for your pains. Soldiers moved and held themselves differently to other men. They learnt to advertise their calling in very physical ways, ways that were easy to parody if you were so inclined, and since soldiers were renowned for causing trouble and being something of a social nuisance, many people felt the need to ridicule them as a form of revenge.

So, why the silly walk? There is a small amount of practical justification that derives from the clothes and equipment that a soldier carried, but much of the reason is purely cultural, an interpretation of a perceived need for 'bravado' or 'bravura'. Military manuals frequently refer to the need for men to cultivate an aggressive and proud demeanour, to carry themselves confidently and challengingly, to project an aura of 'bravery' (a word that has slipped in meaning over the years). The 'brave' soldier was a man always ready to fight, poised for action. Such a mindset was considered necessary in order to be effective in what was still a fairly up-close-and-personal kind of warfare, and it was believed that bravery was promoted and maintained by the physical enactment of appropriate body language.

The feet apart, or 'legs akimbo', element of this martial posture, whether walking or stationary, harked back to the days of knights in heavy armour seated on horseback. It was a stance that both chainmail and plate armour had previously forced a man into; likewise, the heavy clothing that protected legs from chafing when riding. However, changes in warfare meant that armour became lighter and less all-encompassing, and fighting on foot became more common. Military clothing and armour could still encourage a wide-legged gait for the cavalry, for example, but unarmoured musketeers and others had no such excuse.

Our most famous image of Henry VIII has him standing with his feet apart, despite wearing court dress in a completely non-military context. His feet face forwards and slightly outwards but are well separated, in line with, or even beyond, his shoulders. It was a visual reminder that he was commander-in-chief. Indeed, he owned several sets of plate armour, took part in jousts (a seriously anachronistic pastime akin to historical re-enactment) and was well practised in several of the martial arts; he also rode well and hunted often. But this stance was about conscious display, projecting himself as a man of action, a knight of old, a player on the European stage of warfare. In short, it was a load of bluff. The posturing was the thing. Henry was good at the posturing; not only are his feet firmly and aggressively placed but his weight is in just the right spot with shoulders held open and back, and chin tucked in. Get it wrong and the power of the posture is quickly eroded. Any sort of bend at waist or hip reduces the impact severely. If the chest shows the slightest hint of collapsing inwards the illusion is lost, and if you fail to tuck in the chin you look like a nervous upstart who is trying to cover his insecurities with arrogance by staring down the length of his nose. Of course, when the King makes a habit of standing in this martial manner, everyone else copies him, whether they are soldiers or not.

Henry VIII in a manly martial pose. When the King chose to project such a military image with his posture and gait it was inevitable that men and boys would follow in a similar vein.

Erasmus, in his advice to children at this time, was clear that such a stance was wholly inappropriate in small boys – but he also knew that he was fighting something of a losing battle: 'see that thy knees and thy feet be close together, also when thou doest stande, that at least ther be meanly open'. If he couldn't persuade the lads to a completely civilian stance, he was willing to settle for a toned-down version of the kingly legs akimbo posture. Boys could be permitted to aspire to a manly, soldierly set of body language so long as they didn't adopt the full form. Boys being boys, I imagine many of them took great delight in such mimicry.

Moving while maintaining the weight, shoulder, chin and feet-apart combination is a learnt action that requires practice.

The gait you are aiming at is a swaggering one. Strides need to be long and fairly slow. Maintaining that distance between the feet throws your body into a slight roll from side to side. If the speed, stride and emphasis are right this looks like a confident swagger, but if the steps are too short you start to waddle, and oh what a fool you look then. One trick that helps bolster your manly, martial pride is to use an inverse curve to your stride. As your foot leaves the ground allow it to swing naturally inwards to the centre so that it passes under you, then as the stride reaches forward force it back out a little to the side. Don't overdo it, though, unless you want to be laughed at. Erasmus is quite scathing, and not a little xenophobic: 'be not wavering from one side to the other, and therefore let us leave it to the menne of warre of Swicherlande', he writes. Arms get in the way with this wide walk, so tucking your thumbs into your belt, or placing hands on hips is helpful. Again, Erasmus has something to say about this, claiming that to set your hand on your side was to 'smell of a manne of warre'.

An elbows-out posture commanding as much personal space as possible

Swiss mercenaries were famous across Europe for their military prowess and their extravagant clothes and strutting.

adds significantly to the confident, challenging and aggressive look. Think of it rather like the 'manspreading' that happens on public transport, where aggressive young men sitting on bench-style seats spread their legs wide, encroaching upon the seats to either side, daring people to object to their unfair command of the available space (and yes, Erasmus advises against this, too; although clearly not in the context of buses and trains).

The military walk was very capacious; it impinged upon other people even when the soldier was unarmed. The addition of a sword and buckler (a type of small shield) permitted the swagger to become 'swashbuckling'. Both sword and buckler were worn upon the left hip. The sword was held in a 'hanger', which hung off your belt and kept the sword at a useful forty-five-degree angle with the hilt resting on the ball joint of the hip at the top of the thigh. Such positioning made it easy to draw and also held it fairly steady as you moved. The buckler could be tied or hooked firmly to the belt just behind the sword where it too would be steady, but many a young man preferred to allow it to hang more loosely so that it clattered and 'swashed' against the sword as they swaggered down the street drawing plenty of attention.

Imagine the scene then: a young man full of martial pride, striding along, head held high, shoulders back, with a wide swaggering gait, turning heads as he goes, tailed at a distance by a woman with a wooden spoon and a gang of boys all wagging their hips from side to side, almost falling backwards from the extremity of their lean, elbows as pointy as can be, gales of laughter echoing down the street.

If you were willing to put your soul at risk rather than your physical safety, mimicking the clergyman's walk could be just as much fun. This group, too, cultivated a distinctive method of locomotion – almost the polar opposite of the man of war. It's generally described as a 'halting' walk and, in contrast to a soldierly gait, the steps are small. Elbows are tucked in and hands are generally employed holding something, ideally a book of godly content. It's all about visible humility, the antithesis of 'bravura'. Of course, it can easily verge on 'holier than thou' territory, and it was this interpretation that made it so deliciously ripe for mockery. Many a parishioner riled by the contents of a sermon, or young chorister admonished for inattention, relieved their feelings with a parody. Again, the walk was a long-standing habit; Erasmus, writing in a still-Catholic era, says that he has seen bishops who 'glorify' in such a 'manner of going', and mystery plays mention friars and other 'halting' clergymen. In a later, Protestant age, Thomas Nashe in 1595 describes hypocritical Puritans that 'have Bibles always in their bosome' and are 'heaving uppe their eyes to heaven'. It was a very recognizable set of physical habits that distinguished them as members of a godly community, one that was utterly separate and distinct from that of war, conflict and earthly pride.

Dress played a part here, just as it did for the martial gait. Whatever the details of true liturgical dress prescribed by the Church at any one time, the ordinary streetwear of divines tended towards the black, ankle-length gown. Such a garment was a symbol of learning, authority and gravitas, and it wasn't restricted solely to the ordained minister of religion but encompassed anyone in senior, sober authority. Mayors and aldermen wore full-length gowns (usually in a variety of shades of red); older, wealthier merchants, scholars and lawyers also wore black and dark-coloured versions. The use of such clothing among civilians allowed them to be acceptable clerical wear even for those religious sects that favoured simplicity of dress over ceremonial robes. A minister of severe Calvinistic leanings could wear a black full-length gown with a clear conscience as much as a Laudian High Church Anglican could.

The gown, of course, does not dictate a halting, faltering step, but it does encourage a shorter step. Large strides in a heavy gown are quite wearing as you are forcefully knocking against the fabric with each step, and nor do those movements look elegant in such garb. The gown hangs in one full sweep down from the shoulders, obscuring waist and hips, and discouraging any elbow pointing or tucking of thumbs into belts. Since hanging your arms by your side tends to leave you rubbing and getting caught up in the loose fabric, it is

Ankle-length gowns were the preferred clothing of learned men of all professions.

generally more comfortable to keep the arms up in front, and holding something makes this feel much less awkward.

But again, just as with the military walk, practical considerations are only part of the story. Culturally, it made sense for this group of men to make themselves visibly unique in their movements. Standing out in a crowd was part of their calling as leaders of their flock. Ministers frequently defined themselves as 'men of peace', so it made absolute sense for them to avoid the aggressive elbows and swaggering stride of 'men of war'. The 'halting', however, was frequently seen by hostile contemporaries as an affectation. It may be relevant here to remember a verse from Richard Weste's *The Book of Demeanor*, written in 1619 for the use of upper-class lads:

> *In going keep a decent gate,*
> *Not faining lame or broken,*
> *For that doth seem but wantonnesse,*
> *And foolishnesse betoken.*

The clergy were in just such danger; they had taken, it seemed, a natural gesture of the humble mind and formalized and magnified it into a regular and deliberate tick, a counterfeiting of humbleness rather than the real thing.

During the latter half of our period, the walk spilled over from the ordained community and became the signature of the newly confident and 'Godly People', whom many called Puritans. Men, and some women, who wished to emphasize the legitimacy and sincerity of their newly emerging religious positions found this public form of expression ideal. The halting walk was immediately recognizable as one of heightened spirituality and was eminently respectable. A change in dress in order to advertise one's adherence to these rather fashionable beliefs could be interpreted as vanity, but a change in behaviour escaped such reproofs without in any way diminishing their visual impact. A positive rash of halting walks seems to have resulted. A godly fashion.

Almost immediately the walk gained a new reputation: it was affected and dishonest. Those who moved in this way were hypocrites who publicly espoused high morals while privately behaving badly. Mimicking the walk for comedic effect took on political and religious significance. Those who did so, whether on the street, the stage or in print, were declaring their opposition to the rise of the Puritan as a force in society. And it was infectiously funny. At full magnification, as performed by someone seeking to raise a laugh, the halting and the casting up of the eyes to heaven could be made to look like the performance of a demented chicken.

The walk of civic pride.

In London there were other groups whose walks could cause a smirk or two and prompt the mischievous to perform a parody. The ploughman or country bumpkin was sneered at in print and on the stage as well as on the street. There were several ways to spot one: accents and clothes were good indicators, but so was the walk. Ploughing involves a lot of tramping in churned-up mud. Just think of a ploughed field: each and every furrow was individually ploughed by a man who walked behind, up and down, back and forth. Freshly churned up, the mud stuck to footwear making each step heavy. Years of such toil unsurprisingly shaped a man's gait, and boys growing up in the countryside surrounded by ploughmen tended to unconsciously copy the walk of the men around them. Ploughmen 'plodded' along, their walk was heavy, their arms dangled by their sides in a way that manners book writers thought particularly ugly and was easy to mimic.

If you got tired of mocking the rustics, you could always turn your attention to the foreigners. The Spanish above all others were marked out by their movements, displaying a stiffness that seemed completely unnatural to the English. The more upper class and educated a Spaniard, the more exaggerated his bodily control, so that while Spanish sailors stood out only a little, the Spanish ambassador and his senior staff were particularly noticeable. The stiffness came in two forms: a suppression of gesture and a lack of twist. Right across Europe, writers on manners, education and dancing were advocating more restraint, praising self-control and precision of movement. But at different times and places different elements of bodily control caught the attention and formed the focus of authors' works. We have, for example, already noted a shift from table manners to conversation and a rise in the complexity of greeting ceremonies. The Spanish were unusual in the vehemence of their suppression of gestures accompanying speech, while the Italians, although paying extensive lip service to this idea, were generally described by other Europeans as inveterate hand wavers. The Spanish barely gesticulated at all, something that everyone else found rather odd. They were also loath to twist their bodies at waist, hip or neck, preferring to turn with their feet. Yet again we have to acknowledge the influence of clothing here. Spanish fashion adopted very high collars and long stiff body fronts for both men's doublets and women's bodices in the mid-sixteenth century and the Spanish hung on to this style well into the seventeenth century, far longer than any other nation. Indeed, the fashion for such things in England was a deliberate copy of Spanish fashion at times when the countries were politically close (the reign of Mary I and the early years of Elizabeth I) and faded away when England's political alliances began an eastward shift to first France and then the Netherlands. Whether the clothing dictated the posture or the posture encouraged the clothing style to show off the fashionable deportment is a difficult question. It could easily have been something of a feedback loop.

The most popular walk to mock, however, was the walk of fashion. Everyone was keen to get in on the act; popular ballad writers had as much to say as worthy Calvinist preachers, playwrights, poets and pamphleteers. Dedicated followers of fashion came in both sexes, which added to the fun, and fashion's habit of continual change kept everything fresh and amusing. We have already touched on one fashionable walk with Henry VIII's military gait. In truth, elements of the martial walk continued to play a role in male strutting throughout our period in times both of peace and war, but we have also seen one of the additional influences coming into play when we talked about the French-style courtier bow, and we are going to see a couple of other touches come and go. Women's walks have thus far been sadly neglected (apart from a brief mention of the insult 'waggletail'), but fear not: we shall now have plenty of chances to raise a laugh. Making fun of women was, of course, much safer than mocking men, particularly men with clout.

At the beginning of the sixteenth century there was one conventional posture for the portrayal of all ladies of fashion, which was fairly consistent whether the subject was sitting, kneeling, standing or walking, and one that was widely depicted in tapestries, illuminated manuscripts and simple woodcuts. Now, you could argue that it was simply an artistic style, but it does happen to very closely match the few brief mentions of elegant behaviour and ideal deportment for women of the period. It is basically a matter of holding your hips pushed forward and lengthening the back of your neck. Try it standing first to get the feel. Feet together or a couple of inches apart with the toes pointing forwards, now with straight legs push your hips forwards leaving your shoulders behind. From the back of your heels to the vertebrae at the base of your neck your silhouette should form a gentle bowed curve. Now lengthen the back of your neck so that you are looking straight ahead and not down the length of your nose. Looking down your nose at someone has long described the

With her hips pushed forwards and the back of her neck lengthened, tipping her chin downward, this lady is the very picture of fashionable courtly female posture at the beginning of the sixteenth century.

arrogant behaviour of those who pretend to a social position that they don't rightly hold; it's a physical result of copying fashionable posture badly, of only getting it half-right as some upstart or wannabe might do, rather than those who were trained in it from childhood. And the aristocracy certainly were trained in it. Take, for example, Lady Jane Grey's complaint to her new tutor Roger Ascham that her parents corrected her posture with 'pinches, nips and bobs', moulding her into an appropriately fashionable body. Like every other element of fashion, it was important to follow the method to exactly the right degree. In some times and places, the forward placement of the hips needed to be very pronounced; at the very beginning of the sixteenth century, panel paintings indicate that kneeling in prayer was one of those moments, particularly in the Netherlands. Images of English women generally show a more restrained version when sitting or kneeling, but it's still very much in evidence when standing or walking.

Walking in the hips forward position offers two basic gaits: the smooth and the bell-like. The smooth style requires a fairly short stride and a slow pace with a full, heel to toe, use of the foot. While the gentleman was advised to walk slowly so that he didn't look like a hurried servant, he was also advised not to walk too slowly, or he would look 'tortoise like' and 'so stately and affected like ... some lady of quality, or a bride', as the Italian writer Giovanni Della Casa describes. With the hips forward and the shoulders back, the lower ribcage is also pushed forwards and lifted somewhat, creating a very straight-fronted look from the bust down, showing off the smooth-fronted gowns to their best advantage. Hands are most comfortably carried in front, lightly clasped, with elbows bent at a little more than right angles in line with the bottom three or four ribs. It is stately, restrained, demure and also a bit pompous. It was a gait that was admirable for a great lady at court but any merchant's wife who went off to market like this could certainly expect to draw plenty of attention.

While most of the mimicry we have mentioned up to this point was derogatory in intention, designed to puncture egos, undermine authority, point out 'otherness' and encourage onlookers to join with the culprit in laughing at the victim, here we see a different sort of bad behaviour coming to the fore: social climbing. But is social climbing a bad thing? In the deeply hierarchical world of the sixteenth and seventeenth centuries almost everyone said that it was dreadful. God had chosen each individual's place in the world. Social climbing, therefore, was not only disruptive to the status quo but directly challenged God's plan. Of course, it all depended on your perspective. Other people trying to pass themselves off as higher up the ladder than they really were was shocking and wrong. But, naturally, your own attempts and those of your family were just, right and proper, not social climbing at all but simply good people making the most of what God had given them!

Body language is a particularly potent form of status indicator; it's very hard to ignore and affects our responses in a host of unconscious as well as conscious ways. If you are able to deploy it successfully, it is possible to gain many of the advantages of higher social status and greater respect without any further outlay. The woman in the wool gown who walks like a merchant's wife is treated like a merchant's wife, but the woman in a wool gown who walks like a lady is a lady upon hard times, or perhaps she is a lady of unusually humble devotion. Either way, she is likely to be treated with more consideration and respect as she goes about her business. It is easy to see, therefore, why so many people tried to mimic a lady's walk, and also why so many other people resented the attempt. What is less easy is pulling it off convincingly. Try it yourself: a cowboy act, for instance, with that strange bow-legged walk developed after long hours in the saddle. Hard, isn't it? It's fine for ten minutes or so, but then your concentration slips and muscles held in unfamiliar positions become tired. In the sixteenth and seventeenth centuries, there was a lot to be gained from mimicking one's betters at every level of society, but there was also plenty of room for error, for letting it slip for a moment, for getting one bit right and bungling another part. Those with an eye for mockery found fertile ground here. Mimicking Mrs Hoity Toity as she tried, and generally failed, to walk down the street with fashionable elegance could be a most satisfying exercise. Who does she think she is?!

Returning to the hips forward walk, the second option was the bell-like version, which was much sexier than the smooth version. Imagine that your long cone-like skirt is stiff like a bell, then use your hips to set it swinging forwards and back as you walk. Begin in the hip forward posture, then as each foot begins its forward journey let your hips slip back a little, just a fraction for a brief moment, before thrusting them forward again as you make the step. Too much and you look like a 'waggletail', vulgar, awkward and sexually available, but subtly done it gradually builds the momentum in your skirts into a slow and suggestive tolling. It's easy to see how ladies of negotiable virtue in their professional finery would have found the fashionable walk of court ladies very useful indeed upon the streets of London. Easy to see, too, how all that pelvic thrusting could be reworked for comic purposes among our band of mockers.

By the 1560s, many London women had adopted their own fashionable walk quite distinct from that of the aristocratic lady. Eschewing the slow and stately measure of high society, city women who wanted to look good 'tripped' along. The stride was still short but the speed was greater and an element of bounce was injected. Many borrowed a little from the clerical walk to emphasize their godly respectability,

This city miss with her body weight held well forward and head held high is all ready to go 'tripping' along.

'halting' as they went. The grim reaper in the 1569 ballad 'Remember Death' mocks all such vanities:

> *It makes me laffe oft times to see,*
> *their gate, their lookes, their walke,*
> *How halting tryps.*

While Richard Tarleton's ballad of 1592, 'The Crowe Sits upon the Wall', contains the line 'dooth she trip or dooth she taunt', juxtaposing a fashionable but respectable style with a more sexually explicit strut.

Tripping, or a slightly exaggerated version of it, clearly worked very well on stage, providing a visual expression of the stereotypical uppity and overly vocal city maid or wife. The description turns up again and again in a slightly misogynistic manner in so-called 'citizen' plays where the main protagonists are all contemporary London characters rather than kings, queens, historical or fantasy figures. The fact that actors mimicked the walk, or 'going', of women upon stage as well as wearing female clothing was one of the complaints that the preacher Adam Hill cited when he condemned stage players. The theatre provided a good model for those in need of additional inspiration for their street-based mockery.

'Mincing' was another word used to describe the gait of style-conscious city women. It is a word that begins to appear in plays and sermons at about the same time as the first high-heeled shoes. The heels were not all that high by twenty-first-century standards, rarely reaching two inches, but they were completely new, springing from a revolution in footwear construction known as the 'welt'.

Medieval shoes were sewn together and then turned inside out to protect the stitching and give a better look and a more waterproof shoe. Naturally, the leathers had to be soft enough and thin enough to 'turn'. The new system that emerged around 1500 allowed shoes to be much more substantial items. Welts were an additional narrow strip of firm leather that went between the upper part of the shoe and the sole. The upper and the welt were stitched together first and then turned much as before. The sole of the shoe, formed of the very thickest, strongest and most hard-wearing leather, could now be sewn flat onto the welt strip with no need for further turning. Traditional leather shoes are still basically made in this way. The shoes recovered from the wreck of the *Mary Rose* show how, by the 1540s, even ordinary sailors were shod in this new style. As the sixteenth century neared its end this construction method was further embellished for the more fashion-conscious by the addition of an arched heel formed of a leather-covered block of carved wood glued and pegged into place upon the sole. Such shoes tip the body weight forwards, and upon cobbles and other uneven surfaces 'mincing' ensues as the stride becomes even shorter to prevent a person from losing their footing.

The men who adopted heeled shoes were for the most part courtiers. They, and the court women who joined them, were traversing smooth, even floors that had much less impact upon their gait. City girls proud of their new shoes and eager to show off this affordable example of modernity and sartorial extravagance found themselves mincing in the bumpy street where once they had 'tripped' along.

Your walking style was further altered if you invested in pantobles (*chopine* if you were Italian, or *pantoffles* if you were French). These were a form of raised overshoe. They came in a variety of expense brackets, from simple wood and leather to velvet-covered cork, and are best thought of as platform shoes, capable of keeping you up out of the worst of the mud but more reliable as increasers of height and all-round status objects. The puritanical writer Philip Stubbes disliked them, particularly on account of the noise they made. People were 'faine to knock and spurn at every wall stone or poste, to keep them on … with their flipping and flapping up and down in the dirte, they exaggerate a mountain of mire & gather a hepe of clay and baggage together, loding the wearer with importable buthen'. They are prone to slipping off when you walk and it is tempting to surreptitiously push them back onto the foot more firmly against kerbs, steps and so forth. The pair that I have are about four inches high with a solid cork sole so they don't tend to gather muck, but many of the cheaper models had a wooden sole of about half an inch that was held aloft on a sort of open metal stand, and these do get clogged up with mud, leaves and any other street litter.

Helpfully, rather than just moaning about them, the Italian dance master Fabritio Caroso gave practical advice upon how to walk successfully and elegantly in *chopines* as well as some warnings about habits to avoid.

> *Some ladies and gentlewomen slide their chopines along as they walk, so that the racket they make is enough to drive one crazy! More often they bang them so loudly with each step, that they remind us of Franciscan friars. Now in order to walk nicely, and to wear chopines properly on one's feet, so that they do not twist or go awry (for if one is ignorant of how to wear them, one may splinter them, or fall frequently, as has been and still is observed at parties and in church) it is better for to raise the toe of the foot she moves first when she takes a step, for by raising it thus, she straightens the knee of that foot, and this extension keeps her body attractive and erect, besides which her chopine will not fall off that foot. Also by raising it she avoids sliding it along, nor does she make any unpleasant noise. Then she should put it down, and repeat the same with the other foot.*

It is a very unnatural movement and the muscles at the base of the calf quickly become strained and painful, but it does work. With a little practice it becomes possible to move with small steps both quietly and smoothly, even elegantly. Mind you, it is much easier to scuff along with your knees bent – quicker too, and delightfully ridiculous. It must have been a gift for actors playing the parts of comic female characters. Imagine the nurse in *Romeo and Juliet* scuffing noisily across the wooden stage at speed, pausing to knock her pantobles back into place as she passed the pillars on the stage, posture all awry, with knees bent and bum stuck out: 'Now, afore God, I am so vexed that every part about me quivers.'

Meanwhile, as Queen Elizabeth's reign passed its zenith, back among the ladies and gentlemen of fashion everything had gone diagonal. Toes pointed outward, feet and legs were held in a balletic fourth position, the body was turned at an angle to the viewer and the weight was borne unequally with the supporting hip pushed out. Henry VIII's square-on stance had become social death, a faux pas to be smirked at. So too the feminine forward-thrust hips. Movement and emphasis had swivelled to a more lateral plane; suddenly the position of shoulders began to rival feet in importance and twist acquired elegance. The alteration is much more evident in male posture, assisted by more revealing clothes, but a quieter, subtler change is also present in images of women.

When the dancing master de Lauze discusses the female walk he talks first of an erect head and a level eyeline then advises teaching correct walking technique by repeated practice: 'Then make her put her feet close to one another, the toes outwards, and thus holding her by the hands make her take some steps, sedately and in a straight line, in order that she may acquire the manner.' It's not a hugely helpful scrap of advice; except for its insistence on erect carriage of the head and turned-out toes, the actual business of walking is totally ignored. He was telling men to walk with completely straight legs, so presumably women were supposed to follow a similar pattern. The only other clue he gives is his repeated exhortations to smoothness of movement for women. His advice was clearly quite conventional by the 1620s as paintings show.

Around 1590, the hemline of women's skirts rose an inch or two, revealing shoes and feet positions for a period of about twenty-five years, and what we see are a lot of turned-out toes. In general, these pictures show us women standing with their heels about three to four inches apart while their toes are about a foot apart. Many, perhaps most, have one foot, almost invariably the right foot, slightly in front of the other in what could be described as an understated loose fourth position, and despite the closeness of the two feet you can generally detect a favouring of the body weight over the back foot. Shoulders closely mirror the position of the toes. It follows many of the same rules of posture that fashionable men were adopting but with less emphasis upon sideways pushed hips. The forward thrust has completely disappeared. Instead, Italian women were using a lot of hip action, one side at a time. It made for an attractive dance move, known as a '*continenza*', and a method of managing their skirts according to Caroso who clearly found the hip movements both elegant and attractive and far preferable to using hands to control fabric: 'she should never use her hands to lift her

train or the trail of her dress, for this looks most unseemly …
Instead … strutting a little and moving in a snakelike
way with a slight swaying of her dress and the farthingale
[a hooped petticoat] underneath it, thus obtaining the
same effect.' It's great fun to do and I personally have huge
difficulty at weddings restraining myself from running up to
the bride wearing the first full-length dress of her life and
saying, 'No, no dear, like this with your hips.' A skirt worn
over a farthingale, or indeed any other form of framework,
with or without a train, can be entirely managed with the
right wiggle and placement of feet. Even steps, so long as they
are not too steep, can be negotiated entirely without recourse
to touching the skirt with your hands.

If you are an inveterate visitor to Elizabethan and Jacobean
historic houses, as I am, you may have noticed that the formal
flights of stairs are rather shallow with the tread wider than
the rise. In my experience, moving up them while wearing a
floor-length dress can be managed by bringing your foot in
slightly across your body in an arc as you lift it then continue
it round so that it lands on the next step directly in front of
its original position. This crescent movement has the benefit
of engaging with the material of your attire at the centre
point and stretching it out slightly forwards and to the side
ensuring that a fold does not form in front of you. Keep your
body very erect as any forward lean makes the skirt longer at
the front. Just before your foot reaches the upper step raise
your hip. This lifts the fabric just enough to ensure that it
doesn't get between the sole of your shoe and the step. Repeat
the motion for each step. If you make the movement jerky or
try to replace erect posture with additional hip lift it can look

very strange indeed, but done smoothly, slowly and with an impeccably straight lengthened spine you simply sway gently as you rise. It is much easier if some kind gentleman takes your hand.

I don't, sadly, have any evidence of the side-to-side hip wiggling movements described by Italian dance masters in a purely English context, but Italian dancing itself was very popular and influential and French dancing masters (who were demonstrably present in England) were also heavily influenced by fashionable Italian practice. What was taught primarily for the ballroom also informed daily court life more generally. Caroso himself describes the relevant dance move in great detail, insisting that it is the very foundation of grace and decorum in life. The feet do very little, just a small step to the left with the left foot and then bring the right foot to join it. The action is all in the hip, shoulder and the grace of arms and head. It begins with bending the left hip: 'be sure to keep your head erect; and do not drop your left shoulder … strutting slightly toward the side on which you are doing it; this effect is usually obtained by raising your heels a little, and immediately dropping them in time to the music'. Apparently, if you failed to do the hip swagger and simply moved the feet and let your body follow in a jerky manner you looked like you were about to urinate.

Copying foreign movements (possibly including the hip wiggle) inspired irritation and contempt in many observers. In 1588, the author William Rankins moaned that 'English men blinded (with an Italian disguise) and disfiguring themselves (with every French fashion) corrupt their natural manners (by their climate created perfect) with the peevish pelfe of every peacokes plume!' While the historian and writer James Howell around sixty years later was noting how easy it was to spot those who had travelled abroad by their 'gait and strutting, their bending in the hams and shoulders', which does sound rather reminiscent of the Italian dancing master's words.

By the time that Charles I was losing his temper with Parliament and embarking upon his personal rule deep in his belief in the 'Divine Right of Kings' at the end of the 1620s, those wishing to mimic the overly fashionable had a straight-legged, mobile-hipped style of walk to master that required every pause or stop to begin and end with an exaggerated adoption of a diagonal twist to the body. The person you were addressing was faced mostly with your shoulder – usually the right one – over which you peered at them in a deliberately languid fashion with your weight all slouched back over your left hip.

The *Guls Hornbook* has one further, rather unsavoury, comment to make about fashionable walking styles. Dekker advises his men to invest in the very widest topped boots: 'Besides, the strawling, which of necessity so much lether between thy legs must put thee into [the strange, straight-legged, circling walk with the legs kept far apart] will be thought not to grow from thy disease, but from gentleman-like habit.' In short, the high fashion walk of the 1620s gent made him look like he was suffering from the advanced stages of venereal disease, probably syphilis, rotting his genitals.

Just like accents, walking and movement styles could mark a person out as belonging to a particular group, generally one bounded by occupation or social class, but they were also sensitive to geographical factors and generational change. It was a very public mark of separation, too. Whereas an accent is discernible only if one speaks, and then only to a small circle of hearers, the way you move through the streets is open to everyone's gaze. You could spot a halting priest several hundred yards away and tell a mincing city miss from an aristocratic, hips forward lady from across the river. You could also spot who was faking it: the young blood who fancied himself as a soldier, the puritanical zealot trying just that bit too hard to look pious, the Spaniard hoping to pass himself off as a local. All of them provided excellent fodder for alehouse wit, the writers of scurrilous ballads and those who simply pointed and jeered. For some it could be a cathartic release of frustrated ambition to stir up raucous laughter in the street by parodying the behaviour of a newly minted mayor attempting a posher walk. Others used mockery to pursue their political agendas, ridiculing members of the court elite with their Cavalier, 'strawling', straight-legged walk or conversely hounding the puritanical godly crew who 'halted' as they went.

However, if mockery with movement was not your thing, you could achieve much with your clothing choices.

Cross-dressing: an Abomination

Well, technically, yes, if you listen to Deuteronomy, which relates that cross-dressing is an abomination in the sight of the Lord. From about 1570 until 1630 there was an almost continuous trickle of puritanical preachers who thundered from the pulpit upon this theme and had those thunderings printed up for wider dissemination among the populace. According to these polemics, cross-dressing had become a major problem of the age; examples of such transgression were to be seen daily upon the streets, making a mockery of God's law and natural order. Other 'godly' writers, who were not actually members of the clergy at the time, joined in. Even King James I & VI got in on the act demanding that the clergy 'inveigh vehemently and bitterly in their sermons' against the wearing of inappropriately gendered clothing. So how exactly did you go about annoying such high-minded types with your clothing and just how much trouble could it get you into?

Well, you could be prosecuted in the church courts, as

The most famous image of the most famous cross-dresser of the age Mary Frith, also known as Moll Cutpurse.

cross-dressing was considered to be a moral rather than a civil or criminal matter. Mary Frith, who was arrested on Christmas Day in 1611, constituted the most famous case, both at the time of her arrest and subsequently. She was accused of wearing 'indecent' clothing. There was also talk of other immoral behaviour, but it was the 'indecency' that stuck and earned her a session of public humiliation at St Paul's Cross, appearing, as was usual in these shaming rituals, dressed in a white linen sheet. John Chamberland, who witnessed the punishment, observed that 'she wept bitterly and seemed very penitent', but on subsequently discovering that she had turned up for the session 'maudlin drunk' was not so convinced.

It was not exactly her first offence either; she had been

in trouble for theft on several previous occasions. Nor was it the first time she had dressed as a man. By all accounts she had been doing so for some years and not just in private. In truth, she was notorious for such behaviour, with not one but two plays being written and publicly performed the previous year about fictionalized accounts of her life. One penned by John Day, whose text is now sadly lost, was entitled *Madde Prankes of Mery Mall of the Bankside*, and the other, which not only survives but still gets fairly regular airings upon the stage, was entitled *The Roaring Girl* and was written as a joint endeavour by Thomas Middleton and Thomas Dekker. Quite what they tell us about the actual Mary Frith is a moot point; you should perhaps think of them as loosely based Hollywood-style biopics. There are, however, germs of truth in there somewhere if you know where to look. But things are further blurred by Mary's appearance, starring as herself in male costume, for one performance on the stage at the Fortune Theatre earlier in 1611. At a time when no women were allowed upon the stage by law it was an incredible example of self-publicity, public image manipulation and a determined and deliberate flouting of convention. Her subsequent career almost certainly included working as a fence for stolen property and the continued fashioning, by herself and others, of a range of flamboyant adventure stories that formed the basis of several best-selling texts.

Her work with stolen property, tying in with her notoriety in London, is illuminated by a court case involving Henry Killigrew in 1621, which was heard in the Star Chamber. Killigrew had been robbed of his purse by a prostitute and 'heard howe … many that had had theire pursses Cutt or goods stollen, had beene helped to theire goods againe and diuers of the offenders taken or discouered' by Mary Frith. Margaret Dell was arrested for the crime, brought to Frith's house by the constable of St Bride's in Fleet Street, where Dell was identified by Killigrew as the perpetrator in what probably amounted to a form of protection racket. As a fence Mary had a good knowledge of who the local thieves were and their various modus operandi. It is also possible that the goods had already been offered to her to sell on. In the case of Killigrew, and probably several other 'clients', she and the local constable promised to locate the culprit in exchange for a fee. It is likely, however, that thieves who had the nous to make it worth the pair's while were exempt from such public-spirited restitution.

As for the stories that circulated, they were many and various. Take one supposedly written by Frith herself in a pamphlet entitled 'The Life and Death of Mrs Mary Frith: Commonly called Moll Cutpurse' published in 1662, three years after her death. It concerned a wager with another colourful figure, William Banks, a horse trainer. His horse Morocco performed a variety of tricks including mounting the long flight of steps up onto the roof of St Paul's Cathedral. According to Mary Frith, Banks bet her twenty pounds that she would not ride through the city astride Morocco, dressed as a man. All went well, the account claims, until she reached Bishopsgate:

> *where passing under the Gate a plaguey Orange*
> *Wench knew me, and no sooner let me pass her,*
> *but she cried out! Mal Cutpurse on Horseback,*

*which set the people that were passing by, and the
folks in their shops a hooting and hollowing as
if they had been mad; winding their cries to this
deep note, 'Come down thou shame of Women or
we will pull thee downe'. I knew not well what to
doe, but remembering a Friend I had, that kept
a Victualling House a little further, I spurred my
Horse on and recovered the place, but was hastily
followed by the rabble, who never ceased cursing
of me, the more soberer of them laughing and
merrily chatting of the Adventure.*

Unfortunately, the dates don't quite line up. Banks and his
horse Morocco left England in 1601. Mary was born either
in 1584 or '89 (accounts vary) and although she had her first
brush with the law in 1600 she was not a well-known figure
for another few years. Perhaps the crowd reactions, which
sound fairly convincing, occurred at some other moment in
her life.

This, then, was England's most famous cross-dresser.
Following on from the plays, she appears in ballads, poems
and moral fulminations for several generations. If anyone
was going to feel the full weight of society's disapproval
of cross-dressing it was Mary. As a consequence of legal
proceedings, she suffered just this one episode of public
shaming and in much later life endured a spell in Bethlehem
hospital (Bedlam) for 'madness', which may or may not have
been connected to her sartorial habits. How she was regularly
treated in the streets of London we don't know. When I read
the accounts of her character I get a feeling of belligerence

and defiance, the sort of attitude that can develop in the face of regular bullying, but that is just my own gut instinct.

Mary was not the only cross-dresser to face legal proceedings. The numbers are small, just dotted here and there, and punishment as severe as the public shaming ritual, which was the same as that endured by adulterers and other moral offenders, was rarer still. Cases resulting in a small fine and being told not to do it again are more usual. Most seem to involve occasional incidents of cross-dressing as a part of merrymaking and fairly traditional and rumbustious games and celebrations rather than lifestyle choices.

The historian David Cressy highlights a particularly unusual and interesting case of a man dressing as a woman in 1633 in Tew Magna, Oxfordshire, when Thomas Salmon,

A mannish woman and a womanish man. She is wearing boots, spurs and dagger in addition to her masculine styled hat, short hair and skirts; while he is rendered feminine by his display of foolishness, holding children's toys (the shuttlecock and bat).

according to the witness statements, adopted female dress in order to take part in a traditionally all-female social occasion – a gathering in the birth room after a safe delivery. It was potentially a very unsettling incident, breaking some serious social taboos. In addition to pulpit thundering about the evils of putting on gender-inappropriate attire, childbirth and its attendant practices, customs and personnel was strictly female. Men, including the new father, were kept out. This stricture was so vehement that even if a child born alive seemed likely to die, no male priest could be admitted in order to baptize it. This, of course, was a truly serious business, as it was believed that the baby's soul could not pass up to heaven if it had not been welcomed into the Christian fold. The Church, therefore, gave midwives a unique power among women to act as a proxy, to perform a simple baptism. In a culture that held so strongly to the concept of a male-only clergy, it is testimony to the strength of the ban on men within the birth chamber that such an arrangement came into being.

In the case at Tew Magna, the culprit, Thomas Salmon, was a servant in the midwife's own household, who was egged on, dressed and accompanied by the midwife's daughter-in-law, Elizabeth Fletcher. Thomas, we are told, was 'young' – but we are not told how young. Most servants were between fourteen and twenty-six years of age, so he may have just been a lad. They seem to have done a good job disguising Thomas as a woman, as he was not immediately rumbled. In her evidence to the court, the midwife said that it was only when she recognized those particular clothes as belonging to her daughter-in-law that she began to look more closely.

Birth rooms were traditionally rather dark and dingy places as the newly delivered mother and baby were believed to have weakened eyesight and require warmth and darkness in order to recover properly from the ordeal of delivery, but nonetheless Salmon's efforts must have involved a full translation into feminine attire and not just a token effort. Thomas wore the clothes for a couple of hours but was only in the actual chamber for a brief time. According to the daughter-in-law's testimony, they were 'intending only merriment therby'; Thomas claimed that he just wanted to go to the party. The court seems to have been willing to see it as a joke, but one in very bad taste, and ordered Thomas to do public penance.

There are other, perhaps less bizarre, cases of tomfoolery and dressing up that sometimes made it to court, when people went too far, encroaching on sacred spaces and times or involving more sensitive groups. There are records, too, of female prostitutes adopting male dress to entice their prospective clients with an offer of something exotic. And then there are all forms of theatricals, from stagings of *King Lear* in a playhouse to the 'maid' of the Morris dance, where a man dressed as a woman was quite a commonplace sight. The moralists who rushed into print hated it all. 'A woman's garment being put on a man doth vehemently touch and move him in the remembrance and imagination of a woman,' asserted academic and churchman John Rainolds. Thomas Beard thought that men who dressed thus became 'lascivious and effeminate', and satirist Stephen Gosson made plain his disapproval when he wrote that 'to take unto us those garments that are a manifest sign of another sex is to falsify, forge and adulterate, contrary to the express word of God'. People were objecting on a whole host of different, if related, grounds: cross-dressing was a specifically banned activity; it was titillating; it aroused forbidden types of sexual feelings; it robbed a man of masculinity, strength and vigour; it was fraudulent and deceitful; and it overturned the natural order of society, they argued. But it was also part of the traditional repertoire of practical jokes and riotous fun, misrule and May games.

Mary Frith, the 'Roaring Girl', is specifically described and pictured as wearing both doublet and britches, but if you listen more closely to the righteous rants of self-appointed moral guardians, changes in dress need not be so fulsome to raise their ire. Sometimes a simple change of hat was enough. Hats were the first thing on King James's mind when he urged the clergy to preach against women cross-dressing. 'Broad brimmed hats, pointed doublets, their hair cut short or shorn, and some of them stilettos or poniards, and other such trinkets of like moment' were the garments that he was worried about, and they were all worn in combination with full-length skirts. What had annoyed the King so much was not actually cross-dressing but a somewhat mannish interpretation of female dress.

Back in the 1570s when the first texts bemoaning this mockery of God's law appeared, it was primarily the use of buttons that so outraged the commentators. Women's garments up to that date had been primarily fastened with laces and the occasional hook and eye, with large numbers of pins being employed to hold layers and separate items in place. Buttons had been used only on masculine garments.

They became fashion items; male jewellery, in effect. There were buttons covered in elaborately worked silk threads, they could incorporate tufts, be of bright and contrasting colours, come in a huge variety of shapes and sizes, there were gold, silver and even heavily jewelled buttons. Wealthy fashionable men crammed as many as possible down the front of their doublets and along their cuffs. I don't find it at all surprising that some women (including Queen Elizabeth) were interested in mimicking the display. Buttons were primarily seen on doublets, so a female version was soon devised.

Women's doublets were figure hugging, high-necked garments with a tall standing collar, making room down the front for a lot of buttons. The sleeves came in a number of styles, initially close fitting in the 1570s but becoming large and puffy above the elbow in the 1580s, tapering down to a tight-fitting wrist that was often, but not always, fastened with more buttons. There were a lot of points in common with the male doublets of the era: the high collar, the waistline and, of course, the buttons; they were both tailored, well-constructed garments but they were not identical. The body shape was necessarily different, as were the sleeves, and decorative schemes upon surfaces tended more to one set of designs for men and another set for women. There was overlap between the two sexes but the overall look of the garments was distinctly gendered.

In the 1590s, mannish hats rose in popularity among city women. Again, they were more 'inspired by' than direct copies of male headgear and were generally worn in combination with the more feminine linen coif (or cap).

Early on, women took to wearing miniature masculine-style felt hats perched on top of their coifs at an angle, in what is an instantly recognizable perky, even cheeky, manner. Later, the hats increased in size, in line with male styling, and were worn more squarely on the head, which tended to obscure the underlying coif from view, at least at the front.

The short or shorn hair that King James mentioned in his list of abominations was also not always quite what it sounds like. Lots of images from 1615 to 1620 appear to show well-frizzed hair that is just above shoulder length. But on closer inspection you can often see that this is just the front portion of the hair with the rest, much longer hair, being caught up in a bun at the back.

When William Harrison moaned 'that it hath passed my skill to discern whether they were men or women', I am strongly reminded of the wide-scale carping that occurred in my youth in the 1960s and '70s about not being able to tell the difference between the sexes. I found it rather bewildering at the time, as no one could really be fooled, and the gender differences were very apparent. Tight-fitting trousers and jeans revealed rather than obscured figures, particularly on the men. Long hair was generally worn in different styles according to gender, and the choices of colours and patterns varied even when the cut of shirts and jumpers were similar. It was clearly a bogus complaint. Nor could I see why it mattered. Yet the words were trotted out in outrage again and again. Something similar was clearly going on in the late sixteenth and early seventeenth centuries. The young and the fashion-forward were challenging and changing notions of what constituted appropriate dress. One group of people were deeply unsettled by this and others were having fun, perhaps deliberately annoying them.

As a young woman, then, you could ruffle the feathers of your elders relatively cheaply with a few dress accessories. Hats were inexpensive items that could be made more provocative by the addition of a feather or other masculine hat ornament. You could perch it at a jaunty angle, or you could push your coif back a bit and pull the hat forward so that only hat and hair were visible, creating a bold and assertive look while not actually discarding the feminine modesty of a coif. Buttons could be attached to the front of bodices as a false fastening obscuring the more traditional lacings if you couldn't afford one of the new female doublets. You could also play with colour. In modern times, pink is a strongly gendered colour. And so it was in the Tudor and Stuart eras, too, but its gender assignation was the opposite of the twenty-first-century position. Humorial theory dictated that red was the colour of the masculine blood humour and blue was the colour of the watery phlegmatic humour that dominated women's physiology. Pink, as a paler shade of red, was particularly suitable for boys. Many men chose to wear pale pink ruffs that lent a warmer, more masculine tone to their skin, while many women pursued the colder, bluer tones that gave an illusion of paleness. The ultra-fashionable women whom King James was so shaken by with their mannish hats, short hair and pointed doublets in the seventeenth century are often depicted wearing strong elements of red and pink about their persons to heighten this play with gender.

Bright clothing in general, for either sex, had a certain ability to provoke. Whenever someone wished to signal their approval for a man or woman they described their dress as 'sober'. By this they generally meant that it was of more conventional cut and in more sombre colours. Paradoxically, the truly dark shades were expensive, requiring significantly more dyestuffs and longer processes to achieve. So what we might see as 'sober', restrained clothing could actually be more ostentatious than lighter-coloured garments. Deep, strong blacks trimmed with equally black braids, cords, buttons and embroidery, which might seem to us understated, were known by contemporaries to be displays of wealth. The humble person, whether through choice or financial necessity, wore the sort of greys and browns that came from the cheaper grades of undyed wool. All those black clad Puritans of popular imagination are more likely to be prosperous merchants showing off.

Since looking good is a fairly common human aspiration we shouldn't be too surprised to learn that most people did their best to own some of this expensive strongly dyed black clothing. If you trawl through people's wills and inventories, you will find a great deal of black clothing; indeed, if a colour is mentioned at all it is three times as likely to be black than all the other colours put together. The sorts of garments that get mentioned in such sources are, after all, primarily people's best clothes, their most valuable and noteworthy. The popularity of black clothing and its association with Sunday best meant that the social display element of the colour attracted less hostility than marginally cheaper, strong colours of other hues.

If you wanted everyone to notice you and all the local busybodies to start tutting, you got yourself a bit of bright green. A good, strong green required cloth to first be dyed a strong, intense yellow and then over-dyed with a strong blue. It could be tricky to achieve a really vibrant colour; muddy greens were fairly straightforward but clear bright greens needed skill, the right water and plenty of dyestuff. It also faded very quickly as the yellow was sensitive to the light and the blue tended to rub off. These were problems for people using either of the two base colours for anything that had to last, and obviously that was doubly the case when the two were combined to make green. Bright greens were therefore not only expensive to purchase, but wore out very quickly. Few people chose them and this heightened the impact. Many and various were the 'meanings' associated with colours, but a bright green, while it could stand for sickness, envy and longing, was more usually seen as a colour denoting life, springtime and vigour. Bright green was particularly singled out in diatribes against 'gaudy' coloured dress, the very antithesis of 'sober' attire.

Outperforming by far the rants about cross-dressing and gaudy colours was the enormous volume of print devoted to the iniquities of neckwear. All of our most shocked observers of mannish hats, pointed doublets and men being aroused by the wearing of female garb wrote with disgust of people's neck attire, but so too did a lot of less 'godly' authors. Ruffs and collars had no specific religious connotations, so were spared much of the hellfire and damnation rhetoric, but an inappropriate set of ruffs and cuffs aroused a lot of general, society-wide grumbling and disapproval. It was the social climbing that irritated most, particularly as neckwear could circumvent the wealth barrier. Cuffs, ruffs and collars are inherently small garments made not of expensive velvets, damasks and brocades but of much more affordable linen. Their construction required only patience and the sort of fine, straight sewing skills that most of the female population possessed. Starch, the magic ingredient that allowed them to rise and shine forth as symbols of status and fashion, was likewise cheap and the skills associated could be quickly learnt.

Ruffs were initially an accessory of the courtier, supposedly rising to prominence in 1564 when a Flemish laundress arrived in London. She began to teach people how to make the starch and use it in a way that allowed a simple frilled collar that had been shaped around the fingers to grow into the large, wide, stiff ruffs that we think of as typically Elizabethan. As a new and foreign fashion they attracted some sniffyness, but the annoyed voices rose to a crescendo when the ruff escaped the court and started to be adopted by merchants, clergymen and even mere maidservants. In his mock heroic poem of 1630, 'In Praise of Clean Linen', John Taylor puts it thus:

> *Ruffs onely at the first were in request,*
> *With such as of abilitie were best;*
> *But now the plaine, the stitch't, the lac'd, and shagge,*
> *Are at all prices worn by tagge, and ragge.*

He also gives a nod towards the condemnations of the fashion by the likes of Philip Stubbs, Stephen Gosson, John

Rainolds and others whose voices of disapproval we have already heard. He continues:

> *The sets to organ pipes, compare I can,*
> *Because they do offend the Puritan,*
> *Whose zeale doth call it superstition,*
> *And badges of the Beast of Babilon.*

What a wonderful phrase, 'badges of the Beast of Babilon'. I can hear it resounding in my ears as part of a passionate sermon, just as I can feel myself itching with the desire to dash out and get myself one of those 'badges' right now.

It was in the 1590s that those great big wheel ruffs really began to escape the confines of court, sweeping through group after social group. Perhaps inevitably it was maidservants in London who had the edge here. Where most court-inspired fashions moved first to country gentlemen and the wealthiest of city merchants, gradually dropping down the social ladder, accompanied by mutterings about dressing above one's station, ruffs made a single huge social leap at about the same time that the more usual trickle-down was beginning. It was maidservants who were charged with caring for and preparing ruffs for wear. They knew how to make and starch them, how to shape and 'set' them, and they could afford the half a yard of reasonable-quality linen that was required to make one. Naturally, some of the bolder girls made one or two for themselves. *Quel horreur!* In a shocking reversal of the normal rules of fashion, some at the lower end of the social spectrum got there before those nearer the top. Oh, the verbiage that resulted. Anyone wishing to moralize about the dangers of 'aping your betters' called upon the example of ruff wearing. It was, however, a seemingly unstoppable craze. Even those of a puritanical bent – regardless of the 'Beasts of Babilon' style sermons – adopted a form of them in time, inspired by the older, smaller form, in a search for a blend of respectability and fashion.

'You were a horrible puritan th' other day, a very precise Ruff,' one character in a popular play announced. Well, not actually a formal play as such, but rather a jig, which was a short, comic musical with singing, dancing and slapstick. This one was anonymous and entitled *Ruff, Cuff and Band*, an entire entertainment based upon wordplay and social stereotypes through the medium of neckwear. It was clearly written around the same time as John Taylor's 'In Praise of Clean Linen' (1630) when neckwear fashion included several different shapes of ruff or alternatively a smooth, shaped linen 'band' or collar. Within its lines soldiers, gallants, clergymen and judges are all mocked for their neckwear, as well as the Puritans. The jig embodies many of the warring interpretations of ruff wearing. 'Thou art but an effeminate fellow, Ruff, For all th'art so well set.' (The phrase 'well set' referred both to the shaping of a ruff into its characteristic swirls and rounds and to the shape of a fit and sexy body.) Ruff wearers were cheeky upstarts flaunting their sexuality, or they were sober Puritans in 'precise' clean neckwear. They were men of mayoral position, authority and dignity or they were effeminate young idlers who 'make our ruffs as carelesse as we are' ('In Praise of Clean Linen'). Such an expressive garment, capable of carrying so many interpretations so cheaply, was a gift to those who wished to make an impression, good or bad.

Tudor and Stuart society laid far more overt emphasis upon enforcing and reinforcing social order and harmony through the daily visual media of dress and behaviour than that of the twenty-first century. Unlike us with our bulging wardrobes of throwaway garb, the people of the era, even the prosperous, had very few outfits, two or three sets for the most part, which they wore day in and day out, with one set reserved for Sundays. The clothes and the persona were much more closely linked as a result. People knew you, recognized you, by the clothes you wore and every new item that entered your wardrobe would be noted and analysed by your friends and neighbours.

Formal control as well as financial constraints refined things still further. Sumptuary laws, for example, restricted the usage of particular luxury fabrics to finely differentiated social groups, so that the clothes you wore spoke volumes about your precise rank. The clothes of an earl were not supposed to be equal to those of a duke, nor was an apprentice permitted to wear a gown like his master, and woe betide the maid who was mistaken for the mistress. Children were not 'miniature adults' as the popular modern myth would have you believe but dressed in carefully delineated age- and gender-appropriate dress, as family portraits make abundantly clear. Badges, uniforms and signs of office were worn prominently and with pride, something that we, from a society that likes to play down such open symbols of success, belonging and power, can find hard to understand. A town's senior merchants and craftsmen jockeyed for positions such as aldermen and mayors. Those who were appointed were entitled to wear long and distinctively coloured gowns and did so not just for ceremonial occasions but for everyday wear. Indeed, in some towns their wives also boasted certain garments when out and about.

Who you were, where you came from, how successful you were, your age, your gender, your occupation, all were proclaimed by your appearance with a specificity that can leave us somewhat dazed. Making a mockery of this visual representation of stability and order therefore had serious impact. Changes in fashion really did upset people, as the sheer volume of vitriolic rants that survive make very clear. Youngsters got into all sorts of trouble for their edgy clothing choices (including a few actual prosecutions for offences such as wearing breeches that were too big). Playing with gender roles and social climbing were subversive acts, both attacks upon the traditional structures of authority.

In the popular imagination, black clothes and a tall black hat are the mark of a Puritan, particularly the sort of Puritan who emigrated to America as a 'Pilgrim Father'. Yet as we have seen, it was not so much the clothes that marked this group out but rather the public behaviour: the halting walk, the Bible clutched to the chest, the upcast eyes. Because such movements were so marked, so distinctive, because they advertised social groupings so successfully, they were the perfect angle of attack for anyone seeking to puncture the self-confidence or undermine the social standing of group members.

More than any other forms of bad behaviour that we have covered so far, these attempts to humiliate could be aimed at the group rather than the individual. A woman with a wooden spoon in her girdle accompanied by her gaggle of lads lampooning a soldier didn't have to single out the specific soldier who had driven her to action; any soldier would do. The courtier and his entourage who were trailed down the street by a gang of teenage apprentices copying their every move might well be personally uncomfortable and intimidated but they also knew that the insult was aimed at all courtiers, at a way of life – it was just their bad luck that it was their particular turn to be picked on today.

Your clothes and your movements formed the basis of your personal expression, aimed at the wider world. These were the things that people saw first, the basis of their first impressions of you. You could use them to manipulate your public image in ways that contemporaries saw as upsetting and unnerving. The young in particular could deliberately adopt new and outlandish clothing to separate themselves from the older generation or terrify their parents by suddenly abandoning their pretty dresses and elegant manners in favour of sober wools and a halting walk that hinted at extremist religious views. But having made these decisions and changes, having settled upon a public persona, you had to walk the gauntlet of the greater populace, all eager to judge and eager to express their own hilarious opinions.

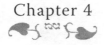

Chapter 4

OUTRIGHT VIOLENCE

We launch now into the rough stuff. There is nothing quite like violence for expressing the vehemence of your feelings. It can communicate your anger, frustration, determination and resolve. It can be explosive and sudden or habitual and relentless, but however passionate outbursts of violence may be there is still an opportunity for control, for twisting and using it to your badly behaved advantage. Violence can be used to bully and intimidate; you can use it to establish your own power and authority or destroy someone else's. Violence can be a defence, a provocation or retaliation and there are numerous different forms that you can employ.

Catfights and Brawls

We begin with an outpouring of vitriol in Winchester one afternoon in the autumn of 1544 when Mistress Foster attacked Mistress Agnes Haycroft in the main street of the city, 'upon whom with the nayles of her finger she had drawn blod'. The start of the fight remains shrouded in mystery, but from this point on several witnesses were able to give accounts of the continued shouting. With her face scratched, Mistress Haycroft left the scene of the fray ostensibly to garner the support of her maidservants, while Mistress Foster was met by her daughter Frideswide, who was naturally upset to see her mother in such an angry state and asked what had happened. 'That brazenfaced hore,' the daughter gasped. 'That meseld faced and skaled hore Haycroft wif she will never be contented till she be driven out of towne with basins as her mother was ... Mother, If I had been there I would have knoked hir furryd cap & her hed together.' By this time Agnes Haycroft had walked up behind them and heard all that Frideswide had said. 'Wold you had don it yow pockye nosed houswife,' she interjected, causing Frideswide to turn to her and shout, 'Agnes Haycroft nay thou pokey nosed hore, feiste thow, thow meseld faced hore, thow camest to towne with a lepers face & a skalled hed. And I defye the utterly, for I wold thow knewist that the fowlest place of myn arse ys fayer then thy face.'

One has to hand it to Frideswide, she had a powerful turn of phrase in the heat of the moment. But we must also thank her, her mother and Agnes Haycroft for a masterclass in the art of the feminine fight. Did you notice that all the violence, both actual and threatened, was directed at the head, with particular mention of head coverings? When Mistress Foster scratched Agnes's face it was probably her hair rather than her face that she was aiming at. A woman's hair was a private and sexualized part of her body, not for common display. Young, unmarried girls might display some hair, but adult women, and especially married women, kept it firmly controlled beneath linen coifs and, when outdoors, beneath an additional hat. Loose hair could very occasionally be on show as a sign of purity and virginity, often in connection with the marriage ceremony (Queen Elizabeth I was crowned 'in her hair' with it combed out loose about her shoulders as a symbol that she, a virgin, was marrying her nation), but in general terms loose, uncovered hair was a mark of prostitution. If you wanted to expose someone as a whore, pulling off her hat and coif produced an instant visual and public effect. It was all about humiliating and shaming a woman in a way that all could see, even if your words were lost in the general hubbub.

Naturally, when someone grabbed at a hat and coif, the victim tried to defend herself, or go in turn for her attacker's headgear. If you managed to dislodge all the coverings, you made the most of your victory by grabbing hold of the hair and attempting to pull and parade your enemy about the

The feminine fight focused upon hair and head gear.

streets in her ignominious, bareheaded state. This is the stock image used in woodcuts of brawling women: hats pulled awry, messy hair loose or in its plaits, women scratching and grabbing at each other's heads.

Remember how Frideswide said that she would have knocked Agnes's furred cap against her head? This was an action that would have required her first to remove it before slapping Agnes around the head with it. It was no simple task to get the headgear off a woman who resisted. For a start, there were several separate elements that were pinned and tied together, secured in place further by being attached to braided hair. Headgear was designed to remain firmly in place even when women rode to market, milked the cows or weeded the garden. The female fight, therefore, required speed in order to get to the headgear before your opponent could fend off your hands, considerable force to yank everything clear, and persistence as piece after piece was wrenched away. Hands and faces frequently came in for a good deal of scratching and women often lost their footing and found themselves rolling in the dirt.

The Winchester fight is one of a small number of recorded physical outbreaks of violence between two women, and is rarer still for occurring outside a household situation. Large numbers of our best insults and slanging matches featured the 'fairer' sex in public settings, but when we talk about scratching, punching, kicking, bludgeoning and stabbing outside the immediate family, we are almost exclusively talking about men acting violently upon other men. Domestic violence was, as it still is, a fact of life for many people. Where that violence followed along the traditional lines of authority – husbands over wives, mistresses over maids, parents over children – Tudor and Stuart society generally chose to turn a blind eye, interpreting it as legitimate 'correction'. So when Joan Jurden stabbed her maid, Marion Grey, in 1565 during a fight over some trampled peas and claimed that it was an accident that occurred when Marion pushed back after being struck with the back of Joan's hands for insolence (they both stumbled, apparently, and the herb-cutting knife that Joan had in her hand found its way into Marion's chest), the jury of the coroner's court probably didn't look that closely before bringing in their verdict of death by misadventure. Had the tables been turned and the maid stabbed the mistress, the response would probably have been very different.

The punishments for such crimes laid down by law were markedly different, too. Murder along accepted hierarchy lines was indeed murder: a husband could be convicted of murdering his wife and be hanged for it. If a wife murdered her husband, however, it was not legally termed murder but petty treason, and the punishment was being burnt at the stake. The same double standards applied to murder across the master–servant relationship.

While murder was pretty uncommon, violence as a means of control persisted across society and is rarely commented upon. Indeed, it only rises to our attention when friends, family and neighbours believed that things had gone too far, that beatings were too regular or too harsh or when the violence went in the 'wrong' direction. Making such judgement calls, deciding when legitimate correction had spilled over into abusive behaviour, was clearly something that worried many people and provoked much talk, thought and debate as the countless pieces of advice from writers upon moral issues indicate.

If we return to the words of Frideswide in Winchester, we can spot a reference to the outcome of such fraught deliberations. She claims that Agnes will never be content until she is 'driven out of towne with basins as her mother was'. This is a reference to a community punishment sometimes termed a 'skimmington ride' or 'rough music'. It was an unofficial expression of public condemnation where the law could not provide redress. Unacceptable levels of domestic violence were particularly prone to attracting this kind of response. Agnes's mother, it seems, was hounded out of town, at least temporarily, in shame by a gang of noisy citizens shouting and banging on cookware.

But outside the home it is men assaulting other men that overwhelmingly dominates the historical record. In 1571, for example, a fight broke out between Thomas Drapier and John Cockes. Both men were servants within the household of Henry Pole and the altercation began verbally in the storeroom. Words led to fists, prompting a maidservant to go and fetch help in the form of Nicholas Harvye, who was able to stop the fight. However, it didn't end there, for later that same day when Nicholas was out running an errand and thus unable to oversee their behaviour, Thomas called John out of the house into the marketplace. John was reluctant at first but Nicholas claimed that he only wanted to talk and was unarmed. When John did emerge, Thomas 'immediately leapt upon him and wrestled with him and violently took his head between his legs'. Locked in this position the two men came up against the side of a building and Thomas Drapier struck his head 'under the ear' and broke his neck.

The fight that happened in the alehouse in Fyfett, Somerset, in 1609 ostensibly grew out of a fairly harmless joke. Robert Parker and William Burrell were spending the evening together when they overheard the conversation of

Male violence was much more common and took many different forms.

a nearby group of men, one of whom was the local minister. The clergyman was moaning about the theft of some of his poultry when Robert Parker took the opportunity to lean over and remark that, 'it was no offense to take awaye a little needed priests cocke'. Clearly the minister must have responded in some way, although the retort is not part of the record. Robert, however, got into trouble with the court for then physically assaulting the minister.

These are just two isolated examples of arguments that turned physical, one with unintentionally fatal consequences and both leading to court cases of one type or another. But there is a great deal of evidence to suggest that such bad behaviour was very commonplace. Evidence of more minor outbreaks of violence, such as fist fights and alehouse brawls, is only patchy. The alehouse assault on the minister is one of a number of altercations within such establishments, but those that are recorded generally have some additional element over and above a straightforward fight that then prompted people to bring the matter to the attention of the authorities. In this case, we can see a large social disparity between the protagonists, critically, an offence against a representative of the Church. In other cases, it is the damage to property that provokes a complaint to the authorities. Sometimes records are the result of a moral crackdown such as we see in Dorchester in the early years of the seventeenth century when a particularly godly and puritanical set of people rose to prominence in local government. Accident could also play its part, as was the case in the investigation into the death of Thomas Drapier. Had the two men fallen a little differently as they fought and Drapier's neck remained intact, it is unlikely that we would ever have known about the incident. But more serious violence is well represented in court cases and this allows us to gain a more general and comprehensive picture of interpersonal conflicts in daily life.

Several historians have undertaken exhaustive studies in different parts of the country into crime rates. Each has found evidence of a considerably higher level of homicide in the period between the arrival of the Tudor dynasty and the outbreak of the Civil War, than that of modern Britain – roughly ten times higher. The numbers of men meeting violent deaths at the hands of other men is fairly consistent across the country in rural as well as urban areas. The 1590s seem to have been an especially bloody decade. Men are killed with knives, swords, bows and arrows, cudgels, staffs, agricultural implements, craftsmen's tools, firearms and bare hands. Many incidents are simply one on one but many others involve small groups of three or four men. Larger groups are rarer but did occur.

The incident that took place at around 5 p.m. on 2 January in 1580 in the small town of Storrington in West Sussex is rather shockingly typical. The two initial protagonists were seemingly respectable and responsible men. Thomas Hutson was described as a surgeon and John Baker as a tailor; both seem to have been qualified masters of their respective trades. John was a local with a local business, but Thomas hailed from Surrey. We don't know what they were arguing about but the fight kicked off when Thomas Hutson launched himself at John Baker, beating him around the head with his fists and 'with a dagger which he held in his right hand'. John Baker was wounded in this attack. The coroner's records say that he 'broke his head' so there was probably plenty of blood. At this point, Thomas claims that he retreated in fear of what John would do in revenge. As he ran away, John's apprentice Henry Emery turned up and, seeing his master on the ground covered in blood and the fleeing form of Thomas Hutson, chased after him clutching a wooden staff. Now a fourth man, William Novis, gets involved. Whether he saw the injured John Baker or not, he did see the young Henry Emery armed with a staff chasing Thomas Hutson and went to Thomas's rescue, using his own staff to beat Henry Emery across the head. Henry fell to the ground and Thomas then stabbed the lad in the chest. The coroner's records sadly give us no more detail. Not only do they omit to tell us what the argument was about or whether there was any other lead up to Thomas's assault of John, they also leave us guessing about William Novis's motivation. Perhaps he was a simple bystander who thought he was seeing an attempted assault by a young fit man armed with an obvious weapon upon an older respectable man. Maybe he was horrified when Thomas Hutson then turned and stabbed the defenceless boy. Both men were charged with murdering the young Henry Emery; William Novis, however, was acquitted while Thomas Hutson was convicted.

Such an abundance of potential weapons and such a willingness to use them is a common theme that runs through accounts of fatal conflicts. It is a typical example, too, of the narrative arc of so many period homicides: an argument that escalates into violence. Murder and manslaughter arising from burglaries gone wrong or attempts to speed up the rate of inheritance are no more common in this period than they are now. It was personal conflict that pushed up the homicide rate. And what this elevated level of homicide shows us is a culture heavily focused upon reputation, of touchiness and a willingness among men to escalate from words to actions.

Our discussion of offensive speech called repeatedly upon the evidence of court cases for defamation of character, something that also highlights the central importance that people of this era placed upon reputation and public respect. It is hard to imagine within our own modern world how a simple slanging match could end up in court; we simply don't take such words as seriously as we once did. The centrality of greetings gestures to the smooth running of society is another such signpost. Honour, respectability and social standing were precious to people; they were worth defending with vigour. Feelings of self-worth were shaped and maintained by the way that those around you treated you. We in the modern world seem to derive much of this self-respect from the ownership and accumulation of things – the car, the big house, the logos and labels of higher status products – but while people of the sixteenth and seventeenth centuries were by no means immune to the allure and status of expensive clothes and goods, they seem to have placed a much higher value upon the behaviour of others towards them.

Perhaps we can draw upon the urban gang culture of our largest cities to see a reflection of this urgent need for visible respect, and the flares of violence, both verbal and physical, that arise when that respect is seen to be missing or neglected. Within both milieus we see cultural pressures to respond energetically and rapidly to any form of perceived slight. Within the historical context, an immediate and vehement response could force respect from attackers and conjure it from bystanders. From women that response tended to be verbal; from men physical violence might well be expected. An unwillingness or inability to defend your reputation in this manner could be seen as humility and godly mildness, but it could also be seen as weakness or an admission of your inferiority. There was also a practical side to the worries about the public perception of one's character.

Money and business were deeply dependent upon judgements of a person's character. No formal banking system had developed so all transactions were personal affairs. In business matters, few of the safeguards that the modern world takes for granted were yet in place. There were no limited liability companies and no insurance schemes. If you wished to order goods or defer payment, take out a loan or enter into a partnership, you needed to be able to inspire trust. If you were looking to sell your produce, let out a spare room or give permission for your daughter to marry, you needed to be certain of the probity of everyone involved. Nor was it just your financial trustworthiness that people were interested in, as different forms of 'honesty' were seen to be linked. A person who adhered to the principles of chastity and obedience within marriage, and who guarded their tongue and followed society's rules of good neighbourliness, could expect support and goodwill in their business dealings, whereas the notorious cuckold would be shunned. Self-control and social conformity in one aspect of life promised fair dealing in others. Even the most day-to-day business could be affected.

Do you remember the woman who needed to clear her

name from an accusation of witchcraft? Several of the town's bakers would not sell to her; her ability to buy food was compromised by other people's slanderous tongues. A good reputation was essential for an economically successful life and male violence could in fact be a positive attribute, not just a defence against slander. The man who was known to be able to hold his own physically was a man who few were willing to cheat. A robust defence of one's reputation told those you had dealings with that you were not going to slink away at the first sign of difficulty; it said that you were willing to invest in your social standing here in this community. The line between good violent behaviour and bad violent behaviour could be rather flexible.

All Tooled Up and Ready for Action

Learning to fight and handle weapons was part of most men's youth at all levels of society, backed up by a patriotic and legal duty to do so. With no standing army to call upon, the defence of the realm was managed through a system of public duty. The aristocracy and gentry saw themselves, at least in part, as belonging to a form of elite warrior caste; their freedom from manual labour allowed them to concentrate upon martial prowess, and the potential for military service served as one justification for a lifestyle exempt from productive labour. Gentlemen, particularly second sons, were all potential professional soldiers and officers, should the need arise. Boys of this social group were expected and encouraged to be more combative than those of humble birth. Even in the advice literature that generally promoted self-control and restraint you find acknowledgement and support for this more aggressive outlook. 'Be manly at neede, begin no quarrel in wrong,' is Sir Hugh Rhodes's admonition. While he didn't approve of boys picking a fight, when provoked they should step up and 'be manly'. His advice to young men in service to a lord includes the line, 'Avoyde murther, save thyself, play the man being compelde'. Stout self-defence might well be an attribute that twenty-first-century men could reasonably advocate, but oh, what a different mindset it takes to include the injunction 'avoid murdering anyone' in a book of modern manners and conduct!

The common Renaissance man could also be called upon in times of crisis. His level of skill was necessarily curtailed by the little amount of training and practice that a life of labour permitted, but led by one of the gentlemanly officers, even the crudest of martial skills could be theoretically brought to bear at the monarch's command. Under Henry VIII, every man from the age of six to seventy had a legal duty to practise with a bow and arrow upon a Sunday afternoon. Men, and those in authority over boys, were required to own the requisite equipment. The hope was that lifelong practice would develop bodies capable of making the bow into a formidable weapon of war. Most communities had areas set aside for the purpose – look out for street names such as 'Butts Close' for evidence of their whereabouts.

The Butts generally consisted of a raised earth bank upon which targets could be set up at the far end of a long enclosure, where men could perfect their aim as well as building the strength and technique required to shoot powerful bows at long distances. Pasture land near the edge of town frequently filled with men and boys on Sundays out enjoying a form of free-range archery known as 'roving'. In small companionable groups they selected a mark, loosed their arrows at it and then ambled up to see whose arrow was closest before choosing the next mark. Rather like a round of golf but without the formal layout. Most men seem to have seen archery practice not as a chore, but as a healthy and worthy form of exercise and sport. By Elizabeth's reign the bow was woefully outdated as a weapon of war, and although the laws remained in place, archery was rapidly fading into a purely sporting context.

After the Rising of the North in 1569, Elizabeth and her advisors saw that the old feudal organization for war, which had come close to failing the Crown on this occasion, along with the use of such old-fashioned weapons, would have to change. Rather than relying upon individual aristocrats to raise troops from among their own tenantry, a new county-based system led by royally appointed Lord Lieutenants was combined with a move to firearms and a push for a little more training. Laws were already in place that required the wealthy to supply arms and armour, including horses and trained men to use them. In 1558, at the bottom end of this scale, men with incomes of between five and ten pounds a year (a moderately wealthy yeoman farmer perhaps) were required to keep one set of armour, a pole arm, a longbow and a helmet. Over time guns pushed out bows but the principle remained.

Meanwhile, each community was also supposed to invest in and maintain a stock of military equipment for use by the poorer citizens. Small-scale formal gatherings (known as special musters) to practise military exercises officially demanded the presence of all the local able-bodied men between the ages of sixteen and sixty, although there was soon to be a division between a selected group of men who received regular training (the trained band) and those who were only called upon to make up numbers in an emergency (the untrained band). Men were to be called away from their ploughs (generally at times of the year when such absence didn't cause too much disruption) for a couple of days of training. They learnt to move in organized formations, recognize the drum signals that would be used upon any battlefield and, hopefully, from the 1570s onwards, learn how to handle the newfangled muskets. The coroner's records of West Sussex list enough accidental deaths from badly handled firearms in this decade to prove both that such gatherings were occurring and to make one doubt the quality of such training. In May 1588, for example, there were 200 men assembled in East Grinstead 'to be trained wit calyver' (a type of firearm). 'Being skyrmysshinge in the said trayninge', Henry Cooper was shot dead, although no one was willing to say by whom.

Other incidents generally involved muskets going off

unexpectedly while being carried, cleaned or stored, and on one occasion, an accident happened at the blacksmith's forge while the gun was being mended on the anvil; unaware that the musket was still loaded, the blacksmith hit it with a hammer and shot his apprentice dead. They all denote a lack of familiarity with guns and safety procedures.

Firearms and knowledge about their usage was spreading rapidly through the male population.

Nonetheless, a significant proportion of Elizabethan men received some military training and were accustomed to handling such weapons as they were issued with.

It was not all guns. Calivers and muskets (both types of firearm) were expensive items and military practice as well as economics dictated that the weapons that many of these men trained with were more traditional variations upon the pole arm, a long sturdy stick with a blade of some sort upon the end. These had the advantage of familiarity, being very similar to the agricultural implements that men used in their day jobs. Maintaining hedges and cutting coarse fodder for livestock taught many men to wield a bill with force, fluidity and accuracy, and hacking down people was not so very different in technique from hacking down undergrowth.

Military training with a bill, or indeed any other style of pole arm, was a matter of learning to use the weapon in such a way as to defend yourself from attack while continuing to pose a threat to the enemy – hedges after all do not deliberately fight back. But such familiarity with a weapon does, of course, go both ways – you really did not want to argue with a farmer who knew what he was doing.

Swords were also part of the standard soldier's kit. Their use upon the battlefield had changed over time into a secondary rather than a primary weapon, but they were nonetheless a very important one. Both projectile weapons and pole arms, whether it was the early combination of bow and bill or the later pairing of pike and musket, required a certain amount of distance between yourself and the enemy in order to be effective; in close fighting a handheld blade was much more useful. Swords represented a second line of defence for foot soldier and cavalry alike. They were intended for use in the more cramped and chaotic stages of a battle when lines and formations had mostly dissolved, and in awkward tight spots where there was little room to manoeuvre. Despite being a rather outdated weapon there were more swords in use than any other weapon type, and they came in a huge array of qualities to suit various pockets. They were widely regarded as tools for personal defence rather than offensive attack: a means of fending off blows from other swords and pole arms. But that didn't stop them being used aggressively as well.

As far as behaving badly goes, the sheer availability of weapons meant that fraught tempers had the potential for serious repercussions. Here, for example, are the shenanigans that upset the peace and quiet of an August day in the town of Lewes in 1585. The accounts come from the various participants and witnesses in a convoluted series of court cases over a six-month period. Naturally, there is considerable variation between people's different statements, even upon simple matters such as the date of the incident. The general picture that emerges from all these documented accounts begins on 6 August with Abraham Edwards heading out into the fields behind his house. He had with him his longbow and some arrows and was intending (according to his wife) to practise his archery skills as a good and patriotic subject should. At about 11 a.m. Richard Goodwin, looking up from his work (he made the 'points' that men used to attach their doublet and breeches together), saw Henry Young leave the house of John Butcher. Richard noticed this because Henry seemed to be trying to conceal a sword and buckler beneath his coat as he headed up the High Street and out at the West Gate towards St Anne's Church. These may have been the personal property of Henry Yonge, who lodged with John Butcher and is described in the documents only as a 'yoman'. Henry is mentioned at one point as having been involved in a previous, if non-fatal, armed affray, so perhaps we should think of him as an example of a swashbuckler serving man adrift in a small town, a type of young man that we are going to meet again later in this chapter. Shortly after Henry disappeared through the West Gate, Mrs Edwards arrived at her neighbour Richard Cheyney's house in a state of alarm, clutching a sword in its scabbard, claiming that her husband, Abraham, was about to be killed and was at that very moment being assaulted by armed men. Richard Cheyney was a man of some standing locally and was accustomed to taking charge; he was accorded the title 'esquire' in the court records, which also mention him indulging in hunting as a sport and mention at least three male servants in his employ. At this dramatic moment he was not wearing a rapier, but snatched up a backsword (one of a number of styles of sword) that, since it is deliberately described as having no scabbard, probably lived upon the wall. His servant Thomas Botcher took the sword and scabbard brought by Mrs Edwards, and with neither man waiting to find suitable belts and hangers to wear the weapons, but simply clutching them in their hands, they left the house through the back entrance to see what was going on. From a distance it seemed clear that Abraham Edwards had been rescued by his shooting companions, so, imagining that all was well, the two men went back inside.

Soon, however, Mrs Edwards was back again pleading for help. Her husband was back in their house and three men were trying to kill him. Cheyney ran out, followed by Botcher who carried both of the swords. When they arrived Abraham was in a bad way, bleeding from three large cuts on his head and another one across his face, with further, probably defensive, wounds on his hands. The three assailants had gone but Abraham and his wife were able to name them. Henry Yonge, it seems, was not alone by the time that he encountered his foe out in the fields; backed up by William Garland and Thomas Brewer, the exchange had begun with a verbal assault. Presumably Edwards refused to back down and a fight ensued. In their own testimony the three assailants claimed that they had no weapons with them at this point other than their daggers and a four-foot 'hawking bat'. Despite the alleged sighting of Henry smuggling a sword and buckler out of his lodgings, Abraham Edward's wounds do seem consistent with those of a one-sided knife fight. The three men also claimed that it was the sight of Richard Cheyney and Thomas Botcher approaching armed with swords that sparked their next move. They dived into a nearby house to hide, found three swords and took them. None of the court cases asked for clarification as to whose house they burgled or why it contained three swords; perhaps it seemed an entirely normal situation and complement of weaponry.

Richard Cheyney, meanwhile, was headed for the local constable's house where he asked for official help in arresting the men who had assaulted 'my man' Edwards. Before any official action could be taken, however, Henry Yonge, William Garland and Thomas Brewer all appeared in the High Street armed with swords, bucklers and daggers. Words were exchanged (the witnesses give varying accounts of exactly what was said by whom and when) and blades came free of scabbards. There were now five people in the street with drawn swords. One of the witnesses, John Holter, ran inside his own house to grab a club, hoping to break things up, but by the time he emerged it was all over. Thomas Botcher was dead, his nose had been cut off and he had a deep stab wound in his shoulder '7 inches deep and 1½ inches wide'.

Counting up the number of weapons involved in this outbreak of violence we find that we have five (possibly six) swords, three daggers, three bucklers, a bow and arrows, a club and a 'hawking bat' that was pressed into service. The daggers are described as everyday wear and the rest of the weaponry was snatched up in a hurry from a series of purely domestic spaces. If Henry Yonge et al. were telling the truth about picking up the swords and bucklers from the house that they were hiding in, we may be seeing an example of military provision within a domestic location rather than a collection of personal weaponry. Three swords and bucklers in one house could represent a large gentry household with multiple sword-carrying male members whose equipment was left with their clothes and other belongings, or it may have constituted a small armoury that the householder was required under statute to provide for the trained bands.

St Mary's Church in Mendlesham has the best and most complete surviving parish armoury in Britain, kept for centuries in a small room above the North Porch. The armour and weapons represent a bit of a mishmash of dates and qualities but are a nice reflection of Tudor and Stuart attempts to provide munitions on a local basis. As instructions went out in the 1570s for parish military provision, local communities were faced with raising the money and finding suppliers. All sorts of old weapons appeared out of the woodwork in order to help fulfil the brief. Professional armourers probably had a boom decade and local blacksmiths did their best to get what public commissions they could. Reports of the musters in the 1570s and '80s tell of a bewildering array of weaponry, much of it ancient.

As time went on, items were broken or lost and periodic bursts of activity introduced new items. The rising tensions across the country in the 1620s and '30s produced a major flurry of rearming and updating, but people still stored the older items, just in case. Meanwhile, items were gradually leaking out of the parish armouries into more general circulation. And then there were all those people who were required by law to provide their own arms and armour, men like John Reyley whose death in 1589 prompted the taking of an inventory of his possessions. He was a tallow chandler based in the small town of New Woodstock in Oxfordshire. His business consisted of manufacturing candles out of sheep fat (all the requisite equipment is listed as being in the 'workhouses' attached to his comfortable but modest three-bedroomed house). The main room in his house, the hall, had a good provision of wooden furniture, but upon the walls, along with a set of painted cloths, were 'one halbarte a byll a hanger'. Here was a very ordinary maker of cheap candles with two pole arms (the halberd and bill) and a sword (the hanger).

Weapons turn up in a fair number of wills and inventories in just such a manner, listed as belonging to exactly the sort of people who were delineated in the regulations as eligible for service at the musters. The Frenchman Stephen Perlin had noted back in 1558 that, 'the servants carry pointed bucklers, even those of bishops and prelates, and the men commonly exercise themselves with a bow. The husbandmen, when they till the ground, leave their bucklers and swords, or sometimes their bow in the corner of the field, so that in this land everybody bears arms.' Twenty years later, Raphael Holinshed was making a similar point: 'Seldom shall you see one of my countrymen above eighteen or twenty years old to go without a dagger at least at his backe or his side.' The attempts to modernize English military organization and practice that occurred in the lead up to the Spanish Armada, and then again as the Civil War approached, simply built upon this tradition, introducing newer weapons to the mix.

Holinshed also highlighted a second reason to be armed: 'no man travelleth by the waie without sword or some such weapon except the minister'. Roads could be the haunt of highwaymen and footpads (highwaymen without horses). Law enforcement was a rather patchy affair that relied upon unpaid elected local constables and required the victims of a crime to take the initiative in bringing culprits to justice. Order and calm within the centre of communities could be supported by the presence of citizens, but out in the quieter reaches you were largely on your own. People felt vulnerable as they moved along the highways, so they took precautions. They travelled in groups and they travelled armed. If you couldn't get your hands on a sword, you carried a staff. Staffs were much like pole arms but without the blade. You should think of seven- or eight-foot hardwood poles, about two inches in diameter, not some flimsy walking stick. Oh, and the butt end was generally shod with iron. Remember that the one carried by William Novis felled Henry Emery in a single blow. A staff gave some protection even when simply waved about by a complete novice, but a few pointers and a little practice could make a huge difference.

If you liked to throw your weight about a bit, maybe indulge in a bit of bullying and intimidation, here was the perfect opportunity. Out in the countryside a significant proportion of men seem to have wandered about their daily lives carrying a staff, ready for action. The initial fight between our violently inclined surgeon and his adversary, the tailor, involved fists and a dagger, but both of the men who became involved later (Novis and Emery) arrived, unprepared, upon the scene with staffs. Both were willing and able to use them.

When you prepared to fight you shifted your grip so that one hand (the right one if you were right-handed) was at the centre of the staff, palm up, and the other one was halfway between that hand and the end of the staff and held palm down. This gave you two striking ends: a short end and a long end. Your strongest hand controlled the movement of the longer section in order to maximize the power of that stroke, while your weaker hand had a much easier job controlling the movement of the shorter end, ready to punch out with the iron-shod butt at short range. The basic position put the staff diagonally across your body with the short butt end in your left hand held back by your left hip and the longer end held at about chest height pushed forward a foot or eighteen inches in front of you. With the staff at the ready like this it was very hard for an opponent to get through your defence. You also had the option of sliding or 'slipping' the

A traveller with his staff. It functioned both as a walking stick and as a useful weapon if you were confronted by highwaymen or footpads.

staff through your hands to lengthen or shorten the fighting end or to deliver a rapid thrust with the tip. Another point to consider when fighting with a staff is that it has no right or wrong side, unlike a sword, which has a sharp edge and a flat side. This means that you can use circular and curving blows rather than just straight strikes.

Imagine for a moment that you are facing an armed opponent and have your staff in your hands. If you pull back, raising your arms to gain momentum for an almighty thwack, there will be a few moments when you have lifted your staff up and out of the way leaving your body undefended. If your opponent is quick he can stab you in the guts before ever you can land a blow upon his head. Those who taught staff fighting advised a different approach. (If you are struggling to follow this next bit, I suggest you get yourself a stick and try it out.) Start in the basic position that we have already mentioned with the staff diagonally across your body and diagonally pointing forward towards your enemy. Now think more in terms of circling the staff like a giant cheerleader's baton. The pivot point of these curving, sweeping blows is halfway between your two hands, about level with your navel. Pull and circle back and down with the right hand and up and forward with your left so that the longer working tip of the staff describes a bigger circle over your right shoulder. Now push round, over and down with your right hand to make the blow, pulling just as strongly back with your left as you do so. Let your right hand slide down the length of the staff at the end of the movement, in effect throwing the end forwards. The momentum of the circular swing adds power, as too does the combined push and pull movement of both hands. Such a blow can have all the force of a wide, open swing but keeps you covered at all times and is much quicker to recover from; you are instantly ready to swing it on to its next blow with no loss of control.

A proficient staff fighter holds the staff quite loosely, with their hands slipping along its length as need dictates, and maintains a momentum of circling blow after blow, sometimes with one end and sometimes with the other, shifting their footwork and position as they do so. Nor do they neglect the opportunity for a sudden thrust, stepping forward, letting go of the staff with the fore hand and pushing the staff into an opponent's face or body with the butt hand before snatching it back and regaining the usual grip. The biggest problem you face when staff fighting is that as all the largest and most powerful swings take time and are hard to abort or redirect once initiated, a nimble opponent with a smaller, lighter weapon can be the more dangerous one – think of Robin Hood and Little John.

Staffs were cheap, easy to home produce if necessary and, unlike swords, which were supposed to be confined to the use of soldiers and gentlemen, there were no laws against owning or carrying them. Men were accustomed to turning to them for self-defence when out and about. The knowledge of how to use them was widespread and backed up both by military practice and the more gentlemanly published manuals of defence. There are scraps of evidence that suggest that staff fighting enjoyed a certain tolerance, at least in comparison to fighting with bladed weapons. A staff was often considered to be not intentionally lethal. It was a formidable weapon that could inflict broken bones and successfully defend a man against swords and daggers as well as other staffs and pole arms, but one that generally did so without actually killing. Maybe the people of Nottinghamshire felt a little differently, though, as nearly half of all the recorded murders in that county between 1485 and 1558 involved staffs, like the death of Henry Pereson of Babworth who was hit on the head by John Strynger 'so that his brains flowed out'. It should also be pointed out that they were something of a favourite among the very footpads that people were so keen to defend themselves from.

The Strutting Cockerel

A small but very noticeable group of men looked to weapons not for defence of the realm or defence from highwaymen, nor to grab in the heat of an argument, but rather as props to shore up their manhood. They were the swashbucklers and braggados who paraded their machismo in the streets utilizing their distinctive, and much mocked, gaits as we saw before, and possibly including, among their brethren, Henry Yonge whom we encountered just a short while ago upon the streets of Lewes. This phenomenon is recorded in Edmond Howes's 1614 expanded edition of John Stowe's great *Survey of London*.

Talking about behaviours that he remembered from back in the 1560s and '70s, he recounted: 'In the winter season, all the high streets, were much annoyed and troubled with hourly frayes, of sword and buckler men, who took pleasure in that bragging fight; and although they made great shew of much furie, and fought often. Yet seldom any man hurt, for thrusting was not then in use: neither would one of twentie strike beneath the waste, by reason they helde it cowardly and beastly.' It continues with a little more detail: 'This field commonly called West-

Sword fighting displays were a popular element of many entertainments. This sword and buckler man comes from a dance manual that gives a choreography for use at balls and masques. It was published at a time when sword and buckler fighting had gone out of fashion and was attracting a lot of ridicule.

Smithfield, was many years called Ruffians hall, by reason it was the usual place of Frayes and common fighting, during the time of Sword and Bucklers were in use. When every Serving-man, from the base to the best, carried a Buckler at his backe.'

The violence could erupt anywhere at any time of day or night. The more organized and staged encounters may well have taken place at West Smithfield where people could choose to either avoid them or flock to watch (as it seems many young women did), but swashbucklers were not always so considerate. Street corners and marketplaces could suddenly and without warning become places of whirling, naked blades as men, women and children backed quickly away.

Everyone, even the most moralistic of divines, was willing to acknowledge that military skill was a useful attribute. 'The knowledge in weapons may bee gathered to be necessary in a common wealth,' admitted Stephen Gosson in his 1579 book *The Schoole of Abuse*, but the 'cunning of fencers applied to quarrelling' made such skill noxious, 'every Dicke Swashe a common cutter', turning to violence at the slightest pretext. 'Fewe of them come to an honest ende,' he concluded with an air of rather helpless resignation.

Armed serving men are a group that we have heard of before, back in 1558 in the words of the travelling Frenchman who was clearly rather shocked that even the serving men who worked for high-ranking clergymen were armed. Please, before we continue, clear your minds of the social status, work and lives of nineteenth-century serving men, of footmen, valets and butlers, for such images of stoic domesticity will only mislead you. Instead let us return to the last blast of the feudal armed retainer. These men did indeed get involved in serving dinner, but they were also expected to follow their lord into battle. They were young men from relatively wealthy and high status families. Second sons and third cousins of gentlemen, and occasionally the sons of wealthy and ambitious yeoman farmers, filled their ranks. Their practical household duties were light and mostly ceremonial, for their true worth to their lord lay in the status that they lent to him. Under the old order, the more armed, trained men that a lord could support, train and equip, the more power he had in the land.

Stripped of its mystique and fancy clothing, medieval aristocracy was ultimately a system of hereditary war-band leaders, thugs with swords who could bring a lot of mates along to the fight. The lord advertised the size of his war band by dressing them all alike in 'livery' and never went anywhere without a sizeable proportion of them in tow. Under the Tudors this style of living was slipping away as the Crown tightened its grip, stamped out military competition among the aristocracy and rewarded a different set of behaviours with power at court. The serving men were becoming increasingly decorative, human status symbols more than actual fighting men, but the mindset lingered on for several more generations. Young men in service had little to do, but a great deal of pride to support. They were provided with good clothes and weapons so that they would cut a dash as they followed their lord around and much was made of their high birth and 'natural superiority'. Is it any wonder that they liked to fight?

A sword and buckler man elegantly attired in the service of his lord.

If you fancied swanning about town swashing your buckler in search of a fight, to the consternation of fuddy-duddy aldermen and city elders, then you needed to know how to handle yourself in the affray. It was all very well for outside commentators to say that there were seldom fatalities, but those swords were not blunted stage weapons – they were sharp.

Sword and buckler was an old combination, tried and tested for generations upon the battlefields of Europe and England alike by foot soldiers, their usage refined over the years. The sword had a flat, broad blade, sharp on both edges and generally of short to medium length. The buckler was a small round shield, rarely more than a foot in diameter, often sporting a point or spike in the centre (the spike was an English speciality). It was used to protect the sword arm, to deflect blows and to punch out with. There were two main styles of fighting with this combination of arms in use across Europe: the German form, for which we have manuals going right back to the thirteenth century, and the Italian method, delineated in a couple of sixteenth-century texts. There is just one manual covering sword and buckler fighting written by an Englishman, but it went unpublished until the manuscript was uncovered in the nineteenth century. Of all of these texts, only one was available in a printed format in English during our period, that of the Italian Giacomo di Grassi, but even this did not appear until 1594, after sword and buckler fighting had gone firmly out of fashion. The manuals, then, are an extremely useful record of sword and buckler fighting by our countrymen, but people did not use them to learn from. Fighting was learnt not from a book, but from practical instruction within the households of great lords or in lessons given in fencing schools run by the newly legalized 'Masters of Defence'.

Earlier, kings had been very concerned about ordinary men learning to use weapons that could be used in civilian life to rob and intimidate and had tried to curtail any attempts to teach the arts outside of the supervision of lordly households, but Henry VIII felt rather differently and deliberately set up and authorized a formal system that was theoretically open to any man. Masters of Defence were able to set up schools and were required to teach the use of a range of weaponry, including several sorts of pole arm combat and several sorts of sword fighting (but not archery or firearms, which were not considered as weapons that needed specialized skilled tutoring, a quick demonstration and some solo practice being sufficient). Anyone paying for such hand-to-hand fighting tuition was termed a 'scholler'. If they reached a certain level of proficiency, they could choose to enter a public contest (known as a 'prize' or 'prize fight') fighting several bouts, firstly in front of a panel of masters and then in public in six separate sword-fighting styles using blunt swords. If they conducted themselves with sufficient skill, they were entitled to be called 'free schollers'. Seven years at this level and another set of public formal bouts upon the raised 'scaffold' (we would call it a stage) and they became 'provosts', who were entitled to teach but only under the auspices of a full Master of Defence. It took seven more years and yet another set of public performances to attain the rank of 'master' with the right to run your own school. The rules don't always appear to have been strictly adhered to; at least one of the known masters progressed up the ranks a little quicker than the fourteen years, but the spirit of the system largely held.

To know what exactly it was that they were teaching, we return to the one English manual that talks about sword and buckler fighting, that of George Silver. Although it was not published until much later, it was written and prepared for publication in around 1599 to accompany his more argumentative work *Paradoxes of Defence* in which he argues that the old-fashioned sword and buckler style of combat was better in battle than the new-fashioned rapier and that men should stick with it for all their fighting needs.

Silver's approved method was to hold both hands out in front of you, close together, the buckler held to shield your sword-holding hand. This is firmly within the German style of usage and indeed much of Mr Silver's method follows that of the 'Fechtbuch', the thirteenth-century manuscript that is our oldest complete fencing manual in Europe. In many ways it is a completely counter-intuitive method of fighting and wholly unlike the sort of sword play that you generally see upon the silver screen (most of which would have got you killed in very short order). To make your body move and posture like this when under pressure requires an enormous amount of drilling and practice. If you are to survive a sword fight, it must become second nature, unthinking and automatic. No one emerges from such intensive training without their previously normal movements, posture and gait being permanently modified, hence the soldier's walk that we mocked earlier. The body is held flexed with a slight bend at knee and elbow, and the feet are placed a shoulder width apart with one a little in front of the other.

The technique was based upon a series of body positions – much like dance – which you needed to learn to hold and move between. Generally called 'wards' or 'guards', these positions were defensive, making it hard for your opponent to land a blow – almost every angle of attack would first meet your blade. From these positions you could launch your own attack if you saw an opening in your enemy's defence. Fights could involve an almost interminable period of cautious circling or dancing back and forth as both protagonists held their defensive 'wards' and hoped that the other person made a mistake and dropped out of position, or 'dropped their guard'.

George Silver was fond of a position that he called 'open fight': 'carry your hand and hilt aloft above your head, either with the point upright, or point backward, which is best, yet use that which you shall find most apt to strike, thrust, or ward'. He doesn't mention it but images would indicate that the left hand, clutching your buckler, was also raised so that it held the small shield over the wrist and back of the sword-bearing hand. From this position you could sweep your sword down to either the right or the left, in an arc that would block any blow aiming at your head or body, using gravity to lend weight to your own cut with the option of a sharp draw back towards your own body at the end of the movement, turning a chop into a powered slash that would cut through flesh rather than just bludgeon it.

That position which he called 'guardant' also called for the hilt of the sword to be carried above the head, but this time the sword pointed down, diagonally across the body with the tip lying in front of the left knee. This was an overtly more defensive posture, offering speedier protection

Sword and buckler fighting in the Italian manner with the buckler held forwards.

but slower attack. Where the Italian di Grassi would have advocated holding the buckler firmly forward and using it to actively deflect thrusts, George Silver advises us to hold it back in reserve, protecting the sword arm unless you use it against the enemy's blade after his thrust is 'spent' at the end of a strike or he if has foolishly allowed you to get into very close contact with him when it becomes an armoured fist to punch him with. There were several variants on both of these positions with names, like 'bastard guardant' with the same diagonal sword blade but held lower, and 'close fight' with the hilt at your hip or thigh and the point diagonally across your body but with the tip upwards.

Fighting in the street was a major annoyance to large sectors of the population, but what if you wanted to upset your fellow swashbucklers? How could you cheat? What were the social conventions and rules that you could flout? We have met one already in Edmond Howes's words when he claimed that men held it to be 'cowardly and beastlie' to strike beneath the waist. It is also worth noting that many sword masters also thought that a strike at the legs was a dangerous strike to make, as the blow left you undefended across your own head and body.

The formal bouts organized by the Masters of Defence prohibited any form of wrestling, punching or other close quarters action, and making thrusts with your sword was actually outlawed, even when used in self-defence, according to a proclamation of 1538:

> *and furthermore his majesty, being credibly informed that divers and sundry his subjects have lately been murdered and slain in sundry frays happening by chance by reason of sudden foins with swords and other weapons, minding to take away the occasion of such sudden slaying and murdering, doth straightly charge and command that no person or persons in any fray or fight that shall happen of chance between them shall use in his fight any foin or foins* [foin means a thrust].

So, despite using sharp-edged weapons, the swashbuckling bravados, eschewing the biting, kicking, punching and thrusting of actual battle, were engaging in a curtailed form of fighting, something more akin to sport than warfare. Or at least they were if they behaved themselves and didn't 'cheat'.

If you wanted to be considered honourable within the ranks of the swashbucklers, you held to a particular style of fighting, aiming your blows only at the upper body with sweeping cuts. When fighting brought you close together you delivered your blow and pulled back at once to a sword fighting distance. You fought only with fellow members of the sword and buckler fraternity and you held your contests and challenges in the customary locations. By adopting the attire and gait of a swashbuckler you publicly advertised your brawling intentions, allowing all others to keep clear if they chose to, or gather to watch if they liked. Such behaviour might well bring you approval among the young bloods and admiration from some young women, but it was not hard to shock them, to step beyond their slightly cosy form of bad behaviour. If you fought like you meant it, fought up close and personal, if you launched attacks without warning and didn't hold back, you'd quickly find yourself being left out of the jolly backslapping and camaraderie.

From Cockerel to Peacock

Civilian sword fighting, however, was about to undergo a revolution in style, movement, etiquette, social status and outcome. The sword and buckler men were to become neither a source of concern or admiration but the butt of the joke; they became typified as crude, old-fashioned and lower-class fools eager to fight over nothing. According to Fynes Moryson in 1617, 'nothing was more common with them than to fight about taking the right or left hand or the wall' (walking next to the wall being the more honourable position when two men walk down the street together, while if there were three people the best position was in the centre), 'or upon any unpleasing countenance' (he looked at me funny). 'But at this day they scorne such men, and esteeme them of an idle brane who for ridiculous or trifling causes run the trial of single fight.' The days of swashbucklers drawn from the serving-men classes were over; all eyes were shifting to the elegant rapier-trained gentleman. The street fighting didn't stop, it just changed.

The fashion came from Italy and swept all before it. When Shakespeare wrote *Romeo and Juliet* sometime between 1594 and 1596 he gave the servants swords and bucklers to fight with and armed the gentlemen (Romeo, Mercutio and Tybalt) with rapiers; anything else would have looked ridiculous to the informed audience of the Globe Theatre who had seen the change played out in the streets around them. Rapiers were not all that effective upon the battlefield, a fact that George Silver harped on about at length, but that was not really the point. The men who wore them did not intend to use them in defence of the realm; they wore them as fashion statements and as status signifiers.

Legally, soldiers of any rank could wear a sword while about soldierly business, but only those who bore a coat of arms (gentlemen and members of the nobility) were entitled to wear a sword in civilian life. The wearing of a sword thus became a visual shorthand for social rank and everyone wanted one that reflected the latest fashions. And since it was the rapier that hung about their hips it would be the rapier that they turned to for self-defence, for defence of their reputations and to indulge their more antisocial desires. As a result, duelling quickly became a rewarding and effective method of bullying. Or perhaps we should say that the *threat* of duelling facilitated upper-class bad behaviour, as much as the actual duelling itself. Naturally, the swords assisted a young man in his attempts to exploit and intimidate the lower classes most satisfactorily. If your tailor started making too much noise about the need to settle your bill before he embarked upon making your next outfit, or the innkeeper was reluctant to rent you his best chamber once he had repaired the damage from last week, you had merely to allow your hand to drift towards the hilt of your sword to lend a certain immediacy to your claims for preferential treatment. If either of these tradesmen needed a little more persuasion, it was an easy matter to manufacture a supposed slight to your honour ('Do you doubt my word?!') and perhaps draw your sword a little, demanding an apology. A reputation helped, of course. The trick was to have a few very public quarrels with people who you were sure would quickly back down. Of course, you needed to look like you knew what you were doing.

Rapier fighting in the Italian style required completely different poses and techniques to the old sword and buckler. It was all about thrusting the tip of the sword into the other person; cuts and slashes were discouraged as being dangerously slow. Rapiers were slender and long so cuts carried less force than the broader and shorter blades that Silver favoured. You couldn't slice an arm off with a rapier but you could pierce your opponent's eye or stick them in the stomach, and, moreover, if you followed the fashionable technique you could do so very fast.

To frighten the unwary and make the loose-lipped tremble, a gentleman had only to draw his sword and adopt one of the new 'ward' postures. The knees were still flexed but the feet were further apart than those of the old buckler men and well turned out. Arms, however, moved very much less, the action now originating at the wrist more often than elbow or shoulder. Many of the movements required a twist in the upper body to add speed and power to straight-armed thrusts. Once again, we note that we have already met the pertinent elements of this posture and movement in our discussion of fashionable gaits: the turn out, the twist of the shoulders, the increased emphasis upon the diagonal line.

Italian fencing practice was influencing all manner of movement, but fashionable, classically inspired movement was also shaping fencing styles. That which felt good, secure and natural in times of danger was that which felt familiar. Fashions in clothing were playing a part, too. Anyone who has ever worn accurate reproductions can tell you that the cut of late-Elizabethan doublets gives you a decidedly different range of comfortable arm movements to those of thirty years earlier. Rapiers were part of elite male clothing and had to work within the constraints that those clothes imposed. Tight, high-cut armholes, stiff high collars and ruffs combined to make it difficult to hold a sword above your head. The battlefield use of broadswords, backswords and hangers (all types of sword) all called for high held 'wards' but not the gentlemanly use of the rapier, whose arm positions did not extend above shoulder height and were mostly lower than that.

Furthermore, gentlemen found the new person of the Italian fencing master more conducive to their position in life. Of gentlemanly status and education, these men set themselves up in opposition to the Masters of Defence, offering more elite premises and structured, theoretically based teaching. They boasted an exclusive clientele and refused to expose themselves or their pupils to any form of public trial or exam. They claimed superiority over the old forms in matters of social status, honour and technique. Vincentio Saviolo, who ran one of the fencing schools in London as well as writing a fencing manual that was published in 1595, promised that, 'a man having the perfect knowledge and practise of this arte, although but small of stature and weake of strength, may with a little removing of his foot, a sudain turning of his hand, a slight declining of his bodie, subdue and overcome the fierce braving pride of tall strong bodies'.

Agility, lightness and speed were the new watchwords for this style of fencing. We have noted how training involved learning positions and movements linking those positions just as you might learn ballet, but now the relationship between the two heightens. Fencers were to move their feet, with well turned-out toes, from positions that in modern ballet would be called first, second, third and fourth, with the last two as the most common and stable 'wards'. Third, for example, is described by Saviolo as 'his right legge formoste, a little bending the knee, so that the heele of his right foote stand iust against the midst of his left foote'. Footwork receives almost as much attention within the fencing manuals as sword positions, with both straight and circling steps and

Vincentio Saviolo's instructions for fighting with the rapier and dagger called for agility, a flexible spine and a nimble wrist but rarely required a gentleman to raise his arms above shoulder height.

sideways slips, and practice is recommended to know how to 'turne and shift your bodie as well on one side as the other'. Saviolo also borrows dance terminology, talking of making 'these passages' when he advises practising sequences, just as a dancing master would have discussed dance moves.

Saviolo clearly favoured the single rapier, but his potential pupils were initially much more interested in a combination of rapier and dagger. Even the most casual survey of portraits of the era will show you English gentlemen wearing both as a matter of course: the rapier hanging at their side and the dagger tucked into the belt, often at their back (the proliferation of diagonal poses is a big help in exposing them to view) with just the tip of the hilt showing on the wearer's right side. When a gentleman prepared to fight he drew both blades and stood right foot in front, knees flexed with his right heel directly against the middle of the turned-out left foot. He held the sword in his right hand with the point of the sword held up at a forty-five-degree angle and his hand low and drawn back just behind his hip, allowing the right shoulder to twist backwards. The dagger sat in his left hand; when brought out in front, with arm nearly straight, the dagger's tip was just in front of the tip of the sword. He kept his weight on his toes so that he could move quickly and lightly at a moment's notice. The dagger was employed as a defence against his opponent's sword, used to push aside and deflect thrusts; the sword was held in readiness to thrust through when opportunity arose.

It was a very dangerous form of swordplay when fought with sharp, pointed blades. Practice bouts were undertaken with the tips of the blade sheathed in a ball or button, or with specially made training weapons known as 'wasters'. With a sharp point the speed of the play lent a degree of chance and accident to the outcome of any encounter. Whereas the cut and slash of buckler fighting, within the constraints of well-behaved practice, could be countered by skill, rendering the fight generally non-lethal, the thrust of a rapier and dagger fight could be the undoing of even the most able swordsman. A rank beginner could get lucky and spear his more skilled opponent almost by accident. As several period commentators pointed out, the semi-sporting gatherings at West Smithfield died away as rapiers took over: 'And the cause why single fights are more rare in England in these times is the dangerous fight at single rapier' (Fynes Moryson, 1617).

As a keen and responsive observer of contemporary life, Shakespeare uses just such an accidental killing by rapier in *Romeo and Juliet*, where Romeo's attempt to stop a fight between Tybalt and Mercutio – which seems almost playful to begin with – causes just enough distraction for a thrust to go astray. When the English translator of Giacomo di Grassi's *His True Arte of Defence* introduced his work in 1595, he too pointed out the increased danger: 'The Sword and Buckler fight was long while allowed in England … but now being layd downe, the sworde but with Serving men is not much regarded, and the Rapier fight generally allowed, as a weapon most perilous, therefore most feared, and thereupon private quarrels and common frayes soonest shunned.' Even its most enthusiastic proponents acknowledged that rapier fights were deadly and unpredictable.

With the new Italian fashion in swords came a renewed interest in fighting for honour. At the heart of this change was Vincentio Saviolo's influential fencing manual, which came in two books: *The first intreating of the use of the Rapier and Dagger. The second of Honor and honorable Quarrels.* Within its pages he set out all those cases where he believed a duel was appropriate – which included any words or actions

Duelling proved a seductive concept.

that a man of 'honour' found to be offensive. He argued that duelling was not for revenge or punishment but for justice, to prove innocence. Anything that cast a gentleman in an unjustly poor light warranted a duel, and victory in that fight would show the world his true mettle.

Of all offences against a gentleman, 'giving the lye' (accusing him of lying) was the most unforgivable, the one act that almost guaranteed a duel among those who ascribed to the code. It had grown out of the old medieval idea of trial by combat. The Italian Renaissance duel was different in that it dealt only with matters of 'honour', not property disputes or criminal matters as the old combats had. The last decade of the sixteenth century and the first of the seventeenth saw English gentlemen embrace this code of conduct with gusto. The society-wide preoccupation with personal reputation found a new means of expression. The English translator of Giacomo di Grassi's *Arte of Defence* asserted that this use of weaponry is purely for the 'defence of man's life and reputation' and not for any trivial or foolish reason, quite deliberately assigning the same importance to a man's reputation as to his life. If village slanging matches could lead surgeons and tailors to fight with daggers and staffs, as we saw when Thomas Hutson fought John Baker, then words and reputation could just as easily, perhaps even more easily, lead the male elite to draw their rapiers and run each other through. The difference lay only in the more formal framing and organization of such elite fights.

One form of malice was given a decided boost by duelling culture: the accusation of cowardice. As we have seen, men from the upper echelons of society were under additional pressure to physically support the pride and social standing of their families. Military leadership, or at least the potential for military leadership, underpinned their status and this of course required demonstrable personal courage. If you did not step up when insulting words were flung, you could be deemed a coward and all your claims to respect crumbled. The words of drunkards, fools or the clearly malicious could be shrugged off and dismissed, braved out by the socially confident with little harm done, but the duelling codes opened up new ways of making and framing those accusations in ways that were hard to sidestep.

Vincentio's second book, *Of Honor and honorable Quarrels*, was a goldmine for those seeking inspiration for such attacks. Here was a carefully set out series of situations and disagreements where the offended party 'ought to challenge him that offereth that dishonour', presented together with all the codes and formulae of words for escalating the initial encounter into a full-blown duel in which the ill-wisher could trap an unsuspecting innocent. An accusation of cowardice did not, after all, require an actual duel. Indeed, the whole point of the exercise was for the victim to refuse to fight, thus opening himself up to the charge. You needed to manufacture a challenge that would seem serious enough to those hearing the tale that it called for a meeting upon the fields of honour, but not one sufficient to actually provoke a man to such dangerous action. It was a tricky balance, but one that had lots to offer. Remember it is only other people – who need not have been present at the 'offensive' moment – who need to believe in the severity of the insult. Good knowledge of the codes of the duel mixed with just the right level of fabrication and misrepresentation could work to brand a man a lily-livered coward for life.

Another version that smacks more of cruel mischief than deep malice is laid before our eyes in Shakespeare's *Twelfth Night*, where foolish and elderly suitor Sir Andrew Aguecheek is manoeuvred into challenging the count's servant (a young male actor playing the role of a young woman dressed as a man). Both try to back out repeatedly, with Sir Andrew resorting to an attempt to bribe his way out, but they are cajoled and shamed into drawing their swords. It is a theatrical and exaggerated performance and a chance for the audience to laugh and jeer at the cowardice on display, but it points quite nicely to the opportunities for troublemaking that duelling offered.

Duels were illegal, condemned officially by both Church and state. Murder was technically still murder, even when carried out with swords at dawn by prior arrangement. Monarchs made proclamations condemning the practice and demanded severe punishments for those who indulged in it, and many moralists decried the whole idea as un-Christian and inimical to an orderly state. Yet the glamour that accompanied this high-class, Italian cultural import had a habit of overcoming people's scruples. Courtiers flocked to learn Italian fencing moves, and detailed points of 'correct' duelling procedure became topics of conversation. Queen Elizabeth is known to have stopped one duel among her personal circle by reference to those rules, forbidding a duel between an earl and a duke on the grounds that they were not of equal rank rather than simply forbidding it outright as illegal or against her will.

Duels were only supposed to occur between social equals of gentry status and above. In addition, Saviolo instructed his readers to refuse the challenge of anyone lacking in personal honour, delineating 'all theeves, robbers, ruffians, tavern haunters, excommunicate persons, heretics, usurers and all other persons, not living as a Gentleman or a Soldier' as unworthy of a formal challenge.

From its inception, duelling was supposed to be a very visible way of life that was restricted to the most privileged in society and marked them out as substantially different from the merely wealthy. Unsurprisingly, therefore, our badly behaved, upstart heroes embraced the code with alacrity. If a readiness to duel marked you out as a member of this elite club, then it cost nothing but a sword, some half decent clothes and some courage to pass yourself off as a fashionable gent. You had simply to strut around a bit, talk ostentatiously about honour and threaten to challenge people.

Despite the fencing masters' attempts to maintain the exclusivity of their schools and codes of conduct, duelling quickly slipped out into more common practice. Beyond the world of theatre and literature, which took to the concept with great dramatic enthusiasm, real-life cases are not hard to find.

In the quiet town of Rye, far from fashionable London fencing schools, for example, it seems that John Wollffe and John Peerse had the requisite knowledge, courage, ambition and pride to see themselves as potential gentlemen of honour. They were both lodgers within Edward Gryffyn's house, which almost certainly marks them as bachelors. John Peerse at least was decidedly not a coat of arms bearing member of the gentry, but rather he was recorded as a common sailor, while the two men's landlord was a simple brewer. This, then, was far from the world of courtly grace. Hostilities between the two men first broke out in the wee hours of the morning of 15 February 1599, just four years after Saviolo's influential book was published. The time of day hints at a plentiful consumption of alcohol, though we can't be certain, and words led to 'a blowe or two with their fystes'. So far, so conventional – this is just the sort of behaviour that we have encountered among other ordinary men – but at first light they met again at the Mountes in Rye, drew their rapiers and fought a duel.

The glamorous idea of duelling for honour seduced more than just the potential participants. Magistrates were just as demonstrably drawn to its mystique by its varnish of sophistication and manly bravery. Kill a man in a duel and the chances were you would be brought before the courts upon a murder charge, but few were convicted of that charge; rather, a verdict of 'manslaughter by chance medley' was reached in almost every case. Unlike outright murder, this was a verdict that allowed a literate man (who could read or at least recite a particular Latin verse) to plead 'benefit of clergy', thus commuting the punishment from death to branding on the hand and possibly a fine. Such a legal outcome could not have been so common had there not been a degree of sympathy among the more established members of the governing elite. This slightly indulgent attitude even extended down the social scale to men like John Peerse, who was convicted of just such a manslaughter charge after killing his adversary with what appears to have been a thrust that severed the femoral artery, John Wollffe dying 'immediately' of a small wound 'in the right thigh near the belly'.

All Together Now, Boys

The first mention of semi-organized gangs comes in 1598 when Stephen Gosson gave a sermon in London castigating those who were known as 'the Damned Crew', whom he called 'menne without feare or feeling eyther of Hell or Heaven, delighting in that title'. They were 'roaring boys' who had come together, joining forces in scandalous living, taking courage from each other and egging on those who held back. Alone they were just guls and gallants that cosmopolitan Londoners mocked and fleeced, but as a gang they could terrorize a neighbourhood. The Damned Crew also turn up in Nicholas Breton's discourse *The Court and Country*, which seeks to contrast all that is good about country living with all that is bad about the life of the fashionable courtier, who will not 'endure a lye without death, challenge for a frowne, and kill for a fowle word, adventure all for nothing, or perhaps worse than nothinge, lose lands, goods, life or foule all in a murther, or a bloody bargain to please a Punke, and to be counted a Captaine of the Divels army, or a Gallant of the damned crew'.

Poems and plays of the era give them a name check here and there, highlighting their highly visible status as the seventeenth century dawned. They were odd, exotic and newsworthy. Back in the 1560s and '70s, loose groups of swashbucklers had wandered the streets. For the most part they were high-born servants in livery, and upon the streets they tended to be clumped together according to the familial and political alliances of their lords and masters. If they got out of hand, the authorities could demand that they be hauled back into line by the heads of their various households. But the Damned Crew were a gang in their own right, without such restraining hands. They were an independent fellowship of like-minded, wealthy and independent young men who turned their backs upon the usual rules of society, exploiting all the privileges of their rank but taking none of the responsibility that was supposed to accompany it. As gentlemen's sons (or at least as men pretending to be gentlemen's sons) they exploited their right to wear rapiers and daggers, dressed flamboyantly and employed the 'strawling' walk of the courtier. They gathered together to gamble over cards and dice, they publicly flaunted their mistresses in the city's inns and taverns, they were loud and intimidating, hurling abuse at those around them. And they could be violent. Quickness of temper and a ready willingness to draw those swords on the slightest pretext formed the very basis of their reputation.

Initially, they began as a very loose and informal grouping (or possibly a set of groupings) who then adopted the insult by which others knew them – a damned or cursed crew. Over time they crystalized into a single entity with a subculture of their own, at least in the eyes of outsiders. Perhaps the best records that we have of the Damned Crew and their exploits arise out of a court case in the Star Chamber in 1600. The reason for the matter reaching such a prestigious court was the social status of the main offender. Sir Edmund Baynham had been newly knighted by Lord Essex during his Irish campaign, and three years previously he had served a term as a Member of Parliament; yet, at just twenty-three years old, he had been apprehended as a leading figure of the Damned Crew.

It happened on 18 March, when six wealthy young men and their servants gathered at the Mermaid Tavern in Bread Street, London. The leader of their gang, called 'Capten' by his fellows, was Thomas Dutton from Isleworth in Middlesex and they had met at what was probably the poshest public drinking establishment in the capital. Taverns in general served wine rather than beer and catered to a middle- and upper-class clientele. The Mermaid was one of the best known and was frequented by a very famous assortment of people, including most of the poets of the day. Trouble first broke out when 'Capten Dutton' and his crew tried to break one of the house rules by sending out for some musicians. The keeper of the tavern, William Williamson, wasn't having any of it. As he explained to the court, he had stuck to his policy to 'usually debarr & deny Musitains & Such lyke Company to enter or resorte unto his said house at any tyme by day or night'. When the argument got out of hand, Williamson summoned the local constable and his watchmen to restore order. It didn't go terribly well.

The Crew, now out in the street, stripped off their cloaks, hats and other loose garments, handing them to their servants to hold. They drew their rapiers and daggers and 'with a great Noyse, outcry and clamor' launched themselves at the hapless

Calling for some musicians to join them in the tavern served as the spark that ignited an evening of violence that saw the Damned Crew fight their way across the city.

watchmen who were put 'in great danger of their lives'. The commotion had drawn a crowd, which the Crew then taunted, Sir Edmund Baynham grabbing one poor old chap by the beard and yanking it back and forth. The watch withdrew as the Crew carried on loudly through the streets. As they neared the churchyard of St Paul's Cathedral, Constable James Briggs, alerted probably by the defeated men at Bread Street, had stationed four of his own watchmen before hurrying off to round up some more men. The watchmen, this time, were 'armed with halberd or Bille as the manner of watchmen is'. Thomas Badger took the lead among the Crew 'pressing forward before the rest' and demanding to know why they had brought weapons, telling them to stand aside and threatening to 'runne them through with his rapier'. Baynham made a grab for Hugh Williams's halberd, wrenched it from him and struck him, inflicting 'a great wound in the head, whereby blood did issue out'. Thomas Dutton made a stab with his rapier that tore through Williams's jerkin, but miraculously missed his stomach. At this point, Constable James Briggs arrived with reinforcements. Edmund Baynham, fresh from having floored Williams, now swung the halberd again and 'struck a great blowe on the head of the same James Briggs & therewith felled him to the ground giving him one sore wound on the head, and afterwards two other wounds on the body'. But the Damned Crew were now outnumbered and nursing wounds of their own (the records are much quieter about the nature of these injuries, sustained while resisting arrest). It was over, bar the shouting – although there was plenty of that, especially from Baynham. As the wounds on both sides were being bandaged by the local barber surgeon, Sir Edmund caught sight of Constable James Briggs being treated. 'Art thou alive yett,' he called out, 'I thought thou haddst bene killed or ells I would have runne my rapier upp to the hilte in thee.' As the Crew were taken away he began threatening Briggs with both further violence and bogus lawsuits brought by his friends in high places.

John Grymes and Gregory Fenner managed to escape arrest, but Sir Edmund Baynham, William Grantham,

Watchmen were traditionally equipped with lanterns, bells and pole arms of some description.

Thomas Dutton and Thomas Badger were all tried for their crimes. In a further move that follows the pattern of behaviour that people came to expect of the Damned Crew, the four men pleaded that it was all the fault of the drink and just a bit of fun. They got off with a fine – a very large fine, of £200 – but these were rich men.

The Damned Crew, despite their notoriety, did not last long, but the idea of elite gangs did. In 1623, the 'Tytere tue' gang, for example, were being investigated by the Privy Council. Building upon the tradition, they adopted quite formalized, and certainly ritualized, structures with titles and hierarchies and a very clear sense of shared identity. The evidence presented to the Privy Council spoke not just of ranks and titles but also of an initiation ceremony whereby members swore eternal brotherhood by dipping their daggers into wine and making an oath of secrecy, to aid and assist each other. It was a singularly well-heeled and educated gang – the name comes from the opening words of a Latin poem by Virgil and translates as 'You, Tytrus', a fortunate youth who had managed to hang on to his land when many others were ousted from theirs. The principal members wore a black bugle, while their followers (servants and persons of lower social rank) sported blue ribbons. Drinking, shouting, swearing, beating up members of the night watch and breaking people's windows seem to have been their specialities.

Roving gangs of upper-class louts were a uniquely London experience. Only in the capital was there a sufficiently large population of the idle rich. Smaller knots of riotous apprentices turn up at frequent intervals in the records of numerous towns and cities, as well as London, but their activities came in short spurts, outbursts of action interspersed with more studious and business-like peace. Members of the Damned Crew or the Tytere tue had no workshops to return to and much less daily supervision from their elders.

The outbreak of war changed things. Suddenly these idle, rich young men had acquired a new outlet for their violent tendencies, and new allegiances and groupings formed as the nation erupted into full-blown civil strife.

August 1642: King and Parliament were at war, Ireland was awash with blood, fighting in England was intensifying and Sergeant Nehemiah Wharton was writing home to his former master, the merchant George Willingham. 'Every day our soildiers by stealth doe visit papists houses and constraine from them both meate and money they give them whole greate loves and Chesses which they triumphantly carry away upon the points of their swords.' It wasn't an isolated incident. Extorting goods and money at the point of a sword was endemic throughout the Civil War. In comparison to the horror of battle perhaps it seems minor, but this particular form of dubious behaviour spread misery far and wide. Sometimes it was a matter of policy, expressly ordered by military commanders. 'Tuesday our soildiers by commission from his exelency marched [7?] miles unto S[i]r William Russels house and pillaged it unto the bare walls'. At other times it arose out of more general hostility to the religious and political allegiances of people the soldiers encountered. 'Thursday august the 26th our soldiers pillaged a malignant fellowes house in this City'. Often it was simply for food, or better food, as supply lines and pay frequently failed. Nehemiah's regiment had a particular taste for venison, and plundered deer parks wherever they could. But there was also the simple business of robbing and terrorizing other people because you could.

The records are full of examples of people's homes being raided by soldiers of their own political and religious affiliations, who smashed and destroyed that which they didn't take. William Prynne, for example, was a well-known Puritan and a vocal and ardent supporter of Parliament, yet thirty Parliamentary soldiers turned up at his house in Swainswick, Bath, 'climbed over my walls, forced my doors, beat my servants and workmen without any provocation, drew their swords on me'. They went on to take all the clothing in the house, drink all the beer, throw all the food to the dogs, break all the cups and dishes and then forced the women to do their laundry and demanded money. In other incidents, whole flocks of sheep were slaughtered and left to rot. Furniture was smashed up and burnt when perfectly good stocks of prepared firewood stood alongside, barrels of beer and wine were broken open and poured onto the ground, mattresses thrown into muddy ponds, and so it went on. Excuses were often rather thin, with soldiers claiming that their victims were papists or 'malignants' on little or no evidence. 'We are all the most abominable plunderers,' Colonel Arthur Goodwin, governor of Aylesbury for the Parliamentary side, wrote. 'I am ashamed to look an honest man in the face.' As well he might have been, since by one report four out of five houses in Aylesbury were looted, in a town that was well known for its strong Parliamentary bias.

Towards the end of the conflict the Royalist side earned a particularly bad reputation for this sort of behaviour. One typical report relates how 'a great party of Cavaliers came into

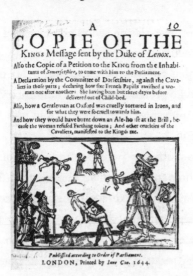

A
COPIE OF THE
KINGS Meſſage ſent by the Duke of *Lenox.*
Alſo the Copie of a Petition to the KING from the Inhabitants of *Somerſetſhire,* to come with him to the Parliament.
A Declaration by the Committee of Dorſetſhire, againſt the Cava-
liers in thoſe parts ; declaring how five French Papiſts raviſhed a wo-
man one after another: She having been but three dayes before
delivered out of Child-bed.
Alſo, how a Gentleman at Oxford was cruelly tortured in Irons, and
for what they were ſo cruell towards him.
And how they would have burnt down an Ale-houſe at the Brill, be-
cauſe the woman refuſed Farthing tokens ; And other cruelties of the
Cavaliers, manifeſted to the Kings me.

Publiſhed according to Order of Parliament.
LONDON, Printed by *Iane Coe.* 1644.

War brought accounts of terrible deeds upon both sides of the conflict, some of which sound now like baseless propaganda and others ring horribly true as the chaos unleashed the worst of behaviours.

Chipping Norton, where they were quartered, and, at their going hence, to show their impartiality (though there was but one Roundhead in the town) they plundered every house therein of whatsoever was of value'. Many people, however, could see little difference between the two. One stanza of the ballad 'A Somerset Man's Complaint' lamented:

> *Ize had Zixe oxen tother day,*
> *and them the Roundheads stole away,*
> *a Mischeif be their speed.*
> *I had six horses left me whole*
> *and them the Cavalieers have stole,*
> *Gods zorcs they are both agreed.*

One of the best-selling woodcuts of the day pictured a soldier dressed not in armour or carrying weapons but draped in looted goods. There was even a term, a 'straggler', for someone who pretended to be a soldier in order to wander about the countryside terrorizing people into handing over their possessions.

War, as ever, allowed people to indulge their less savoury side and swords proved to be the perfect tool for such extortion. Sixteen-foot pikes were clearly useless in a domestic setting and muskets, too, could be tricky in small spaces and in rapidly changing scenarios (they were cumbersome and slow to load by modern standards), but a sword in the hand was a very visible and immediate threat.

The end of hostilities ushered in a return to previous shenanigans and exploits. 'There was no sooner an end to

A soldier as envisaged by a war-weary soul.

the Wars of England, but a great company of Officers and Soldiers being discarded, they repaired to the famous city of London, in hope that new troubles would arise, to maintain them in the same disordered course they formally practised in the Armies, but missing fewell to feed their desires, they began to study living by their wits.' So declared the opening lines of a pamphlet in 1652 entitled 'A Notable and Pleasant History of the Famous Knights of the Blade, commonly called Hectors'. The pamphlet described rituals, initiation ceremonies and riotous, frequently violent, escapades of a gang of ne'er-do-wells who refused to settle back into a respectable life. 'All that I can say to their manner of life is, that it consists much in cheat and cousenage, gaming, decoying, pimping, whoring, swearing and drinking, and with the nobler sort, in robbing', our pamphleteer continues.

Notice how it is the gentry element, the 'nobler sort', who are turning to robbery. Pistols now were backing up swords as sources of bully power. Gentlemen, the cavalry in particular, had acquired and learnt to use them upon the battlefield. Many, too, had practised the art of plundering and extortion up and down the country, discovering pistols to be especially useful from horseback. Such skills were not to be forgotten. John Evelyn called the Hectors 'a sort of perfect debauchee' and accused them of drinking blood. The blood drinking was probably derived from an infamous, sensationalist account of a group of defeated Royalists in Berkshire recounted in the May 1650 edition of *A Perfect Diurnall*. Supposedly, they decided to drink to the King's health using their own blood and proceeded to slice bits off their own buttocks in order to do so. It was not something that the London-based Hectors had actually done, but it must have seemed to Evelyn like just the sort of thing such men would do. Swaggering through the streets intimidating the citizenry, loudly and publicly engaging in almost every form of bad behaviour possible, they quickly became infamous.

About town they increasingly indulged in 'scowering', arriving together at a tavern or alehouse, forcibly driving everyone else out, eating and drinking to excess and leaving without paying, stopping only to beat up anyone unlucky enough to catch their attention. They were well known enough for 'Hector' to acquire a new meaning: to bully, intimidate or shout down.

As our period ends, these London gangs of high-born men were about to separate out into two of the great scourges of the late seventeenth- and eighteenth-century world, with those of the highest birth becoming self-indulgent, syphilis-pocked rakehells, and the less financially secure slipping into the short and brutal life of the gentleman highwayman.

It's clear that violent transgression was something that changed in style and focus considerably over time but was also tightly bound by issues of gender and social class. Violence might well often be considered bad and contrary to the social norms, filling whole forests-worth of paper diatribes against swashbucklers, brawlers, duellists, plunderers and Hectors, but most of those who burst into illicit action were actually conforming to a set of largely unwritten rules. Primarily, they observed the stricture that fighting was a man thing; women who fought were rare birds who largely stuck to scratching faces and pulling hair. When men fought, they did so in styles and with weapons that were considered appropriate to their social position, that emphasized their bravery and manliness. Rapiers were for gentlemen, staffs and agricultural implements for commoners, sword and bucklers for servants. Quick and immediate violence for the defence of ordinary reputations, delayed and formalized duels for lordly ones.

Chapter 5

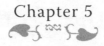

DISGUSTING HABITS

Let us step indoors for a moment and see what's going on in the domestic or semi-domestic sphere. While fighting, shouting, gestures and mockery do all have a place indoors, their major expressions reside outside in public places; personal habits, however, are much more noticeable at close quarters. Indoors, where you can corner someone in a room, is the very best place to display all those annoying little ticks, lapses and repetitive movements. It is easier to ignore or pretend to be unaware of a gentleman scratching at his genitals when you are both out and about, one can simply walk on, but in the pub, visiting friends or in your own home people have to work much harder to cope with your behaviour. The impact is magnified both by the physical closeness and by the implied intimacy of the situation.

At the Trough

It was at dinner that you had the finest opportunities to disgust people with your personal habits. All faults were magnified during the dining ritual, and a whole host of food-specific examples of bad manners came into play.

Messy eating of any sort was disgusting. Spreading, slopping, spraying or spilling food caused lips to curl, nostrils to flare and faces to be turned away. The disgust increased the nearer to your mouth the food got. Egg dribbling down your ruff was nastier than egg on the tablecloth, but letting it slip down your chin was worse still. Guffawing with laughter was never considered gentlemanly behaviour, but to do so at table when your mouth was full of food was a heinous breach of manners. Scratching yourself was likewise generally seen as mildly unpleasant, but do so at table and people shuffled away from you. The more personal, bodily and intimate the habit, the less people were willing to tolerate it in the dining room.

Cleanliness and control were never more valued than when eating. Before you even entered the room it was considered polite to spend a few moments tidying yourself up and adjusting your attire – and washing your hands was absolutely essential. Attention to the cleanliness of fingernails was required and hair was to be combed. Those clean hands were to be kept as clean and grease-free as possible throughout the meal by judicious recourse to your napkin. The same went for mouths and lips, again utilizing the napkin at frequent intervals to 'oft wipe and make your mouth full cleane'. Mouths were not supposed to become overly greasy even as you ate between napkin wipes. Children were issued with instructions to eat small, controllable mouthfuls, not to overload their spoons, not to gnaw on bones or lick their fingers. Small, dainty mouthfuls, chewed with the lips firmly closed, was the polite way to eat, and as for slurping or making other noises as you ate, most authors expressed zero tolerance: 'sup not lowde of thy pottage, no tyme in all thy lyfe', admonished Sir Hugh Rhodes with more than usual vehemence.

Dinner and, to a lesser degree, supper were central, pivotal activities in any household. It was not just a matter of eating. Dinner occupied a quasi-religious position in daily life, carrying echoes of Holy Communion. Echoes that were quite deliberately called upon by the clergy of all denominations in their sermons when they evoked images of harmony and the importance of obedience and adherence to the 'natural' and 'god given' hierarchy. Prayers both at the start and finish of the meal set the tone, marking the activity out as separate from and more significant than the hours either side.

To give you some idea of the heights to which the nobility took this ritualistic approach, let me outline the first few minutes of the table-laying ceremony in Viscount Montague's household at the very end of the sixteenth century. At ten in the morning, the gentleman usher was to assemble the senior staff of the ewery (table linen and hand-washing department), pantry (bread), buttery (drink) and seller (silver, pewter and other tableware). The yeoman of the ewery laid out all his linens, basins and jugs upon a small side table and, once he was ready, he picked up the main tablecloth for the lord's table and the yeoman usher (the gentleman usher's underling) accompanied him as he walked forward 'with due reverence'. They stopped and bowed twice upon the journey, once when they reached the middle of the room and again when they arrived at the table. No one else was in the room yet; they were bowing to the place where the lord would later sit. The yeoman usher was then required to kiss his right hand and lay it on the table, and then the yeoman of the ewery laid the still-folded tablecloth on the spot that had been kissed. The two men then carefully spread the cloth. In some households this was done with special rods so that they handled it as little as possible. The two men then retreated back across the room, pausing to bow again on the way. And that is just the tablecloth! Much the same ceremony accompanied all the other necessities: the salt, the napkins, any cutlery and the trenchers.

In addition to the ewer board laid with its basins and jugs, the cup board had to be prepared for drinking cups and vessels of wine and beer, and the carvery table with its knives and towels. Friends and I have re-enacted the full service on numerous occasions and despite plenty of practice, so that it all runs smoothly and seamlessly, it still takes us half an hour before we can begin to bring the actual food onto the table.

The seating plan and the food served closely echoed one's social position within the gathering. Your place at dinner was a direct reflection of your 'place' in the hierarchy. Within this framework, small acts of deference to those in authority were carried out and a very physical form of largesse was distributed. People waited, for example, for the head of the table to begin eating before they started their own meal, and the best food was placed in front of him (or occasionally her). As public and personal marks of favour, small portions of this best dish were often distributed to selected diners to enliven the plainer fare meted out to lower-ranking members of the household and signal a lord or master's approval. Younger and junior members of the company usually undertook different parts of the preparations of the table and serving of the food. Even those of noble birth might do so when young as part of their education and training for a life of power and privilege.

Manuals of household management (such as that which gave us the account of Viscount Montague's table laying) give us more detail. These are mostly handwritten manuscripts that could act as practical guides for senior staff. Each member of the household is instructed, in turn, a little about their general duties and in great detail about their involvement in the preparation of the dining areas, the laying of the table and their part in serving the food. They delineate when and where each individual in the household eats their meal, from kitchen boys to grooms of the stable. Grooms, for example, ate in the great hall of most of these lordly houses but were the last group to be served and were seated nearest the door. Kitchen boys, on the other hand, were almost always kept in the kitchen for their meal.

This daily enactment of social relationships and lines of authority, with its pauses for prayer, demanded the most formal manners. The controlled nature of the space and the uniformity of the approved activity made any deviation from the formal code stand out. Small insults and slights could have large impacts within this setting. Usurping someone else's place, for instance, could be very effective in an ongoing war of attrition. You wouldn't get away with too great a social jump – a groom who tried to sit at the top table could expect a sound thrashing – but if one groom routinely made a play for the senior of the two available places, the other groom would be sorely aggrieved. Spreading out along the bench or holding your elbows out wide, restricting other people's personal space, was another annoying and aggressive tactic. Leaning on or across the table worked, too.

The details of food-sharing etiquette gave enormous room for manoeuvre. We have talked a lot about various conduct books and their advice upon speech, movement and general management of the person, but if we look at those that were published before, say, 1620, we would be struck by how heavily they are focused upon the precise manner of doling out morsels of food. Well over half of their content could be described thus.

At the top end of the social scale a trained carver was employed. This was an honourable position in its own right and generally reserved for someone of high birth. When he had finished carving the lord's food, he was assigned a place at the gentleman waiter's table within the great hall, along one side but near the top end of the room. His job required different techniques for each type of meat brought before him, each with its own specialized words: mallards were 'unbraced', herons were 'dismembered' and quail were 'winged', while the humble chicken had three different carving terms and methods depending upon what particular type of chicken it was – a hen was 'spoyled', a castrated cockerel known as a capon was 'sauced', and a young bird that we might call a pullet (but was then known as a chicken) was 'surched'. He performed his art at a prominent side table at the upper end of the hall with great ceremony, wearing a special, long 'arming towel' that draped around his neck and whose two ends were tucked into his belt as a badge of office.

If you carved – or perhaps I should stick to the correct terminology and say sauced – a capon, you first lifted and cut off the legs, then the wings, and poured a little wine or ale over them as a light sauce. The wing had then to be 'minced' before being served up. Woodcocks or baby herons (heronshrews) were first unlaced (breast meat carved off), then the pinions and neck were 'broken' before the legs were removed, with the feet still on. All the various bits were then laid neatly upon the serving dish and the appropriate sauce was poured over. The cooking method, as well as the species, could alter the carving technique, but ultimately it was the carver's job to reduce all meats cleanly, elegantly and in public into manageable bite-sized pieces.

Lower down the social scale, whether among those of lower rank within a great household or in smaller, humbler establishments, the majority of different foodstuffs arrived on the table either as something that could be eaten with a spoon ('spoonmeats' was the period term) or already cut up into bite-sized morsels served in communal vessels, the carving having been done without fuss or ceremony back in the kitchen. The diners helped themselves from these common bowls using a combination of fingers, spoons and knives, so sharing etiquette quickly came to the fore.

Fishing about for the best bits was decidedly rude and so was randomly planting your spoon or knife all over the bowl. You were supposed to stick to the bit nearest to you, mentally dividing the dish up into sections like a pie. Oh, and turning the dish around so that the good bits were now

Sharing was central to the dining experience.

upon your side of the dish was also 'scarcely honest'. If the luck of the draw set some especially good small dish of food right in front of you, then setting to and devouring the lot could breed plenty of resentment. Your failure to offer the dish around and serve others before yourself would not go unnoticed. Even choice morsels within a dish could be used to snub fellow diners. Remark with delight how all of the kidneys within a steak and kidney pie had fallen to your side of the dish, and fail to spear them one by one and hand them out to your fellows, and everyone would know how little you cared for them. To leave out one person from a sharing event could be very pointed.

Giving the whole bowl a bit of a stir was liable to make your fellow diners cross, as was anything that involved fiddling about or playing with the shared food. Such behaviours went beyond rude and into the realm of disgust, alongside the smearing, spreading and spraying that we began with. Food was appetizing when it was kept in distinct and discrete sections, and subject to careful control. Anything that broke those boundaries, that allowed the food to flow or fall out of its allotted space, was dirty and stomach-churning.

Putting unwanted morsels back in the shared bowl after you had lifted them out was another off-putting gesture, but returning a bit of gristle after it had been in your mouth was so disgusting that no one would eat with you. Several texts warn against returning anything that had touched your teeth. '*Dentibus etacta. Non sit buccella redacta,*' wrote the anonymous author of one manuscript fragment entitled '*Ut te geras Mensam*' – or in English: 'let not the piece of food, when it has been touched by the teeth, be put back', from 'How to bear yourself at Table'. Generally, when broaching this subject authors spoke of not returning bread to the dish after you had bitten into it, rather than meat. People could also be put off their dinner by finger licking or by a spoon covered in slobber being returned to the dish for a second helping. If mess became more distressing as it neared your mouth, like the egg on your chin rather than on your ruff, then food passing the lips represented the point of no return. Once food entered the mouth no one wanted to see it ever again. Or hear it. Chewing with your mouth open was one of the most widely reviled habits.

Open mouths were repellent in their own right, even without partially chewed food in them. Yawn, gape, sneeze, burp or cough without at least a token attempt to mask the action and people looked on askance. If you had the time and control to get a handkerchief up in front of your mouth so much the better, but the sudden nature of several of these explosions meant that the simple act of raising the hand to obscure the sight of an open mouth was acceptable. On a purely practical front, open mouths held the possibility of bad breath issuing forth where it might revolt those forced to breathe it in. A hand or handkerchief disrupted such airflow and could help to spare people the smell. But the sight of the open mouth was also to be avoided, regardless of breath.

Open mouths offended for the most part because they, like bodily fluids, breached the inside/outside boundary. To look inside was both overly intimate and faintly disgusting. The bodily interior was private. Only within marriage, when two people's flesh became spiritually one, was there supposed to be any penetration or sharing of this internal realm. The wetness of mouths was also repellent, being closely linked with corruption, decay and filth. Cleanliness, by contrast, was always linked with dryness. William Fiston in his 1609 *Schoole of Good Manners* called the 'driveling' of the mouth 'loathsome' and warned 'beware of this beastliness'. Remember, too, all those insults based on the open mouth: 'frog mouthed', 'flounder face', 'slack jawed' and so forth that called up thoughts of wide, spreading orifices of all sorts. The mouth lolling open was also used as an image of the mindlessness shared by drunkards and idiots, the very antithesis of wit and self-control. It is no coincidence then that the gate to hell was always depicted as a gaping maw waiting to swallow people up.

When the writers of conduct books for elite children wished to dissuade their young readers from certain rude behaviours they often claimed that the common people were prone to such errors – wiping your nose upon your sleeve was 'like a fishmonger', for instance. But was that really true of table manners? Could you still offend and annoy a fishmonger by messy eating? Would a wheelwright have cared if you had greasy fingers or swiped the best bits from the bowl?

On a practical front, some of these rules were easy to follow even in the depths of poverty, if you so chose. Keeping your mouth closed when chewing is not expensive and can be mastered by very young children, for example. But there were some elements of polite behaviour that would have been out of reach.

Napkin use is all very well if you have a napkin and the facilities to launder it regularly, but how many people did? It's not an easy question to answer. We do have a large body of evidence about the contents and equipment that people had at home in the form of inventories taken after death, but such inventories contain a number of problems for the historian. Survival of the documents is a bit patchy – good in some areas and almost non-existent in others. The records are much more fulsome among those who were wealthier with more to pass on to their heirs, leaving us with only a scattering of records for poorer people. Married women technically owned nothing, so what we have in practical terms are inventories only at the demise of household heads: men, widows and spinsters. The people making the lists were also a varied bunch of officials, friends and neighbours who all had a different idea of just what should be included in the list at all, what level of detail was appropriate and just how items should be grouped together. So one inventory will group the entire contents of a house together with the description 'all the household stuff' and another will list every spoon separately. As napkins are small items of fairly low value, there is a strong possibility that not everyone thought that they were worth mentioning at all. Inventories, therefore, can give us an idea of a minimum. They tell us some of the things that were present, but leave us guessing about how much has gone unrecorded. Absence of evidence, as any historian or archaeologist will tell you, is not evidence of absence.

Bearing all these issues in mind, let's take a quick peek at a few inventories to give us a (necessarily rather vague) sense of napkin ownership. Looking in this instance at just the 130 surviving wills and inventories for the medium-sized market town of Banbury, Oxfordshire, for a twenty-year period, from 1591 until 1611, we find that fifty-three out of that 130 list napkins among the household goods. Another sixteen simply refer to 'all the linen' or 'the napery', which may or may not have actually included napkins. A retired vicar was the most enthusiastic napkin owner in this sample, with ninety of them in his house at the time of his death, while the barber surgeon was not far behind with a stock of eighty-four. Most people, however, had far less. The most common stock was half a dozen, and two people had a grand total of one each. More common than napkins by far was the ownership of tablecloths – almost double the number of households – and there was only one example of someone who had napkins but no cloth for the table. It should come as no surprise that the larger stocks of napkins were found in wealthier households, but the presence of small numbers across a very wide cross-section of wealth brackets is more illuminating. Thomas Beste, for example, was a day labourer who left a wife and three small children. They had a small house with a tiny patch of land attached and a very basic range of furniture. His entire worth at his death was £2 1s 8d, but it still included one solitary table napkin.

The impression we get, therefore, is that a sizeable proportion of the population had some table linens, but few owned large enough stocks to use a clean napkin at every meal. There would appear to have been strong social pressure to participate in some of the niceties of elite dining manners, at least upon special occasions. Tablecloths and napkins add very little to the practical survival of a family and yet many people who will have known food shortages were willing to invest in them.

A wider survey of inventories over a longer period and in multiple geographical locations shows table linens to be one of the first luxury goods to be present in ordinary homes. In the 1550s, they are rare outside the homes of the gentry and merchant class but they spread rapidly as soon as people have the wherewithal. Only beds and bedding seem to have commanded a higher priority among the wider population. If you rank inventories by value, the spending hierarchy becomes clear. At the very bottom layer people concentrate their assets upon very simple practicalities: a couple of cooking vessels, a stool or two, a single set of clothes and a few basic tools. If the good times roll, they begin to add bedsteads and bedding with maybe a table and chest. Linens occupy the next layer of comfort: firstly sheets for the bed, then a tablecloth or two, then a towel for hand washing, a 'drinking cloth' (which I think is a cloth used to wipe the rim of a communal cup between users) and a set of napkins. Only when people had amassed a suitably large stock of these linens did they start to branch out into other luxuries and status indicators, such as pewter vessels, cushions, more elaborate furniture and so forth.

Good table manners clearly held significance for lots of people, not just the wealthy. So there is a definite possibility that you could offend the local wheelwright, miller or even a simple labourer and his family by flouting the basic rules of good table manners. Perhaps if they only had a very small stock of table linens, they were especially concerned about hand washing and small non-messy mouthfuls in order to avoid unnecessary laundry and heavy wear and tear on the few linens that they did have. It's impossible to know for certain, and presumably standards varied from household to household, but upper-class sneers about ordinary manners should not be taken purely at face value. Very humble people cared about dining rituals and were willing to part with hard-earned cash in order to enact them. Just imagine how much upset you could cause by arriving in such a household, demanding food, chucking unwanted bits over your shoulder, belching, farting and smearing greasy hands all over the precious tablecloth.

We do have some fairly broad hints that there were two groups of people who routinely exhibited rather lax personal habits. The older, richer and most importantly, more powerful members of society enjoyed a certain licence to be as objectionable as any of Mr Dekker's guls. 'Eate as impudently as you can,' he instructs, 'for that's most Gentlemanlike.' The very same conduct texts that instruct young serving men in the niceties of polite life also contain frequent reminders that they are not to take offence or even register disapproval at the behaviour of their 'betters'. Social superiors were under much less pressure to behave with formal politeness and consideration to their underlings. The elite were encouraged to modulate their manners according to the company they were keeping. When in the presence of their own social superiors the full formal code applied; among equals it could be adjusted according to how intimate and familiar you were. In front of inferiors, you really didn't need to bother, unless you were particularly fastidious or wished to show them some special consideration. Indeed in some situations, a degree of informality towards lesser beings was interpreted as a mark of favour, of condescending intimacy and friendship. Rather than being distant and exacting, the nobleman who farted along with his henchmen and made a joke of it was temporarily allowing them licence to relax in his presence.

It was, as ever, all a matter of degree and context. A gentleman in a tavern who indulged in fart jokes, slurped his pottage, blew his nose on the tablecloth and monopolized all the choicest delicacies on offer might think that he was presenting a display of his power and superiority, and might feel that he was stamping his authority over the humbler citizens present, but Thomas Dekker's readership were drawing up their own conclusions and quietly adding a few figures to the bill. (Mr Dekker actually includes a section telling his guls never to question the bill or pay too much attention to the prices listed.) They felt the insult implied in the boorish behaviour. They were aware of the formal code and knew when it was being flouted and that such bodily laxity held an aggressive, arrogant edge.

The other group who made a habit of flouting the rules were to be found among those of an especially godly persuasion.

We have met before people who felt that dissembling disguise and outward show were fundamentally immoral. Just as some of them refused to conform to the socially required displays of deference and respect in terms of hats, bows and curtsies, so could they be unwilling to follow other aspects of good manners. For Quakers and Puritans alike it was a matter of separating out the 'empty ceremony' of fashion that could be thought of as deceitful performances from the 'natural honesty' of behaviour that came from genuine care about other people's well-being.

Interpretations of just where this divide came provided great potential for cultural dissonance. Nicholas Breton, for example, was clearly a devout man, well within the religious mainstream, someone who would be marked out as 'godly' and maybe as 'a hotter sort of Protestant' but not 'Puritan'; and yet, overly fussy and precise manners cut little ice with him. In his 1618 discourse *The Court and Country*, he contrasted 'the dainty fare, sweetly dressed and neatly serued' of the socially pretentious and courtly, with the 'holesome fare, full dishes, white bread, and hearty drinke, cleane platters and faire linnen, good company, friendly talke, plaine musique, and a merry song' of a supposedly honest and more worthy country dwelling sort. Aristocratic dining rituals he condemned with obvious distaste as belonging to the court and the past:

> *I remember I haue heard my father tell of a world*
> *of orders … a Trencher must not be laid, nor a*
> *Napkin folded out of order; a dish set downe out*
> *of order, A Capon carued, nor a Rabbet vnlaced*

> *out of order; a Goose broken vp, nor a Pasty*
> *cut vp out of order; a Glasse filled, nor a Cup*
> *vncouered nor deliuered out of order; you must*
> *not stand, speake, nor looke out of order ... but*
> *in that there is difference of places, and euery*
> *one must haue their due, it is méets for good*
> *manners to kéepe the rules of good orders: But*
> *how much more at rest are we.*

It is very interesting that he carefully puts 'cleane platters and faire linnen' into his list of good country manners but the folding of napkins sits within his sneer about the overly elaborate. Clean eating is something that he endorses as simple, honest courtesy among people in genuine harmony with their fellow diners. Fashionable, sculptural napkin folding, however, goes beyond this, in his analysis, into the realms of empty and unnecessary ceremony.

There is not a great deal of evidence for napkin folding as an art in England, but in Italy, home to so many fashions aped across Europe, the practice was becoming a very notable aspect of the elite dining experience. It was not the personal napkins laid out for each diner that were subject to this art, but a separate set sculpted especially for show. The elaborate meal described by Vincenzo Cervio in his book *Il Trinciante* (1593) began with a huge centrepiece formed of concertina-folded white napkins arranged to form a three-dimensional castle. The towers and courtyards of this starched linen castle contained live birds and rabbits wearing coral necklaces. When the guests entered the room to the accompaniment of music and fireworks, the napkin-formed gates were opened, releasing the wildlife to fly and hop about the room.

The first book to be published, in 1629, upon the technique was *Li tre trattati* by Mattia Giegher. He worked at the University of Padua where he taught young men of high social standing the arts of carving, serving and napkin folding. These young men were also instructed in the rules of heraldry and the symbolism of emblems, so that they could use Giegher's techniques to design sophisticated and meaningful table centres. Such exhibits were much prized for displaying the education and erudition not just of the men who made them, but also the diners who appreciated them and commented upon the structures' various allusions and meanings. Such moments within the dining ritual emphasized the exclusivity and social prestige of the occasion. It was a great opportunity for snobs to exploit when boasting to their less privileged brethren about the fashionable, napkin-festooned events that they had attended. But napkin folding also provided good ammunition for others, such as Nicholas Breton, to lampoon, to dismiss as outrageous examples of empty ceremony and vain posturing.

If the gap between napkins used for cleanliness and napkins used for witty sculpture seems a fairly straightforward one when discussing the morality of good manners, other issues can be more obscure. Imagine yourself faced with a guest who belches loudly at table. You could take offence at their bad manners, their lack of consideration for other diners' sensibilities – but if your guest chose to wrong-foot you, they had only to call upon

God and the value of plain honesty in daily life. How very embarrassing, when you thought it was you who occupied the moral high ground, to be challenged with placing outward forms above religious rigour.

As we have seen, worries about the legitimacy of masking, disguising, hiding and pretending were common in the first half of the seventeenth century. Many forms of polite bodily control could be seen as hypocritical. William Gouge's summing up of puritanical objections in 1622 included phrases such as: 'many that have not a sparke of Gods feare in their hearts are able to carry themselves very orderly and mannerly' and 'Good manners are a hindrance to grace'. (He ultimately thought that these were bad arguments but still took the time to outline and refute them.) But were these behaviours – covering up a yawn or belch, turning away when you coughed or spat, or inventing falsehoods to divert attention from the fact that you were leaving the table in order to urinate – things that a devout person should do?

There would seem to be a second divide in the nature of good or bad behaviour here. Those elements of bodily management that consisted of covering nakedness had strong biblical support, and those that comprised disguising or covering actions did not. It would be much easier for someone seeking to follow God's law, free from man's artificial codes, to be polite and modest in terms of clothing his body than it would to find justification for suppressing a belch.

What we do encounter are numerous complaints about the overly devout indulging in 'affected' manners. 'When Puritanism grew into a faction, the zealous distinguished themselves both men and women, by several affectations of habit, looks and words,' remarked the writer and poet Lucy Hutchinson, with decided hostility. Along with the halting walk, clothing, hairstyles and speech, being more visible and public aspects of a separate and distinctive mode of self-presentation, form the focus of many of these complaints and descriptions. But one is left with a general feeling of ruffled feathers and discomfort aroused by low-level bad manners wrapped up in holier-than-thou attitudes.

Those who felt strongly about projecting a 'godly' image often described themselves as 'plain speaking', 'honest dealing' or 'plain in manner' – phrases that for me carry echoes of a modern set of behaviours found in the person who begins a sentence with the phrase, 'No offence, but …' and invariably goes on to say something that they know to be highly offensive, daring you to respond. The 'I speak as I find' comment at the end of something rude and personal functions in much the same way. Both of these phrases claim the right to bypass kindness and good manners by calling upon the greater moral authority of 'truth'. Now, I am well aware that this is a wholly subjective interpretation based upon nothing but my own culturally informed modern response, but I do not think we can rule out the possibility that 'plain in manner' fulfilled much the same role. If you do manage to slip back in time one day, please try it out for me.

A Powerful Thirst

To drink or not to drink, that is the question. Whether it is ruder in the pub to suffer the slings and arrows of outrageous refusal, or taking up the pot, drown your reason in ale. Both options could be construed as bad behaviour. Refusing a drink could be an insult and blatant provocation, while drunkenness could be bestial and foul. It was all in the context and the degree. Everyone drank some alcohol. Weak forms of ale and beer were the everyday drink of almost everyone. Water was drunk by people in the very depths of poverty and proverbially by Cornishmen (which may in itself be simply an indicator of regional low living standards) and it was generally out of necessity rather than preference. It was widely understood that ale and beer had some nutritive value and that water could be 'bad' and unhealthy.

Such 'knowledge' came not, of course, from modern scientific analysis, but from simple experience. Stagnant, stale or polluted water was frequently blamed for sickness and general ill health. According to Andrewe Boorde's very popular medical manual for laymen, the *Dyetary of Healthe*, for example, 'water is nat holsome sole by itself for an Englysshe man'. The only water that he would countenance drinking was watered wine, and he advised filtering and boiling the water first before adding it to the wine. Ale (made from malted barley, yeast and a variety of traditional herb flavourings but no hops), on the other hand, he regarded 'for an Englysh man is a natural drynke' and 'maketh a man stronge', while beer (made with added hops to give flavour and a preservative effect) was the 'naturall drynke of a dutche man', but 'it doth make a man fat'. This was written in the 1540s when beer was still regarded as a foreign import and largely confined to the metropolis. As the beer habit spread, ousting traditional ale in all but the most rural regions, worries about its ability to make people fat drifted away. That reference to watered wine, meanwhile, is a good reminder that most people most of the time drank very weak forms of wine, ale and beer. When we hear of soldiers or farm labourers being given eight pints of ale a day, we must not think in terms of modern standards. The exact alcoholic content of historical brews is very hard to pin down but contemporaries were quite clear that there were two basic types of drink: a weak ordinary version suitable for men, women and children on a daily basis, and a much stronger one for celebrations and social occasions.

When I have attempted to follow sixteenth-century ale and beer recipes I have had very varied results, but in general terms I would say that my household brews (or 'small ales') were about a quarter to a third of the strength of modern draught beers and my 'strong' ales varied from that of modern draught to bottled beers. Spread over a day of heavy manual labour, eight pints of small ale probably didn't even make a man merry, let alone drunk, particularly when you take into account the tolerances of a body brought up on such drink. When the question of drinking or not drinking was raised it was generally assumed that it was the strong ale, beer or unwatered wine that was being discussed; the ubiquitous consumption of the weak brews was uncontentious and taken for granted.

Outright drunkenness annoyed a lot of people from all walks of life. It comes as no surprise to hear the well-known Puritan William Prynne describe drunks as 'odious, swinish, unthrifty and state-disturbing', but the deep hostility voiced in the popular ballad of 1624, 'A Statute for Swearers and Drunkards' is indicative of disgust and anger unrelated to class or religious affinity. The second part begins:

> *You that sweate out your life*
> *in beastly drinking;*
> *Untill your bodies*
> *and breathe be stinking:*
> *You that sit sucking still*
> *at the strong barrel,*
> *Till into tatters rent*
> *turnes your apparel:*
> *You that by guzzling*
> *transforme your best features,*
> *Changing your selves from men*
> *to swinish creatures.*

The ballad is accompanied by a woodcut of a man at a table outside an inn or tavern. His hat is shown askew and his nose is drawn large and cross-hatched in an attempt to indicate a heightened colour in this black and white image. He stands straddling a piss pot, as if incontinent, and a great stream of vomit issues from his mouth.

It was a fairly popular theme for ballads, allowing people to laugh at the idiots who slipped from honest merrymaking and good fellowship into disgusting habits. 'Some were carousing while others were singing, / others like sots lay dead drunk on the floor, / Some at their fellows Glasses were slinging, / Another vomiting behind the door', ran one verse of another ballad accompanied by its own gleeful image.

The same rather cruel enjoyment of the more physically disgusting aspects of heavy drinking can be seen in the real-life example of Thomas Marsh of Layer Marney in Essex (uncovered by the historian Mark Hailwood in his book *Alehouses and Good Fellowship in Early Modern England*). Thomas Marsh was one of a group of men drinking one Wednesday evening at Turner's alehouse, a group that included the parish constable, John Lufkin. It was Lufkin's involvement that brought this particular instance to the attention of the courts when charges were brought against him for failing to discharge his duties. John Oultings, who was the witness in the case, arrived at the alehouse at 6 p.m., by which time the merry crew were already assembled. At around 9 p.m., John Lufkin dramatically called for the landlord to bring them the 'fowler', a huge 'stone pot' that Oultings estimated must have contained nearly two gallons of strong beer. It may have been refilled at some point, for when our witness, who was staying in one of the chambers overnight, came down at dawn, Lufkin and several of the others were still 'playing'. Thomas Marsh, however, was 'so drunk he fell fast asleep at the table, hanging down his head, foaming, slavering and pissing as he sat'. His compatriots thought this was a great joke, fetched a sack and placed it

The drunkard revealed in all his less pleasing aspects.

over Marsh's head. When Thomas Marsh made no response, clearly unconscious rather than asleep, John Lufkin then took the opportunity to shout in his ear that he would henceforth be known as 'fowler' and then undid his codpiece, exposing his genitals to view. It would not be until the following morning that the last of the drinking party left the alehouse, after a forty-eight-hour session.

When the largest vessel in an alehouse goes by the established name of 'the fowler' it is apparent that binge drinking on this scale was not unknown in the parish of Layer Marney. Individual pots or cups of ale or beer could be purchased in such establishments, but it was more common for a group of people drinking together to buy a shared jugful and perhaps bring their own cup with them. This eased the pressure upon landlords to invest in large numbers of drinking vessels and made drinking together a much more communal activity, but it also makes it very hard to gauge just how much Thomas Marsh consumed. Perhaps it was just that lack of precision that was Thomas's undoing.

Besides passing out and vomiting, drunkards were easy prey to a host of other vices, from gambling, smoking and fighting to making fools of themselves through the medium of dance.

Drinking so much that you pass out, throw up or piss yourself is a fairly foolproof way of repulsing other people. Loudly singing and shouting late at night, reeling down the street bumping into people and picking fights were all reliable methods of causing offence and anger, just as they are today. Then there was the long-term disapproval if you spent all your money on booze and were unable to support your wife, children and yourself. In such cases, even your old drinking buddies could fade away and give you dirty looks, as the 1615 plaintive ballad 'Nobody Loves Me' bewails:

> *Now that I have no Chinke,*
> *With the ducks may I drinke,*
> *All my friends from me shrinke,*
> *Nobody loves me.*

Moderate your drinking, however, so that you remained 'merry' and good company without tipping over into full 'drunkenness' and you were sitting pretty. Rather than upsetting or annoying people, the moderate drinker was considered to be an honest fellow. For every ballad that sings of the evils of drunkards there are two that extol the virtues of sociable gatherings with a glass or two, even if some of them have a rather defiant tone. The early seventeenth-century ballad 'To Drive the Cold Away' paints a picture of warmth and harmony: 'Old grudges forgot, are put in the Pot' when neighbours get together over a pot of ale. More elite poems and songs focus upon the value of wine (rather than beer or ale) for inspiring witty conversation and flowing verse. The poet and playwright Ben Jonson and his circle of friends were especially prolific in this arena. Helping people cope with the stresses and strains of life is another virtue frequently cited in the humbler sort of pro-drinking literature. People are encouraged to 'cast care away' or drink, laugh and sing 'in spite of all your woes'. But it is friendship, neighbourliness and camaraderie that provoke the biggest vote of approval for social drinking.

The difference between heavy and moderate drinking is quite explicit in the ballad 'A Health to All Good Fellows', which begins, 'Be merry my hearts, and call for your quarts, / and let no liquor be lacking', but adds a note of caution in verse two with:

> *We cannot be termed, all drunkards confirmed,*
> *so long as we are not unruly,*
> *weele drink and be civill.*

Being 'civil' was the key. Drinking was not in itself bad behaviour; drinking was good behaviour so long as you were still able to follow the general rules of sparing other people your bodily fluids and the sight of anything too personal and intimate. If you controlled yourself you were a 'good fellow', but if you didn't, or couldn't, then drinking was a disgusting habit.

The references to drunkards so far have all been male. However, women, naturally, also drank to excess. Elizabeth Clarke, née Kyffin, was a particularly desperate example. She lived in the parish of Myddle, Shropshire, in the second half of the seventeenth century, and Richard Gough, one of her neighbours, records how one evening her husband Francis 'went to fetch her from the ale-house in a very dark night, but shee, being unwilling to come, pretended it was soe dark that shee could not see to goe: hee told her hee would lead her by the arme, and gotte her away almost half way home, and then shee pretended shee had lost one of her shoes; and when hee had loosed her arme, and was groaping for the shoe, shee ran backe to the ale-house, and boulted him out, and would not come home that night.' Elizabeth was not the community's only habitual female drunkard. Judith Downton 'went dayly to the alehouse' where she 'spent her husband's estate soe fast that it seemed incredible'. William and Judith Crosse were a husband and wife team, 'both overmuch addicted to drunkeness', who also ran through their money at speed.

Alehouses and drunkenness were not restricted to the male half of the population, but nonetheless there is plenty of evidence for a more limited tolerance of female over-indulgence than that accorded to men. The German traveller

Thomas Platter was somewhat surprised that female public drinking was countenanced at all, commenting that it was in his view 'particularly curious that the women as well as the men, in fact more often than they, will frequent the taverns or ale-houses for enjoyment. They count it a great honour to be taken there and given wine with sugar to drink; and if one woman only is invited, then she will bring three or four other women along and they gaily toast each other.' Notice how the women are 'invited' to join in and that it is seen as something of a treat. If we take a look at one of the (small number of) ballads celebrating female good fellowship at the alehouse, we see a similar tone emerging, one that suggests that such gatherings were acceptable, but were surrounded with provisos.

> *So let the health goe round about,*
> *this day weel take our pleasure:*
> *Our husbands were last night all out,*
> *and well goe home by leisure?*
> *For sack and sugar let us joyne,*
> *you see it is cold weather?*
> *And blithely let us spend our coine,*
> *wee seldome meet together.*

This ballad, 'Fowre wittie Gossips disposed to be merry' (c. 1630), is a rather defiant piece, full of excuses. When the historian Amanda Flather analysed the references to people present in drinking establishments in Essex court cases in her book *Gender and Space in Early Modern England*, she found that 36 per cent of them were female, which puts it well within the bounds of normal, socially acceptable behaviour. We can't ignore, however, the way such behaviour came with additional caveats and restrictions for women drinkers. The case of Jane Boone, Anne Malabourne and Elizabeth Bagg, who met in a London tavern in 1631, is a clear reminder of the double standards in operation. The three single women, having enjoyed a quiet drink of burnt wine (fermented wine such as brandy) went up to the landlord and tried to pay the bill. He was furious, saying that his servant should not have served them and that they would never be served again in his establishment. Elizabeth protested that they were perfectly able and willing to pay for their drink, but the landlord called her a 'Jade' and continued saying that 'they were all jades that kept her company'.

But what about not drinking? We have already met the relevant concept 'a health to …' The drinking of 'healths' was to all intents and purposes compulsory. When one man (it was usually a man) stood, raised his glass and said the magic words, every other man in the group had to drink. The preacher Thomas Thompson may well have offended a room full of men himself by refusing. One of his sermons in 1612 rails against the custom and reeks of personal discomfort as he describes how someone who will not join in the drinking 'is accounted no good fellow, but a meacock, or a puritan'.

In Henry VIII's reign, the custom was a fairly innocuous one with one or perhaps two healths at a celebration or other important occasion, generally dedicated to the King and the host of the evening, but by the time Charles I ascended the throne in 1625 it was becoming a major phenomenon.

Everyone was getting in on the act. The 'lively lads' of one ballad all drink to each other in the alehouse: 'Here honest John, to thee I'll drinke and so to Will and Thomas', it proclaims. While, 'Here's to thee kind Harry' is in fact the chorus line of another ballad requiring everyone to drink at the end of each verse (there are over twenty of them). Nor it seems would a token sip do. 'What a disgrace is it held for a man to leave a drop in the bottom of his cup? What an affront is it to the company, not to pledge every man his whole one?' and skipping one or two in a string of healths, well, that was 'the greatest disrespect and Injury can be offer'd to the person in remembrance', remarked Clement Ellis in 1660, adding that such omissions could lead to duels.

One of the defining aspects of health drinking was its binding nature. Once the ritual began it was very hard for anyone involved to back out. For those who were having fun that was part of its appeal. Propose a toast and the fellow across the table who was beginning to shift in his seat and start talking about work in the morning was now obliged to stay a little longer. A couple more and he would be in no fit state to think sensibly about the consequences. Healths held a group together, turning casual meetings for a quick pint in the alehouse at the end of the day into long, late-night drinking sessions. Richard Younge describes exactly this in 1654, although he was clearly not happy about it. 'They will winde men in, and draw men on by drinking first a health to such a man, then to such a woman my mistris, then to everyone's mistris, then to some Lord or Ladie; their master, their magistrate, their Captain, Commander, &c. And never cease.'

The toasts also enforced a form of social glue, with public exchanges of dedications: the etiquette of the drinking party requiring that compliments towards one of your party or personal circle had to be returned in like form. Formal and formulaic, they provided an easy to acquire social language for those who might not know each other very well. Within this framework, different social classes could mix with little difficulty or embarrassment, something that several gentlemanly commentators, including Clement Ellis, found very unsettling.

When the tide had turned in the Civil War and Royalists began to see their cause crumble, the drinking of healths turned political. A health to the King (or Queen) had long been one of the most common toasts, but to continue the practice at this point in history carried an utterly different meaning. In the 1640s and '50s, toasting the monarch was a public declaration of partisanship; to many eyes it was seditious, even treasonous. But it was a simple action, a traditional action and could take place almost anywhere. It was a form of protest open to anyone of any social station within the usual structures of daily life. You could do it quietly in trusted company or shout it out in a public taproom. You could do it in sorrow and forlorn disappointment or you could bellow it in hopeful defiance.

By the late 1640s, such politically motivated toasting was making its way into print, with a raft of Royalist drinking songs appearing as ballad sheets. 'The Courtiers Health' was one of the first and begins, 'Come boyes fill us a Bumper, / wel make the nation Roare'. In addition to calling for 'a Brimmer to the King', the political nature of the drinking song is spelled out in the lines:

We Boyes are truely Loyal,
for Charles wel venture all,
We know his Blood is Royal,
his Name shall never fall.

Not content with celebrating Charles, the ballad also pours scorn upon Parliament itself and on its more visible supporters. I imagine those performing the line 'Pox on Phanaticks' positively shouted it.

It was not without its dangers either. There are countless cases of people getting into trouble with their toasts to the King. The Red Lion alehouse on the High Street in Bristol, for example, was the location of a vicious fight when a group of Parliamentary soldiers overheard a health being drunk to Charles and the Marquess of Ormonde in 1649. Two men died as a result. The number of people making such toasts and the scale of the disruption and worry they were causing led Parliament to ban health drinking in all its forms in 1654, prompting the poet Alexander Brome to write:

They vote that we shall,
Drink no healths at all,
Nor to King nor to Common-wealth,
So that now we must venture to drink 'um by
stealth.

Not that much stealth seems to have been necessary, though; the ban seems to have barely slowed the flow of Health ballads and there is little sign of a drop in the number of people getting into trouble over them.

So, to drink or not to drink? You could annoy people either way. You could offend people's physical sensibilities with your puking or urinating, or their moral scruples by forcing them to partake. You could sin against good neighbourliness by refusing to drink or attack their politics by calling healths, or, just as effectively, by pointedly walking away part way through. You could undermine their reputations by branding them as drunkards for drinking or as 'meacocks' for not. It was fertile territory indeed.

A Stinking Air

'[L]othesome to the eye, hateful to the nose, harmful to the brain, dangerous to the lungs': King James I thought that smoking tobacco was a disgusting habit. Mind you, he rather liked the taxes that it raised and the support that it gave to the attempt to colonize America in his name. From the 1580s onwards, widespread tobacco usage furnished large numbers of people with three new ways to annoy the neighbours. Most obviously, you could smoke or snuff it up, producing the sorts of sights and smells that offended the King, or you could sell it in taverns, alehouses, apothecaries, grocers, host rowdy parties of people who disturbed the neighbours, or, finally, you could grow it and deprive the King of his taxes.

The first wisps of smoke drifted onto English shores from sailors with Spanish connections when Henry VIII was still king. By the mid-1560s the whiff of tobacco was a common dockside smell but it was in the 1580s that it wreathed around the bodies of captains with political clout at court. Drake and Raleigh were names to conjure with and their adoption of the American Indian habit ensured that tobacco made the big time. By 1588, William Harrison was noting the popularity of the new habit, describing, for those who moved in less fashionable circles perhaps, how 'the taking in of the smoake of the Indian herbe called Tobacco, by an instrument formed like a little ladell, whereby it passeth from the mouth into the head and stomach, is greatly taken up and used'. A German visitor, Paul Hentzner, who visited London a decade later, commented in a rather surprised tone, 'At these spectacles [plays and bear baiting], and everywhere else, the English are constantly smoking the nicotine weed, which in America is called tobacco.'

They smoked it in tiny little pipes that took a good deal of care to manage. Anyone who has smoked a pipe, or been around people who smoke pipes, knows that even with modern grades of tobacco and pipes shaped by centuries of experimentation there is a degree of 'business' involved. The tobacco must be lit, any spent ash knocked out, and bowls refilled. Keeping a pipe lit is still something that people take a while to master. Faced with the tiny bowls (about two centimetres long and one centimetre in diameter) of sixteenth-century pipes, with the bowl tipped only thirty degrees from the horizontal, and a lack of matches or cigarette lighters, even the experienced pipe smoker can be flummoxed. So when we hear of people at the turn of the seventeenth century having lessons in smoking perhaps we shouldn't laugh so hard. Or, then again, perhaps we should, for it is Ben Jonson who encourages us to in his 1600 play *Every Man out of his Humour*, saying of one character, 'He comes up every term to learn to take tobacco and some new motions'. The 'new motions' were party tricks with smoke. There were smoke rings, of course, and a series of little puffs or 'smoke globes', and breathing the smoke out of your nose seems to have been particularly fashionable.

It is another playwright, Thomas Dekker, who provides us with the most detail about smoking culture. He really hated it and gives it as a trait to all his most foolish, empty and antisocial inventions, calling them at one point 'stinkards'. At this early date smoking was still an expensive habit (which is why the pipes were so small), with all of the weed arriving through Spanish or Portuguese hands, and to enhance the prestige of being a wealthy, fashionable smoker it was possible to invest in very costly paraphernalia. Firstly, you needed a box to keep your tobacco in. It would need to be fairly watertight and preferably fairly airtight. You would also need a means to light it, so that meant a tinderbox with its flint and steel, again of sufficient quality to keep your tinder dry. Many smokers relied upon a set of special small tongs to carry a lit ember from a fire or brazier up to their pipe. You would also need a cleaning tool for when the pipe became blocked. Thomas Dekker, with a sneer, suggested that you could have them all made of silver or gold so that you could at least pawn them when you had bankrupted yourself.

Some places and times were more effective than others when you wanted to blow your smoke up someone else's nose. Church was one. The Catholic Church on the Continent banned smoking in church and in all 'holy places' as being a disgusting and ungodly habit. The English Church didn't adopt that particular tactic but clergymen felt very justified, indeed obligated, to thunder against the 'lascivious' nature of smoking and its perceived close links with drunkenness and general vice. If you failed to find the courage to smoke in church, the next best opportunity to make lips curl was at the dinner table, where the smell would turn all tastes 'to ash'. Endless talk about tobacco – its different types, whether the 'cane' or the 'pudding' form was superior, which merchant had imported it, where it had been grown, the colour, texture, dryness and purity, the fineness of the 'mincing and shredding' or the various diseases that some (not all) medical men believed it could cure – could also serve, in several commentators' minds, to add irritation to the growing smog. Others complained that smoking made men silent, that the dull-witted used it and all its fiddle and faff to cover long gaps in the conversation when they could think of nothing to say. Either way, most detractors agreed, smoking made you into very boring company.

In 1614, the first commercial crop to arrive without Iberian involvement was put upon the London market by John Rolfe of Jamestown in Virginia. The early settlement of that colony had been dogged by disaster. In 1607, a number of men (and boys, but no women) had set out, inspired by what has been called the first true advertisement campaign in history, and like a bunch of our own guls they seem to have taken the exaggerated claims completely at face value, travelling with next to no farming equipment or expertise. Some rather poor luck (arriving during a drought) and a fulsome dose of bad behaviour that led them to squabble and fight among themselves and with the locals did not bode well. Despite a shipwreck and crisis in funding, further men, supplies and equipment (and eventually some women) arrived in dribs and drabs over the next few years, but it was a close-run thing, hundreds of the settlers dying of starvation, disease, drowning and military conflict – there was even some cannibalism.

John Rolfe's eventual arrival, after surviving shipwreck and the loss of his wife and child in Bermuda, marked a turning point, closely followed as it was by the arrival of the fourth supply fleet. In this improved environment he managed to plant a form of tobacco that was saleable in London. Previous samples sent back from the colony had been of the local variety that no one liked much, but this new form was grown from seed smuggled from Trinidad. Barnaby Rich, a soldier turned author, estimated that in 1614, as the first Virginian crop arrived, there were already 7,000 retail outlets for tobacco in London. This must be a bit of an exaggeration, but gives some indication of the size of the market that the colony could tap into. In many of the numerous outlets tobacco was merely an additional product. Taverns and apothecary shops seem to have been the main suppliers, but there were others for whom tobacco became the main or indeed only product. Customers were often encouraged to stay and smoke on the premises, producing new venues for socializing.

Many of the local London records over the next couple of

decades contain complaints about the new habit and the new establishments. The judges of Sergeants Inn, for example, made several attempts to shut down a business 'near adjoining' that was annoying them 'with the stench and smell of their tobacco'. The smell is something that turns up repeatedly when people object to tobacco, but it's not the only thing that they found disgusting about such emporiums. 'His shop is the Randevous of spitting, where men dialogue with their noses, and their communication is smoake,' wrote John Earle in 1628 when he sought to characterize the tobacco seller. We noted before how tobacco had a reputation for bringing up the phlegm – claims regarding its medical benefits all relied upon this characteristic. In addition, the combination of the types of tobacco and the shapes of the pipes meant that tar was drawn up from the bowl of smouldering leaves, along the length of the pipe and into the smoker's mouth, where, dark and bitter, it had to be spat out. The premises of tobacco sellers must have quickly acquired a very noticeable look and enduring smell.

And so to taxes. This is a story far from the capital, out among the green, rolling hills of Gloucestershire around the small town of Winchcombe. Here, an enterprising bunch of people started growing their own tobacco. Not the best quality perhaps, a more hardy variety to suit the climate, but with substantially cheaper transport costs and no import duty it was a commodity that could be sold at bargain prices. It was additionally rumoured to be mildly hallucinogenic, which may have increased its appeal. Unfortunately, the King saw it through different eyes. Back in 1604, the same year that he penned his personal diatribe against the evils of the weed, 'A Counterblast to Tobacco', James upped the tax on tobacco from the very modest 2d a pound of Elizabeth's reign to a whopping 6s 10d (representing a rise of around 4,000 per cent). In 1619, he ordered all tobacco, regardless of origin, to pass through the port of London to facilitate collection of these monies and banned the growing of the crop on home soil.

This probably came as music to the ears of the folk of Jamestown, inconveniencing as it did the trade via Spain and Portugal, much of which used Bristol, as well as cutting off local supplies. Buoyed up by rapidly rising sales and a king who favoured them, the colony took the opportunity to splash out and purchase twenty African men and make payments for a boatload of British women. The men, who had been baptized upon the journey, were initially taken on as indentured servants but that early equality with poorer Englishmen was soon eroded, and later merchants took care to avoid any spiritual teaching that might have afforded the subsequent Africans a Christian leg to stand upon. Cash was paid for the men, but the women were in effect purchased as 'wives' for 120 pounds of tobacco each. (The women were not technically enslaved; they were offered free passage to the colony on the understanding that they had forfeited their right to choose or refuse a husband and upon arrival the male colonists took their pick of them and paid the company.)

The people of Winchcombe, meanwhile, were having none of it. One of the large-scale growers, John Stratford, did indeed follow the King's wishes and ploughed up his crop that year, but his smaller neighbours carried on regardless and the next year he too was planting tobacco once more. It continued in this back and forth game of attrition for the next eighty years. Local records indicate that during the 1630s, fourteen areas of land were producing tobacco, the parish tithe barn was being used to dry the leaves and a couple of houses in North Street had been pressed into service as stores of the cured product. Soldiers were sent – several times – by subsequent regimes, to tame the farmers. They burnt fields and fought with locals and got precisely nowhere. The 1653 attempt generated a rather plaintive letter from the commander in the field:

> I got together 36 horse and went to Cheltenham early and found an armed multitude guarding the tobacco field. We broke through them and went into town but found no peace officer but a rabble of men and women calling for blood for their tobacco so had there been any action blood would have been spilt. The soldiers stood firm and with cocked pistols bade the multitude disperse but they would not and 200 more came from Winchcombe. Major Clarke is not come and I want advice. Ten men would not in 4 days destroy the good Tobacco about Cheltenham. The Cornet would not act and some of the County troops are dealers and planters. I was forced to retreat; the Justices rather hinder than help us.

You almost feel sorry for him, don't you? Almost. Twenty-three years later it is clear that nothing had changed, as Samuel Pepys recorded in his diary that another company of soldiers had been dispatched to Winchcombe, 'to spoil the tobacco there, which it seems the people there do plant contrary to law, and have always done, and still been under force and danger of having it spoiled, as it hath been oftentimes, and yet they will continue to plant'.

If you need any more pointers upon annoying the non-smokers, I suggest that you peruse that most wonderful of illustrated broadsides, 'The Armes of the Tobachonists', published in 1630. Two thirds of the sheet is filled by an image laid out like a full, formal coat of arms, devised, so the text beneath claims, by a group of bawds, whores, panders, brokers, knights of the post (customers of the whores), roarers and ordinary guls, which 'smoaky crew with oaths and smoak, all in a roome close sitting, / with huffing, puffing, snuffing, spawling, spitting / after a slavering haulk, and drisling hem' produced the perfect visual representation of their art.

If you are not practised at reading the complex visual messages of formal heraldry, some further text at the base of the image helps to illuminate some of the finer points. But suffice to say that, flanked by a pair of foreign chimney sweeps and topped by a crest formed of a 'moorish' man with two pipes breathing out great clouds of smoke from his nostrils, the shield itself depicts a naked man, legs astride and bent double with his backside towards us and his head between his legs. Two more pipes issue from his lips and a plume of smoke from his anus in what was probably to be read as a 'new motion' (pun most definitely intended).

Chapter 6

REPULSIVE BODIES

Many of the bodily rules, taboos and injunctions of our Renaissance forebears have remained in place and unaltered. There are a few instances where we would have a few more scruples, such as a reluctance to spit in public, and there are conversely a few areas where our laxity would cause consternation, particularly in matters of bodily exposure, but on the whole, that which our parents drum into us in childhood is much the same as that which was drummed into our predecessors. Such common ground makes it remarkably easy for us to understand and emulate the badly behaved of the past.

Snotty-Nosed and Drooling

Let us start with noses. These were supposed to be kept clean by the judicious application of handkerchiefs while turning 'the body a little if there is any honest man there', so that the action was at least partially obscured. Noses were never to be picked in public, especially not at the dinner table. Inspecting the contents of your handkerchief after blowing your nose was a particularly disgusting habit. Nor were you ever to emulate those who 'thrust their fingers into their nostrils, and make pellets of that they pick out' (a translation of *Il Galateo* by Giovanni Della Casa). Such manners are intimately familiar to us today and yet there are elements that might still fox a time traveller.

Not everyone, it was acknowledged, had a handkerchief to hand. If that proved to be the case, then it was preferable to blow your nose between a pinch of your finger and thumb and cast the offending matter onto the ground where you scuffed and ground it into the soil with your shoe rather than leaving a globule for other people to step in. You did not, if you wished to be seen as well mannered, wipe your nose on your sleeve (reminiscent of fishmongers) or upon your bonnet or gown, 'being rustical and rude' in Erasmus's mind. In his manners book for boys, Sir Hugh Rhodes demanded that lads blow their noses first thing in the morning, upon waking, and again at the very beginning of their morning cleansing ritual before dressing. Across the board, the writers of manners books were keen for you to keep your phlegm out of other people's business as much as possible. Loud nose blowing was condemned as 'a filthy thinge', while snorting and sniffing were worse.

The ideal was to be discreet and quiet about such actions, neither drawing attention nor leaving a mess that might dirty or inconvenience those around you. The bodily functions of the well behaved were to be kept as private as possible. Giving your nose a good blow first thing in the morning before venturing forth from your chamber reduced the chances of you needing to attend to it when you were out and about among other people. Turning aside from those present when you did need to blow both actually and symbolically removed the actions from other people's immediate presence. These two simple principles of discretion and distancing informed much of the practical advice upon managing the body.

If, in another example, you had to fart – and it was best not to do so at all in company – then you should do so quietly and without making any movement or comment that alerted people to it. Such simple precepts made it very easy to manufacture offence when the desire took you. Placing your left hand upon your stomach, lifting your right buttock off the bench and sighing loudly, with or without the actual accompanying fart, could embarrass and discomfort a whole room full of fellow diners. Talk of ear wax, the fullness of your bladder or a persistent itch could be enough to make listeners uncomfortable, and if, having thus drawn their attention to the subject, you then proceeded to scratch at yourself, stick your finger in your ear or jiggle about from one foot to the other, discomfort could quickly turn to active distaste.

As we implied earlier, spitting was taken to be rather less rude throughout this early period than it is now. We have largely forgotten that spitting was as much a part of our cultural response to bodily processes as nose blowing (in preference to nose wiping or sniffing). Medical advice used to maintain that an occasional expectoration was necessary for health, expelling corrupt matter from the body. Certain medicines were available to stimulate the production of saliva in order to encourage the action. In the eighteenth and nineteenth centuries, chewing tobacco was actively advertised in terms of its 'beneficial stimulation of the saliva gland'.

For many of us, the only memory of this cultural phenomenon is found in the Western, where saloon bars have a spittoon in the corner. Their presence in such a setting, in the early years of the twentieth century, is apt, for they were indeed one of the last places that you would have found them. Pressure to stop spitting began in the second half of the nineteenth century in the cities of Britain where desperate overcrowding made tuberculosis a particularly virulent hazard, in part because of spit lying on streets and floors. Medical persuasion soon translated into strong social pressure and the change in manners rolled out across the nation and over the Atlantic. But even without this understanding of contagion, in the sixteenth and seventeenth centuries spitting could still carry some potential for offence.

Erasmus was most concerned that, as with nose blowing and snot, a person should turn aside in order to spit, that they should be careful not to spit on anyone and that they should take the time to grind the resultant mess into the ground so that 'it trouble no mans heart nor stomacke' – a comment that makes it very clear that discarded bodily fluids provoked physical revulsion. Handkerchiefs were again to be deployed if you needed to spit in formal indoor situations, and it was considered a particularly gross habit to spit across the dinner table.

Yet to not spit at all, to swallow a mouthful of spit, was also considered 'fowle' and 'uncleanly'. Spitting was felt to be a necessary and unavoidable action that needed to be managed with discretion. Your duty as a well-behaved person of breeding and good reputation was to spare other people, as Richard Weste's little ditties in his *The Booke of Demeanor* make clear:

> *If spitting chance to move thee so,*
> *thou canst it not forbeare,*
> *Remember do it modestly,*
> *consider who is there.*

There was also a worry that some people had allowed the action to become more than a necessity – that they had got into the habit of regular, frequent spitting, almost as a sort of punctuation to their speech.

Numerous Elizabethan texts mention 'unnecessary' spitting, and indeed coughing, peppered through people's social interactions generally in a mildly reproving tone as if it was a bit annoying and not perfectly well mannered, but not all that objectionable either. So long as the action was well managed, with turning aside, handkerchiefs and so forth, frequent spitting could be overlooked. The line between necessary and unnecessary spitting, however, was clearly one of personal opinion. Context probably played a part in making this judgement; it certainly does today. Jogging, for example, appears to be an activity that excuses public spitting, as does some outdoor team sports, such as football. Interestingly, other forms of heavy exercise do not seem to generate the same tolerance and the same people usually refrain from spitting when they are out and about engaged in other activities.

Disgust and distaste in the face of slack bodily control was often expressed in terms of the animal kingdom. Belching, yawning, scratching and stretching all made people think of the behaviours of farmyard creatures. It was argued that God had given us bodies that carried out many of the same processes as beasts, but that he had also, uniquely among his creations, given us reason so that we might exercise control and choose to comport ourselves in a manner closer to the angels. Our expulsion from the Garden of Eden, theological thought proclaimed, had taught us shame and shown us,

Men turned into beasts by drink.

through the adoption of clothing, a new way of marking out our humanity. A godly person accepted the physical processes of their body but tamed, ordered and covered them in modesty. By doing so they learnt the lessons of original sin and indicated their willingness to strive for a better state in the life to come. Physical bodily discipline could help us to learn spiritual discipline. When we let physical control slip, we allowed the bestial to come to the fore; we became less human. Scratching yourself was 'doglike', yawning excessively made you into a frog, drooling was 'swinish' and those who farted resembled cows. This descent into the behaviours of the animal kingdom degraded and diminished an individual. When you spat or blew your nose without consideration of others, or ate with your mouth open, making slurping and wet chewing noises, you revolted people in a visceral manner, and at the same time you made yourself less worthy of consideration as a fellow human being – you became subhuman and unfit company. The offence was multi-layered.

Arse

As an allusion to the dirtiest of bodily functions – but without the actual excrement – farting and talking about farting were just naughty enough to provoke the more sensitive listener while raising a laugh in a more rambunctious one. One of my favourite subversively sly forms can be found in Timothy Kendall's *Flowers of Epigrammes* from 1577:

> *She would not misse her fistyng curre* [farting dog]
> *for any thing: and why?*
> *Forsoothe when so she letts a scape,*
> *she cries me, fie curre, fie.*

If you are struggling with the language there, don't worry – an emblem engraved by George Glover around the same time makes it much clearer. The image is of a fashionable lady with a flower and a small lapdog under the title 'oderatus'. It is intended to be a visual representation of the sense of smell and the accompanying verse says:

> *Wee that are Dames of the most dainty nose,*
> *Sometimes the Violet sent, and then the Rose,*
> *But if about us all things prove not well,*
> *Our doggs are neere, that can excuse the smell.*

Blaming your farts on the dog wasn't always entirely effective, it seems; then, as now, people were wise to it.

Talk of farts was in this case used to repurpose one of the usually worthy and rather ponderous renditions of mottos, emblems and 'devices'. It was also perfect for political satire. 'The Parliament Fart' of 1607 was one of the most popular and long-running political commentaries of the time, regularly added to and updated well into the 1630s. Inspired by a real

fart – a particularly loud and opportunely timed one, let loose
by Henry Ludlow – that had the House of Commons in fits of
laughter, it begins: 'Never was bestowed such art, / upon the
tuning of a fart'. Puns abound throughout the poem, as do
the names of all the prominent MPs of the day:

> ... *a very ill motion,*
> *not soe neither quoth Sir Henry Jenkin,*
> *the motion was good; but for the stinking.*

(Motion, of course, is the word generally used both for a
bowel movement and for a formal proposal in Parliament.)
The poem may have enjoyed so long a life because of its robust
humour, and a simple, predictable structure that lent itself to
being turned into a popular ballad and sung to a well-known
tune. The ease with which anyone of a suitably scatological
wit was able to compose their own additional lines to fit the
format surely helped as well.

'Thanke God quoth Sir Edward Hungerford / That this
Fart proved not a Turdd', continues 'The Parliament Fart'. For
talking turds was just one step further down the repulsive road
than talking farts. When Thomas Dekker, in his evocation
of terrible gul behaviour, decided to portray the very worst
of table manners at a tavern, he did so by reference to bare
bottoms and defecation. 'Call for a close stoole, protesting all
the gentlemen that it costs you a hundred poundes a yeare
in phy-sicke', he began. This offended against the 'don't draw
attention' rule in dramatic fashion. All the conduct books told
youngsters to make sure they went and relieved themselves
before a meal in order to avoid having to leave the table mid-

meal. To call for a close stool (a chair with a built-in chamber pot and a lid that you could drop after use to contain the smell) was to loudly announce your intention to the whole room, and a close stool was worse than a mere chamber pot, implying defecation rather than just urination. The mention of physic expanded the theme by bringing purges and loose bowels to mind; for after blood letting, medicine to induce 'the shits' was the physician's basic stock in trade.

In addition to verbal discretion, polite people, in total contrast to Mr Dekker's guls, were also discreet about any behaviour that might draw attention to bodily functions. 'It does not befit a modest, honourable man to prepare to relieve nature in the presence of other people, nor to do up his clothes afterwards in their presence. Similarly, he will not wash his hands on returning to decent society from private places, as the reason for washing his hands will arouse disagreeable thoughts in people.' These were Giovanni Della Casa's instructions in 1558 requiring gentlemen to make a thorough job of cleaning and redressing themselves in private, emerging only when bodies were once again 'sweet and neat' and fully covered. The whole process was to be conducted in private, giving people no clue as to where you had been or what you had done there.

Attempting to shock, revolt and wickedly amuse his readers, Thomas Dekker did not stop with talk of visits to the close stool but advised his guls to 'invite some special friend of yours, from the table, to hold discourse with you as you sit in that withdrawing chamber'. Having alerted everyone to your least savoury bodily functions, he advised you to put social pressure upon someone to join you as you left the dining room and went into another space where the close stool had been set up. This was the equivalent of inviting someone into the public toilet cubicle with you.

Relieving yourself was supposed to be a private activity. In fact, it was so firmly associated with privacy that the image of a man upon the privy with his breeches around his knees is one that Wenceslaus Hollar used to illustrate his character 'All-hidd', or 'he that absents himself not to be chidd', on one of a set of themed playing cards. In a world of almost continual company, where even beds – never mind bedchambers – are shared spaces, the one and only place where solitude could be guaranteed, where you could hide from social disapproval, was upon the privy or close stool. (Indeed, the

Upon the privy. Note the presence of a long shirt pushed up out of the way, but there is no sign of any drawers or underbreeches.

word privy is a shortening of the term 'place of privacy'.) Even our outrageous Mr Dekker felt the need to back up the instruction to obtain an audience by quoting a supposedly real-life, admittedly foreign and infamous example. For when he instructed his guls to invite a friend along, he added the phrase, 'as your great French Lord doth'. Seeking to pile on more gullish misdeeds and extend the topic, he finished by recommending that upon returning to the dining chamber you raised the question of which literature would be most suitable for wiping your backside with, allowing yourself the opportunity of metaphorically smearing excrement all over other people's literary efforts.

Dirty, smelly, leaky and shameful, human bodies were best kept firmly out of the sight and minds of polite people. Arses, of course, were the most likely of the 'private' parts of the body to be exposed in the usual course of the day. Men had the option of untying their codpieces (rather like unzipping one's fly) if they just needed to urinate. Turning one's back successfully hid the nakedness and there were things that you could do to mask the sound and smell. Every now and then one comes across references, for example, to pissing in chimneys, fireplaces or chimney corners. This was a smell reduction tactic, particularly if aimed into a chamber pot. The draught of the chimney tended to carry odour up and away along with the smoke. The smell of smoke additionally worked to cover any lingering hint of urine. Less polite men, or those caught short, might urinate directly into the fire or ashes where it would quickly evaporate. This does smell bad for a few moments before dissipating (yes, I have been subjected to it). If the fire is out, or the number of men so indulging themselves is too high, it is a foul and very smelly option. In high concentration the smell of urine is not so much masked by the ash as turned into a potent, almost sulphurous version that lingers and lingers.

Relieving yourself outdoors was supposed to involve the strategic use of a bush or tree, as the German traveller Thomas Platter's commentary makes clear. He was writing about some extraordinary behaviour at Balaruc near Montpellier that he witnessed in 1595. The tone of his remarks is somewhat gleeful as he enjoys a good sneer at the foreigners. Balaruc was one of the first of the spa towns where people drank the waters for therapeutic purposes. Having drunk their allotted glass the wealthy patrons walked abroad and 'as the water acts promptly, and causes abundant stools, it is a curious spectacle to see everyone firing off in full view, and even vying with each other; for there is no bush or tree to give cover'.

Female evacuations could be managed more discreetly than male operations with no overt nakedness by dint of long skirts and no knickers. One simply placed the chamber pot in a convenient location, stepped into position and lowered oneself in a squat surrounded by a tent of skirtage. If one was within a privy, a quick hitch of petticoats sufficed.

Men wishing to defecate, however, did have to bare their backside and, depending upon the fashion of the time, this could be a right palaver. The man of sartorial elegance, just like his poorer and more practical-minded brethren, suspended his trunk hose or breeches at the waist from his doublet. This was a continuation of long-standing male clothing tradition where full-length leg coverings had been supported by a short and simple waistcoat-like garment worn beneath the coat or gown. Holding up your lower garments with a belt is a much more modern habit. In the early years this support was achieved by means of a series of ties, known as 'points', while later on hooks and eyes became the main form of support. Surviving garments indicate a number of different strategies. Sir Rowland Cotton, Member of Parliament and wealthy gentleman, for example, had a cream satin suit that he wore when he had his portrait painted in 1618. The suit is now part of the Victoria and Albert Museum collection in London and boasts forty eyelet holes around the waist of both the doublet and breeches. The two would have been fastened together using twenty points. Each point would have consisted of a length of cord or ribbon around eight inches long with metal 'aglets' at the ends to make it easier to thread them through the eyelet holes. Each point was first passed through one eyelet upon the doublet, from the outside towards the body, then it went through a corresponding eyelet upon the waistband of the breeches, again heading inwards, along to the next eyelet and outwards through this one and the corresponding doublet eyelet. Now the two ends were secured with a single looped bow. Twenty such fastenings ensured that Sir Richard Cotton's suit lay evenly and smoothly upon his body with no pulling or sagging at the waist and absolutely no chance of any embarrassing slippage.

Both the aristocratic Swedish Sture brothers (famously murdered in Uppsala Cathedral where the clothes they were wearing at the time of their deaths were kept as memorials) and Cosimo de' Medici, ruler of Florence, were happy to trust to twelve pairs of eyelets to keep themselves secure, but one anonymous German gentleman had thirty-nine. Now, just imagine yourself in the privy trying to deal not just with numerous bows to undo and then poke back through those eyelets and retie, but having to do so when half of them are around the back of your clothing.

Your first line of defence was the regular morning evacuation. From Erasmus onwards, all the writers of practical instruction for elite boys and gentlemen advise a profound visit to the privy, close stool or chamber pot first thing in the morning before you got dressed. Hopefully, that would deal with the business so that once 'trussed' you had no further need to bare your backside during the day. But if you did? One possibility for the powerful (and arrogant) was to have a lowly personal servant accompany you in order to untruss and retruss you, even if they left or turned away during the actual event. Forcing them to remain, or even wipe your backside, was grossly bad behaviour, but nothing like as bad as that of our gul who forced a social equal into that very position.

Without a raft of lowly servants, the pressures of elegant court life or utterly reliable bowels, most men went for a less pointed approach. Ordinary men seem to have had far fewer pairs of these fastenings joining the two garments – they were not so worried about achieving a perfect look – but the basic problem was much the same whether you were rich or poor and gave rise to two fairly simple and practical solutions.

Breeches generally stay up quite well when supported mostly at the sides and front. If you thought that you might have to manage alone, you just didn't tie up the points at the back. When you wished to drop your breeches, you simply loosened off the side fastenings, which allowed you to slip your rear end free in the manner of the 'All-hidd' character. When you had finished you had merely to tuck yourself back in and retighten the side points, which had remained threaded in position. Mind you, such a strategy can give a somewhat saggy-arsed look when you stand up. Those wishing to retain elegance and independence could instead unbutton their doublets and shrug the whole suit off their shoulders in one, still fastened, piece, to fall crumpled at their ankles. Re-dressing involved hauling it back onto the shoulders and doing up the buttons. Your tailor probably thought that this was extraordinarily bad behaviour, as a well-cut and perfectly fitted suit was put under major seam-damaging pressure during these manoeuvres. (Most of the men of my acquaintance who regularly wear Elizabethan clothing go for this approach, which they assure me is quite straightforward and relatively speedy.) However, it not only preserved your sartorial elegance but prevented you from exposing another offensive reminder of bodily functions: dirty shirt tails.

As we briefly mentioned in discussing female evacuations, women generally didn't wear knickers, and nor did many men. There is a small body of evidence for knicker-wearing men, but it is even smaller for women. Italian courtesans, for example, are described and pictured as wearing large, bloomer-like undergarments for additional titillation, and the effigy of Elizabeth I in Westminster Abbey has a pair of linen drawers that may or may not be original, along with a more convincingly original corset. The account books of the Newdigate brothers, John and Richard, during their time as students in Oxford in 1619 mentions male drawers twice, once when they are laundered alongside some stockings and once when they are mended. In 1688, Randle Holme, describing articles for use in heraldic representations in his *The Academy of Armoury*, defines drawers as a pair of linen under-breeches that some men wear. But it is all pretty scanty.

Images of bare arses, male or female, within an English context often also portray the clothing that has been pushed aside. Shirts, smocks and stockings are much in evidence; knickers, bloomers and drawers are not. Even the Newdigate accounts are not quite as emphatic as you might think. The drawers are mentioned just twice, in close proximity to each other, as if the laundering highlighted a problem and was closely followed by the repair work. In addition to laundry bills, the accounts, which roughly cover a three-year period first at Oxford and then at the Inns of Court in London, mention the making of new shirts for the two men on five separate occasions and around a dozen payments for new stockings, numerous purchases of ruffs and cuffs, but no new drawers. When they were worn, drawers were not meant to be seen, so perhaps their appearance was unimportant. Equally, they might have been made of particularly hard-wearing stuff and therefore didn't require frequent replacements. The other possibility is that the Newdigate brothers, although unusual in recording their possession of drawers (there are almost no other such incidents among account books or inventories until later historical periods), were not all that unusual in their daily habits. Perhaps they didn't feel the need to wear drawers every day; perhaps such items of clothing were additional extras when donning one's very best embroidered shirt. For it was shirt tails that provided most men's washable posterior coverage.

Both surviving shirts and the cloth requirements mentioned in various accounts for making up shirts indicate that the basic shirt was intended to reach down to just above a man's knees. There was a slit at both sides that ran from the hemline up to the top of the thigh allowing the material to be quickly and easily tucked around one's nether regions both front and back without impeding movement. Any unpleasant 'skid marks' or 'accidents' that might occur did so upon the shirt tails, keeping the lining of the breeches clean. Shirt tails, therefore, were considered to be inherently dirty, and allowing them to hang out was filthy upon two levels. Visible shirt tails not only brought the whole business of the privy to mind, but, in addition, the presence of shirt tails on the outside of the breeches implied the lack of shirt tails within the breeches.

Girls Aloud

Let's talk about periods, ladies. Boldly, loudly and publicly. This was one bodily function that caused widespread repugnance. To this day people are much less willing to talk or joke openly about menstruation than they are about farting, defecation or urination. The generalized advice that bodily processes be kept private and that their management be discreet in both speech and action have consistently been more closely and conscientiously followed here than in any other aspect of body management. While popular ballads abound in references to people pissing, farting, vomiting, shitting, spitting, belching and even ejaculating, I have yet to find one single mention of, or even a vague allusion to, monthly flows in this format. Plays, poems, joke or jest books, letters and court cases all maintain the silence. Only in a small number of medical texts can the menses be regularly found. Even here many try to skip over the subject of female bodies, presenting the male form as the pattern for mankind and shying away from discussing the female form in fear of 'lewdness', as if sex was located purely in the feminine.

From Avicenna (the Persian scholar more properly known as Ibn Sina, who died in 1038) onwards, the majority of male medical authors drew together a variety of ancient Greek, Roman and Arabic sources that described the womb as a sewer that channelled the toxins and filth of the female body out and away in the form of menstrual blood. A 1586 text, for example, claimed, 'It is agreed by all Physicians, that the womb is like dregs and a drain.' Ancient religious beliefs had also held that menstruating women were 'impure', and that their presence could curdle milk, turn wine sour, cause mirrors to become cloudy and make ivory 'obscure'. While this was not official Christian doctrine, such beliefs were widely held among the populace at large. Not all medical men, however, were convinced; as the herbalist Nicholas Culpeper wrote in his *Directory for Midwives* in 1651, 'Writers disagree about this.' Certainly Thomas Raynold, the author of the first full gynaecological text in English, *The Birthe of Mankinde*, published in 1545, felt very strongly that menstruation was not intrinsically dirty. 'I know nothing in woman so privy ne so secret, that they should need to care who knew of it; neither is there any part in women more to be abhorre'd, than in man,' he stated.

Thomas Raynold was a practising physician who had translated the main body of his text from a book originally written in German, but he added and amended freely where his own understanding and beliefs differed from the original, and this positive, if strongly defensive, attitude towards the female reproductive system was one of those changes he introduced. Nicholas Culpeper, a man who followed Raynold's way of thinking, neatly laid out the two opposing arguments. One group of physicians characterized menstrual blood as 'venomous', a concentrated concoction of various waste products and outright poisons. Much of their medical practice revolved around ensuring that it was fulsomely cast out of the body at regular intervals as the retention of even trace amounts could have dire consequences for a woman's physical and mental health. They promoted a range of remedies that 'brought on a woman's flows' (remedies that incidentally often contained abortificants such as the herb pennyroyal). Yet mainstream medical theory also held that during pregnancy this same menstrual blood ceased to flow out of the body because it was diverted to nourishing the growing child through the umbilical cord. Moreover, after the birth the menstrual blood was converted into mother's milk and continued to provide sustenance to the newborn. These two medical 'facts' led other physicians to argue that the blood could not be 'venomous' but could 'offend only in plenty', as in only when there was too much or too little. That it could and did go wrong quite frequently was an article of belief that Culpeper, despite his championing of the natural healthiness of the female reproductive system, was quite willing to go along with. Mixed with 'bad humours' or 'kept too long in the body', menstrual blood became 'corrupted' and caused 'great symptoms'.

The casebooks of John Hall (Shakespeare's son-in-law) show the typical medical man's response to female patients. He included ninety-three female patients within the selection that he presented for publication, fourteen of whom he treated for menstrual problems, with approximately half of them diagnosed as having too heavy a flow and half as having too light a flow. Very crudely put, his cure for both 'disorders' were different sorts of purges, and in the case of his own daughter he records the number of stools she produced after each dose. Such a high percentage of menstrual problems among a group of patients suggests that John Hall was actively looking for such issues, that questions about the state of a woman's 'courses' was one of his standard questions during a consultation. He was expecting trouble in this department. His daughter, for example, was suffering from 'convulsion of the mouth' yet much of the treatment was centred around the fact that her courses had also ceased. The restarting of her menses is closely linked within the account with her recovery. Whether a physician believed that the menstrual blood was positively venomous or not, the general feeling that this was a difficult and dangerous area pervaded society.

The casebooks of Simon Forman show similar thinking.

A significant proportion of his patients were female. His practice was based upon a mixture of astrology, Galenic mainstream medicine and the more alchemical works of Paracelsus. According to the historian Lauren Kassell's analysis, 44 per cent of his case notes upon female patients mention the reproductive system with particular emphasis upon 'the stopping of the matrix due to congealed humours' (retained menstrual blood), prompting him to write a treatise upon the subject. Both his astrological charts and his observations of 'diverse women that have bine troubled herwithe', as well as his readings of medical texts, had led him to the conclusion that a large percentage of female health problems, physical, mental and emotional, were ultimately traceable back to the proper regular cleaning out of the womb. His investigations of the matter led him to record some of the astonishingly rare female voices upon the subject of menstruation. 'I have made diligente inquisition amonge grave matrons and midwives and others to knowe wher the matrix doth exempte himself of any thinge that yt receyveth of man more than once in a month or noe. And they have told me yea, that yt doth exempte yt selfe of any thing that yt receiveth of man and doth vomite out wind (like as the stomacke doth) at the vulva.' This little nugget of practical information, that semen is not held within the womb from one month until the next, that menstrual blood is not packed with rotted seed, was one that he had been unable to find in any medical text.

Such understandings and misunderstandings of the nature of menstruation lent a distaste and disgust to the subject in non-medical circles. A reluctance to speak of the issue was one response to this uneasy state of affairs. When one vicar, Ambrose Westrop, made mention of 'matters concerning the secrets of women' in the pulpit, his parishioners considered that he had profaned the 'ordinance of preaching' and were heartily offended. It was cited as a major complaint against him in the sequestrations of 1643 when he was removed from office. Public discussion, particularly in a religious context, of such female bodily functions was not to be endured.

But there was much more to such revulsion than worries about the physical corruption inherent in menstrual blood. There were also the religious and spiritual connotations to take into account. In the sixteenth- and seventeenth-century mind, the entire female reproductive system was overshadowed by the special spiritual disgrace associated with daughters of Eve. Adam, too, had sinned in the Garden of Eden, but his sin was considered to be less wicked and the ongoing taint was correspondingly thought to be milder. The fall of mankind from God's grace was firmly blamed on Eve tempting Adam. For those not brought up within the Christian, Jewish or Islamic tradition, the idea that the person who breaks the law (don't eat the apple) is less guilty than the one who tempts them to break the law is an odd one, but the power of that interpretation cannot be historically overstated. Religious-minded men of every hue and in many different formats marked women out as particularly prone to sin, to lapses of morals and poor judgement as a result of their descent from Eve. Women's words and women's actions were not to be trusted. Lifelong supervision by fathers, brothers and husbands was considered essential by the majority of the population. Women, too, surrounded by such messages from early childhood, accepted and usually actively supported this analysis. Femaleness was inferior and suspect, and the menses were the very essence of this difference from the stronger, purer male pattern.

As an inherently female experience, the majority of men could dismiss menstruation, if they so wished, as something that happened to weaker, lesser beings – something linked to the sinfulness of Eve and her shame. Silence about the subject suited these men admirably. Even as fathers and husbands, men could choose to distance themselves from the 'taint' of menstruation by insisting that these were 'women's matters', never to be discussed in front of men, and that the practicalities were kept from their sight. The mess and the pain were to be dealt with discreetly and silently. How individual men responded to menstruation in private is, of course, unknown; there may well have been many who were supportive and unembarrassed within a family context, but society and the ideologies of the day permitted and indeed enabled responses of guilt, shame and secrecy.

The pain and danger of childbirth, which was certainly more widely spoken about, was presented by the majority of Protestant divines as God's rightful punishment of women, an opportunity for them to atone for their original sin. The pain was supposed to be accepted as 'a mercy' that allowed them to approach nearer to a blessed state. Prayers for women to use in the birth room frequently included phrases thanking God and accepting the agonies as 'just reward for my manifold sins'. Concerns about spiritual purity and concerns about physical purity frequently became intertwined in these outpourings. John Donne's 1618 sermon in St Paul's Cathedral, celebrating the successful delivery of a child to Lady Doncaster, for example, made the commonplace connection between the physical mess, bloodiness and 'filth' of childbirth with the spiritual impurity of original sin and Eve's part in the fall from grace. 'Our mothers conceived us in sin, and being wrapped up in uncleanness there, can any man bring a clean thing out of filthiness?' he asked, continuing with long references to dung, blood and human excrement.

Now, technically none of these concerns, misunderstandings and worries apply in the modern Western world. Doctors have long accepted that menstrual blood is not poisonous or rotten. The presence of a menstruating woman, most people would agree, does not curdle milk. Wombs full of retained blood are not the root cause of female mental illness, nor indeed of many physical complaints. Very few religious leaders hark on about women's additional burden of original sin (at least, not to the same degree or with the same vehemence of their forebears). And yet embarrassment and secrecy persist. Even adverts for feminine hygiene products remain rather shy and coy creatures, with their iconic blue liquids to demonstrate absorbency rates and lots of healthy young women tripping lightly through sunlit meadows. Start a conversation about menstruation in a public place and people try to shush you; men often blush, turn away or leave. Often it is those men who most loudly indulge in crude language and misogynistic jokes that are most perturbed by such talk. I can't be the only woman who has spoken deliberately to disconcert and subvert in such a social situation. But if, in our supposedly enlightened world, talk of the monthly flows can be seen as behaving badly, just think how very offensive public mention of such matters was when all those worries seemed justified, when doctors of medicine and men of the cloth agreed wholeheartedly that the womb and its cycles were potentially dangerous, morally, spiritually and physically.

No wonder then the silences that greet those in search of information about women's periods. What ballad writer would wish to include a line that would upset his clientele so absolutely? He could write of almost every other bodily function and expect to raise a smile among at least some of his potential audience. He could rail against almost any transgression, from adultery to thievery, witchcraft to heresy, giving graphic descriptions of repulsive and shocking behaviour, but there were no words that he could use about menstruation and still expect to sell copies.

So how did women manage their periods? It's a question that I am often asked, although usually only when older, more confident women can catch me in a more retired and private environment. And I can only guess. The silence is almost total. Two possibilities spring to mind: belts and pessaries. With no tradition of underwear wearing, any absorbent pad would have to be supported by a belt of some kind. Now this is certainly what happened within the nineteenth and early twentieth centuries where we have both surviving examples and women's accounts. Such pads could be folded cloth or a cloth bag stuffed with other disposable absorbent material. The cloth elements required laundry, much as baby's nappies do, beginning with a soak in cold water, followed by a vigorous scrub. If modern – or at least recent – practice is anything to go by, this particular type of laundry happened outside of the normal household routine. Women's accounts of twentieth-century practice, including those of my own family, tell of rinsing and scrubbing such articles separately and privately, each woman dealing with her own. The idea that these scraps of stained fabric might be seen, even by one's immediate female family, was shameful. Indeed, my family discussions of 1940s and '50s systems caused otherwise forthright women to blush and become decidedly agitated at the idea of adding feminine hygiene cloths to the general whites wash.

Pads and belts are rather cumbersome and uncomfortable contrivances, which may have led a proportion of women to turn to the pessary option. We today would use the word 'tampon' in this context. The use of medicinal pessaries at the time is well recorded; take, for example, this remedy for an insufficient flow included in Culpeper's book: 'If she be no Virgin, put Mercury bruised in a Bag for a Pessary, with Centaury flowers. Or Garlick beaten with Oyl of Spike.' The proviso 'if she be no Virgin' is an important one. It makes clear that this pessary was intended to be inserted into the vagina and it indicates the assumption that cloth would play a part. It also highlights the cultural importance of not inserting anything into the vaginas of virgins, in order to preserve that vital moment of wedding-night 'deflowering'. Tampons, if they existed (and I can't categorically prove that they did), were for experienced, married women, not young girls.

Two practical methods are, however, possible. One is to extend the medicinal pessary form, imagining a small linen cloth bag that was packed with absorbent materials of one sort or another, although this option leaves open the possibility of bags breaking, which would not be all that pleasant. The other option is the single strip of linen wound tightly into a cylinder. The shape receives some historical validation from its presence among the range of bandages, plasters and cloth bolsters and wound packers used by medical men. John Taylor's mock heroic poem of 1630, 'In Praise of Clean Linen', helpfully talks of the fate of worn-out shirts, sheets and handkerchiefs:

> *Which though it be but thin and poore in shape,*
> *A Surgeon into lint the same will scrape,*
> *Or rolles, or bolsters, or with plaster spread,*
> *To dress and cure, all hurts from heele to head.*

He doesn't, of course, mention menstruation as such, but the use of rolls of old, worn and thus especially absorbent linen to staunch blood flow is suggestive. This usage is much closer in form to the tampons of today and carries much less risk of difficulties than a bag. A small strip of linen would be easy to launder – more so than the pads or bags of other methods. In the spirit of historical experimentation I have tried all three of these options, and it is most definitely this linen-strip method that gets my vote. It was more secure, more comfortable and easier to manage cleanly than the others.

The Naked Truth

Mere nakedness was considered rather less repulsive than the display of menstrual cloths or public discussions of such practicalities. Nakedness was wicked and shameful, but also titillating and not beyond the pale of discussion. You could talk about nakedness, preach about nakedness, publish accounts and even pictures of naked people, so long as you did so with some semblance of reprimand – rather like the newspapers that go to great lengths to dig up scandals so that they can indulge their readers with exciting and juicy details of bad behaviour. Pretending to hold the moral high ground and condemning the transgressions of others, they have a licence to vicariously roll in the filth, to fantasize with impunity.

Most famously in this vein were the mid-seventeenth-century accounts of Anabaptists, Ranters, Diggers, Quakers and Adamites, religious and political extremists in an age of intellectual and philosophical experimentation. Religious and political opponents of these groups (virtually everybody) commonly accused them of practising nudity. It was a highly effective slur containing, as it did, just a germ of truth along with a hearty helping of fascinated and gleeful repulsion.

Preachers of various opinions had been harking on about 'naked truth' and condemning the vanities of fashion and the evils of disguising one's true nature for decades. Remember, too, all the worry and anguish about falseness in greeting rituals, table manners and misleading dress. Deciding to abandon clothing as a gesture of spiritual commitment and

Adamites at worship – allegedly.

purity, therefore, held a certain resonance. But, on the other hand, bare bodies were suspect, uncontrolled, lewd and sinful.

In 1641, when censorship of print had effectively broken down, the first of a series of pamphlets describing and denouncing religious deviation appeared, complete with graphic woodcuts of nudity during worship. 'A New Sect of Religion Decryed Called Adamites' pictured a naked man standing upon a stool while preaching. A naked woman with a luxuriant mane of untrammelled hair stood nearby with her discarded smock at her feet. The sight has clearly had an effect upon the preacher, who is shown sporting a large erection. Before him stands a second naked man armed with a long pole beating at his upright penis. A speech bubble issues from the pole man's mouth containing the words, 'Downe Proud Flesh Downe'. Such an image was bound to attract attention upon the bookseller's shelf or in the ballad seller's pack. The body of the text accompanying the image described a supposed group of ardent Protestants who stood naked before God during their prayer meetings and refused to follow the usual forms of marriage, permitting men to have sex with any woman they felt desire for (women were not granted the same agency). It is hard, in truth, to find any hard evidence that this sect existed or operated in this manner outside of tabloid-style exposés, but the publishers and public were loath to let go of the idea.

The same year that 'A New Sect' was published, a second version of the Adamite creed went into print with another, particularly crudely carved woodcut featuring eight naked figures, an erect penis, some sticks and the words 'Downe lust' within a speech bubble. Both woodcuts were to enjoy

And more naked worshippers.

long, active careers, appearing upon various pamphlets for the next fifteen years or so. 'Downe lust' accompanied, for example, a text called 'Love one another' in 1642, 'A Sermon preached the first day in Leaden Hall St' in 1643 and 'The Ranters Religion' in 1650. A further development of the theme amalgamated several scenes, including a woman upon her knees kissing the bared arse of a man and a small mixed-sex group of naked dancers celebrating the banned feast of Christmas.

Sometimes the people accused of such practices were Adamites, sometimes Ranters and sometimes the Quakers, such as in one entitled 'The Quakers Dream' of 1655. Anyone with odd or unusual religious beliefs seemed to be fair game. There was certainly no shortage of odd and unusual religious beliefs around, as sects divided, merged and divided again. Debates raged, even at the heart of government, about what form of Protestantism the country should follow. Popular confusion upon the issue is well expressed in one rather exasperatedly amused ballad:

> *The Synod have full four years sate,*
> *To find out a Religion,*
> *Yet to conclude, they know not what,*
> *They want a new Edition.*
> *Say all wise men, what shall we be?*
> *Brownists, or else Presbyters?*
> *Of the Antinomian Heresie?*
> *Or Independent-Fighters?*
> *Shall we be harmless Adamites?*
> *And weare no cloaths upon us?*

Historians are divided in their opinions of whether the Adamites ever existed as a real religious sect, and divided, too, over whether they believe that other, better-documented groups, such as the Ranters, actually used nudity in their worship, but there is a strong possibility that, fictitious or factual, the discussion of such antics in the popular press inspired acts of nakedness among slightly later Quakers. 'Going naked as a sign' is a phrase that turns up several times in the early writings of Quakerism, and the denunciation of that form of faith by one who had once been a Quaker himself includes a claim that 'twas usual with him [Abiezer Crippe] to preach stark naked many blasphemies'. Should such hostile comments be taken at face value or with a generous pinch of salt? It is hard to know for certain but there was certainly an opportunity here for scandalizing the neighbours and shaking up their belief systems.

It is supposed to be Ranters, this time.

Working up a Sweat

Even a couple of inches of skin could offend against codes of modesty and cleanliness. And yes, I do mean cleanliness in a physical, bodily sense of the word and not just spiritual or moral cleanliness. Bodies were observed to be fundamentally dirty, exuding sweat, grease and bad smells alongside the more obvious waste products and bodily fluids. Cleanliness, according to the Tudor and Stuart mind, was located in the regular renewing of clean linen cloth encasing the body. It was the 'shifting' of dirty linen underwear for a fresh, clean layer of linen that drew away the bodily filth from the skin, rendering a person 'clean, sweet and neat'.

In popular accounts of Tudor and Stuart life, much is made of the lack of water washing; we are often encouraged to sneer and laugh at courtiers who have elaborate and extortionately expensive clothing covering stinking, festering bodies. But that is not how they saw it at all. If you spend any time reading Tudor and Stuart writings of almost any sort, you will quickly notice the near obsession with cleanliness. Everything good is 'sweet and clean' and everything bad is 'dirty' or 'filthy'. Remember how often the insult strings of words included accusations of dirt, lice and filth. Sermons, too, return time and again to purity, cleanliness and unspotted virtue in opposition to besmirched, soiled, stinking sin. The beautiful are generally described as sweet smelling and neat about their persons, while the ugly are often described as foul and disordered in their dress. It is frequently said that the Victorians believed that cleanliness was next to godliness, that they made housework and hygiene into a veritable idol, but if you read the literature of the two eras, the impression that you are left with is that it was the Tudors and early Stuarts who were the clean freaks. At least in theory.

Achieving clean bodies was another matter. No one wanted to risk soap and hot water. The soap would scour away the natural oils protecting the skin and the hot water would cause the pores of the skin to open. This was considered to be a very dangerous state of affairs, for open, oil-denuded skin made a person vulnerable, according to the medical understandings of the day, to disease. Sources of infection were thought to be carried invisibly through the air in swirling miasmas ready to insinuate themselves into bodies by any and every available means. Noses were clearly the most open orifices through which disease could enter. Luckily, miasmas, although invisible, were thought to betray their presence through smell. The avoidance of bad smells was, therefore, everyone's first line of defence. Cleanliness had a vital role to play here, driving out bad smells from the home and the clothes and bodies of family and household members.

Mouths were the next most vulnerable points of entry, requiring food and drink to be as pure and as cleanly prepared as possible. It also encouraged people to keep their mouths closed, as good manners dictated. Slack-jawed, open-mouthed people were clearly idiots, and probably diseased idiots, too, as miasmas could so easily enter these badly guarded portals. But after mouths and noses it was through the open pores of the skin that people expected disease to enter the body. Experience had shown that the public bath houses of the past had spread some of the most unpleasant and frightening of diseases through their clientele (including syphilis, which was particularly prevalent in this place where so many prostitutes and their clients met) and fear of hot water only grew when the government shut the baths down as a public health measure.

Cleanliness was thus vital to health, but how was it to be achieved without opening the pores? Thankfully, there was linen. Clean linen. For men it came mostly in the form of shirts, the occasional pair of drawers and plenty of hose or stockings, a few nightcaps, collars and cuffs. Between them, these garments provided near total body coverage. For women, the smock did the main duty, reaching down to the mid-shin, where hose or stockings took over. Linen caps were worn both day and night, while an array of cuffs, kerchiefs, pinners, partlets, rails and veils filled in all the gaps apart from the face and hands.

Linen was quite unlike the other two main fibres, wool and silk, because linen absorbed water and grease where wool and silk repelled them. It also becomes more efficient at this job with time and wear. Worn, much-washed linen cloth takes in far more unwanted matter than newer fabrics. There is also the useful fact that the dirt and grease show up well upon white linen, so you and everyone else are aware of how clean or dirty it is. This visibility of filth provided a good spur to vigilance in the battle for hygiene and gave reassurance to others that you really were clean and therefore no danger to their health. The more often you changed your linen clothes, the more often you laundered them, the more waste matter was absorbed and removed.

In the past, I have often recounted (in books and on television) how I have personally experimented with this hygiene regime, living for extended periods without water washing, instead wearing and regularly changing a full set of linen undergarments. And to my surprise, I have found that a quite acceptable level of personal cleanliness can be maintained in this manner. One is not quite as sweet smelling as those following the daily showering regime that modern life promotes, but on the other hand one is not foul and stinking either. There is a light smell up close but the skin remains in good health – better, if I am honest, than with the showering regime.

The old belief in the cleaning power of linen is not at all stupid, but reflects a truth: that frequently laundered clothes are a path to cleanliness. In the sixteenth and seventeenth centuries, most people washed hands, faces and feet with water. A few were able to indulge in private, hot-water baths and steam baths (Henry VIII, for example, had extensive bathrooms built in his palaces), but most relied upon the laundress and the action of clean linen to care for the rest of the body. This was the reality of daily life. Nudity, therefore, could conjure up thoughts of dirt, of sweaty armpits and greasy necks untouched by the exfoliating and absorbing rub of linen, and of dirt left lying upon the surface of the skin rather than being carried away to the wash tub. Bare skin was dirty skin.

This aspect of nudity is well expressed by our friend Mr Dekker when he advises his guls to wander about their chambers in the morning before dressing, 'either in thy thin shirt onely, or else ... strip thyselfe stark naked'. Then, if the weather is cold, he instructs his young fools to 'creep into the chimney corner ... till by sitting in that hot house of the chimney, thou feelest the fat dew of thy body (like basting) run trickling down thy sides'. No one suggested that there was anything unpleasant or dirty about sitting near a fire fully clothed. But imagining sweat left to linger on a naked body was truly repulsive.

Lewd Creatures

There were plenty of different ways to excite or repulse people with your sexual behaviour. Indeed, lewdness formed the core of many of the most vehement rants of the era. Many of the behaviours that we have already discussed were presented in this manner: the flirty suggestiveness of inappropriate clothing, the luxuriating and corrupting influence of skirts worn by men, the sexual invitation implied within the bell-like walk of fashion. Language on the streets was frequently highly sexual in nature and popular literature was packed with smutty innuendo, enough to prompt Thomas Brice in 1570 to publish a ballad entitled 'Againste filthy writing', asking 'is Christ, or Cupide Lord?' and deploring the 'wanton sound and filthie sense' that he found therein.

But sex itself was by no means all repulsive and bad. Enthusiastic, vigorous and pleasurable sex was excellent behaviour, so long as it was within marriage and undertaken for the procreation of children and the strengthening of the bond between husband and wife. Medical men and churchmen both agreed that marital sex was healthy and approved by God. It promoted harmony within the family and a contented state of mind that helped both partners live good lives. Mutual pleasure was an essential component of legitimate sexual relations, according to people in all walks of life; although the idea was perhaps strongest among the most educated and the most religiously committed.

The Catholic Church had always carried a certain ambiguity in its attitudes to sex and marriage, holding up a model of celibacy as the ideal for a spiritual life, while accepting and promoting the institution of marriage as one sanctioned by God for the conceiving and bringing up of children. From the very beginning, however, Protestantism turned its back on the celibate life. Many of the abuses and failings of the Catholic Church which had goaded religious reformers into action were felt to be centred within the enclosed and celibate communities of wealthy monasteries and convents. There would be no monks or nuns following the new reformed faith; Martin Luther himself famously married, raised a family and encouraged other priests to follow his lead.

For many people who thought of themselves as Protestants, the ideas of adult celibacy and popery were intricately linked, providing a subtle pressure upon those with strong Protestant beliefs to embrace marriage and sex. This religious endorsement of an active sex life was backed up by the medical men of the day. The human reproductive system, especially those aspects that pertained to the female body, was subject to a great deal of confusion and uncertainty within the medical community. Did women produce seed as men did? Was the womb simply a receptacle like an oven that cooked the seed planted by men? How long was gestation? Could conditions within the womb change the temperament or physical form of the growing child? Learned men held a range of opinions. If the woman did produce seed, they opined, then surely, just as in men, that seed would only be produced at the height of pleasure. Female sexual pleasure would, therefore, be just as necessary as male sexual pleasure when conceiving a child. Those who were most swayed by religious teachings that held companionship and procreation as paramount, were, therefore, once again being encouraged towards an active and enjoyable experience within the marriage bed. When we think of the more serious godly members of society, we should remember that they were just as keen, maybe more keen, on good sex than their more disordered neighbours.

The perceived problem, of course, was bad sex, and that was most commonly seen as stemming from female insatiability. Medical men sometimes described cool phlegm-humoured women as being desirous of the hot blood humour of men, hungry wombs sucking up the male seed, but they all repeated, as a self-evident truth, that women had a much greater and less regulated sexual appetite than men. The Church, unsurprisingly, saw it as a consequence of Eve's transgression in the Garden of Eden – once a temptress, always a temptress.

Popular culture seems to have been even more convinced of the magnitude of female desire and relished stories of voracious wives out on the prowl. Collections of short stories such as the anonymous *Tales and Quick Answers, Very Merry, and Pleasant to Rede* (1567) and *The Deceyte of Women* (1557), also anonymous, are dominated by storylines focused upon women in search of extramarital sex. Think back, too, to how much of the language of insult revolved around women and sex. Women taking lovers, working as whores, 'waggletails' and 'salted bitches' turning weak and inadequate husbands into cuckolds and wittols. Ballads abound with such subject matter. 'The Seven Merry Wives of London' (*c.* 1681) is a little unusual in featuring a robust all-female cast of women expressing their own desires by complaining about their husbands' sexual inadequacies:

> *The Shoe-makers Wife fill'd a bowl to the brim*
> *Crying out, Here's a Bumper, sweet Sisters, to him*
> *That is able to please a young wife to the heart,*
> *But alas, to my sorrow, the truth I'll impart;*
> *I'm afraid I shall ne'er have a Daughter or Son;*
> *Tho' I labour a Woman's work never is done.*

She attributes her lack of satisfaction to his having 'a short peging aul', a handy tool of his trade as well as an obvious euphemism. The pewterer's wife complains that her husband will 'seldom cast into the mould', while the surgeon's wife demands sympathy since she has been married for over a year and 'Yet he never had enter'd nor found the right Vein'. The pavier suffers both from only having 'one stone' besides being 'the worst Rammer as ever was known' and the fiddler is always 'out of tune'. Only the blacksmith's wife is contented since he 'follow'd his labor with hammer and tongs'.

The insults, the ballads and the stories all express a widespread belief in the lustful nature of women. Maids, it was generally agreed, were shyer and more reserved, but wives could be sexually demanding and widows, having once known the pleasures of the marriage bed, were very eager to 'have a young-man their aprons to brush', according to *The Wiving Age*, another ballad, of around 1625.

The printed matter reflects the male viewpoint, both ballads and other forms of popular literature being, as far as we can tell, penned by men; but invective in the street was frequently feminine in origin and not confined to the ranks of the literate. Women, everyone agreed, liked sex, and being but weak and feeble creatures they were not always very good at controlling themselves.

When you look at much of the literature about female bad behaviour, there is within it a lingering disapproval being expressed towards husbands who had failed sexually, who had not satisfied or controlled the appetites of their wives. For example, one of the women expressing her disappointment in the ballad of the 'Seven Merry Wives' above threatens to find an alternative if the situation does not soon improve, while the very first verse relates the adventures of the washerwoman who does laundry for young trainee lawyers at the Inns of Court and boasts that they supply 'pretty sport' when her husband neglects his duty. The stories contained within *The Deceyte of Women* frequently include unflattering descriptions of useless doddery husbands and make sharp comments such as, 'And if my lorde had biden at home peradventure the woman had never fallen to that'. Even more typical is the jigg *Singing Simpkin* (a short play that was sung and danced by comic actors, often after the main feature at the theatre). A young wife with an old and frequently absent husband entertains a succession of lovers and has to resort to hiding them in chests to prevent them finding out about each other. The action is pure bedroom farce, but of all the characters it is probably the young wife who is portrayed most sympathetically. The men are either stupid, cowardly or both. She is presented as a deceitful but capable woman surrounded by several sorts of idiot. Most of the blame within the jigg is placed upon the situation that she finds herself in – what else is a young woman to do when her husband cannot perform? It seems that a lack of ability, or enthusiasm, for sex among husbands was in itself seen as bad behaviour, a linked but separate failing to that of not exercising control over a wife's behaviour.

It should come as no surprise that any form of sex that did not take place within the bounds of marriage counted as bad behaviour. Taking a lover, a mistress or paying for sex, whether your partner was male or female, human or animal, it was all very bad and there was no shortage of people willing to tell you so. Churchmen thundered from pulpits, neighbours shouted in the street, doctors wrote texts outlining the physical damage that could be expected, courts handed out punishments to those who were caught and made sure that those punishments were as public as possible in order to deter others.

One element of all this disapproval that we, as a modern audience, might note is the lack of precision in the condemnations and descriptions of transgression. We saw right at the start of this book how the language of insult lumped all forms of female sexual misdemeanour together in the epithet 'whore', whether a woman was being accused of selling her body or taking a lover; even suggestive behaviour or flirting could attract the word. The same was true of all forms of sexual 'immorality'. People used a host of words that we now regard as referring to specific sexual practices in a seemingly wide-ranging manner. For example, bestiality is used to describe sex between humans and animals, anal sex between two male partners, anal sex between a man and a woman, and general 'beastliness' is used as a description for all bad sexual behaviour of any sort. The word 'sodomy' could be employed for a similar wide range of behaviours, and in the 1570 ballad 'The Horrible and Woeful Destruction of Sodome and Gomorra' its meaning even extended to describing incest.

What such fluid language reveals to us is a feeling that chastity and good behaviour is all about self-control. God had given mankind certain feelings and drives and marked out a proper and particular sphere for their expression. Holding firmly to that covenant, the institution of marriage was the human and Christian thing to do. Beasts partook of indiscriminate sex; people revealed their nature as creatures with souls by their restraint and discrimination. With a

A loose woman. It is interesting to see how, in addition to loose clothing, smoking is used in this image as a suggestion of bad behaviour. Step outside the bounds of good behaviour in one area, this engraving is saying, and you will be open to them all.

simple boundary set around marriage the chaste and the impure were divided into two distinct groups; you didn't really need to define types of impure or immoral people, all could be lumped into the same category. Immoral behaviour was loose behaviour, and was enacted by people who had abandoned control and self-restraint. The poet and clergyman John Donne, for example, describes a debauched courtier as one 'who loves whores ... boys and ... goats' ('Satire 4', 1597) and links two forms of sexual misbehaviour with dirt and bare skin in the first of his satires: 'But, in rank itchy lust, desire and love / The nakedness and bareness to enjoy

/ Of thy plump muddy whore or prostitute boy.' Once you stepped over the line from chaste to unchaste, all manner of immorality was likely to ensue. A man, according to this way of thinking, who took a female lover probably also took male and animal lovers, too.

We have already encountered numerous loose men and women, or at least many people who were accused of being such. They were prominent among the gangs of elite young men, openly flaunting their mistresses, as well as in the fictional versions of wayward wives and cuckolded husbands who populated plays and ballads. And if angry neighbours are to be believed, real-life naughty nookie lay around every corner in every town: masters taking advantage of maidservants, wives entertaining lovers while their husbands were out, abandoned sweethearts already with child, widows eyeing up all the young men. The church courts are packed with such stories and accusations. One such story was that told by Elizabeth Barwicke in 1627 to her neighbours in London (and she was sued for doing so). She said that upon noticing that Mary Wharton was in a room with Mr Pierson with the door locked she, Elizabeth, had been forced to 'breake open the doore upon them, and there found Mr Pierson ... in a great sweate, and thinke you ... what they were doing'. While in Canterbury Mary Philpott allegedly caught William Atkin as he came 'from the bed of John Knoth's wife' when, suspecting them of immorality she wrenched open the chamber window from the street.

Wherever the church courts met they record numerous similar tales. Most were heartily denied (we are after all generally hearing about them when the accused adulterers sued for defamation of character) but there are also cases where the guilty confessed to their sexual misbehaviour as Michael Fludd did in 1598. His accuser was Margaret Browne who went to quite some lengths to put a stop to the frolicking next door. On 13 May, when Clement Underhill's husband was away and Michael arrived and slipped upstairs, Margaret took herself off to a small spyhole in the wall and watched. At six o'clock Clement shut up shop downstairs and joined Michael in the chamber where the two of them had 'carnal copulation' after which Margaret saw Fludd 'wipe his yard on her smock' and then wash his penis in 'a pail or a tub of water'. Margaret called her husband over to look and he saw Fludd 'with his hose hanging about his legs'. Margaret reported the whole matter to the Lord Mayor and Court of Aldermen who referred the matter to the Court of Bridewell. Clement was 'punished' (probably a whipping) and Michael was fined one pound.

Much of the pressure and rationale for reporting and punishing perceived immorality came from a belief in divine collective correction. The subject of Sodom and Gomorrah was a popular one for sermons both in the pulpit and in print, and the lesson that such preachers wished to be learnt from the tale of God's wrathful punishment of an entire city (save for the one 'just' man) was that the sins of the individual could bring down God's vengeance upon an entire people. The idea was particularly strong in the first half of the seventeenth century. We were our brother's keepers. Plagues, floods and tempests were understood in a similar way, as collective punishments for failing to live as a proper Christian community. Heresy, it was believed, earned very similar community-wide retribution and bad sexual behaviour was frequently closely linked with bad theology.

Take another look at our naked Ranters Ranting, images of threateningly unorthodox thinkers. Their religious errors were endangering their souls, but also endangering the health and safety of the people around them. If their strange form of worship angered the Almighty his response might not just encompass those untrue Christians, but include their neighbours who had failed in their duty to teach, control and guide them along the right path. Displaying their naked bodies and inappropriate sexual excitement along with the accusations of free love, these pamphlets and images are outlining the two great causes of potential public catastrophe. Those erect penises, if permitted to continue unchecked, could cause the heavens to open and pour down fire and brimstone.

The secret, then, to repulsing people with your very presence was to let it all hang out. The more exposed your body was, the more open your orifices, the more you were seen to lust after those you were not wedded to, the more worry and revulsion you could generate. Casually revealing intimate physicality was bad, but you could generate even more offence if you could force the sight, smell or sounds of your body upon people. An accidental, quietly managed fart at the dinner table was considered unpleasant, but people understood that holding it in might not always be possible. A wet-sounding fart repulsed more than a dryer noise, calling to mind bodily waste much more fulsomely and hinted at less control of the sphincter. Lifting a buttock, however, and sighing loudly or making some comment to draw attention not only forced everyone, including those out of range of the smell, to think about farts, but also implied that the action was intentional, that you had farted on purpose. A deliberate fart didn't just produce physical distaste but made people feel disrespected.

Chewing with your mouth open, as we saw in the previous chapter, similarly gave an opportunity for twofold offence, with the lack of care and consideration offering insult while the sight and sound of wet, saliva-coated food in an overly intimate open mouth prompted revulsion. Turn to face someone in particular while you slobbered and drooled and you made the action into something akin to an attack. To this day, most people will pull away when faced with such sights and sounds.

Nudity, too, could be alarming, or even hints of nudity. Think of that scene in Shakespeare's *Hamlet* when the prince presents himself to Ophelia 'with his doublet all unbrac'd; / No hat upon his head; his stockings foul'd, / Ungarter'd, and down gyved to his ankle', or in other words with bare shins, an unbuttoned doublet that shows his shirt and no hat. She thinks he looks 'As if he had been loosed out of hell'. Her father, from this description, assumes that he has gone mad. Naked shins and a flash of shirt! Aaarghhh! It seems such an overreaction to our modern sensibilities until you recall all the beliefs about bodies that we have discussed: the importance of clothing after the fall from grace in the Garden of Eden; the need to set our human selves apart from soulless beasts through our behaviour; the dirtiness of nudity and the understanding of shirts as a filth-collecting layer. This was a play intended for performance upon a public stage, so a man's bare shins were probably as far down the actual nudity road as the play could go without censorship, but it was still sufficient to add a frisson of shock to the scene. The exposed shirt alluded strongly to sweat and, because it was loose and visible, to a loss of control. Sexy, in a rather animalistic way, but do remember that animalistic behaviours were not given such a positive spin as they might be today; think perverse more than raunchy. The loose, untamed body could be a worrying thing indeed.

Conclusion

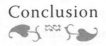

THE COMPLETE SCOUNDREL

By now, I hope you're feeling well equipped with a veritable arsenal of uproar-inducing tactics that would rile any reputable Renaissance character. However, as we have seen, it's not always as straightforward as it looks. There just wasn't a sure-fire way of winding up all people, in all situations, all of the time – you needed to know what you were doing!

Throughout our period, the vast majority of the population would have liked to see people greeting them with a bare head and a bended knee; they found that such civilities eased and smoothed their daily existence, minimizing confrontation. In particular, people in positions of authority wanted to see social structures acted out in the behaviours around them. Those at the very bottom of the social ladder, however, could only dream of receiving such gestures of respect, despite bowing and scraping to everyone they encountered. Longing to receive a share of that consideration, they could, perhaps surprisingly, become some of the most vehement supporters of respect gestures.

High or low, the inhabitants of Tudor and Stuart Britain would generally have been disgruntled, wrong-footed or even outraged by a refusal to remove a hat and perform a bow. And yet we have also seen that there were small groups of people, particularly towards the end of the era, who actively disliked being on the receiving end of such behaviour. For the Quakers, who refused to remove their own hats and bend their own knees in an attempt to follow a more godly way of life, receiving such courtesies from others was an embarrassment.

Likewise, most people felt that a woman should guard her tongue. Silence and modesty were much admired as virtues in womankind, and when women did speak, a mild tone and gentle words were thought to be best; yet there were those who also held a certain admiration for the wife who could hold her own in a street-slanging match. The extended riffs of colourful language in numerous court cases bear witness to the pride involved in picking an apt and cutting phrase. So we must conclude that although any victim of a phrase like 'nitty slitty breached knave' might well have been very upset by the verbal attack, some of the bystanders may have enjoyed the performance immensely. Perhaps there were even some protagonists who rather relished the verbal fencing for its own sake, much as we see reflected in the theatres of the time, where word duels were hugely popular.

If it was hard to annoy all of the people, it was also rather tricky to do it all of the time. Different behaviours shifted from good to bad and back again with disconcerting frequency. Almost any man would have felt aggrieved to be called a knave in 1590, but far fewer would have objected fifty years earlier, or indeed fifty years later, as the term waxed and waned in its offensive impact. We have encountered numerous words and phrases that fluctuated in much the same way, from shouts of 'witch' to 'Puritan'. Nor was this exclusive to words. Swashing your buckler in 1570, despite the disapproval of civic authorities, attracted lots of admiring attention at West Smithfield from young women who thought you adventurous and daringly manly, but if you tried it in 1620 the young women would laugh and sneer at you for being old-fashioned, crude and lower class. Equally, the halting, clerical walk was for many years entirely respectable and acceptable. Yet from the 1620s to the 1650s, the wide-scale fashion for such mannerisms among the vocal, self-appointed 'godly' crowd turned it into a flashpoint of irritation for other members of society.

Other behaviours relied upon context in order to offend. Cross-dressing on the stage or in more local entertainments was both normal and respectable (except in the eyes of a few of the ultra-conservative) so long as it was men or boys dressing as women; but remember the uproar when a young man dressed as a woman to attend a lying-in party in the birth room, or the diatribes against women wearing 'mannish' hats in the street. Morris dancing frequently involved one man dressed as a character called 'the maid', but if any of these men used their female costume outside of the performance, hostility and indeed legal action became much more likely. It is the use of drag in inappropriate places that underlies most of the official records that we have of cross-dressing. Infiltrating an all-female lying-in party may well have been envisaged as a bit of fun but it caused upset and consternation because of the sincerity of the tradition of the birth room. Had it been a girls' night out at the local alehouse that had been gatecrashed by the young cross-dressing lad there would have been little need for official involvement; people might have been a bit miffed, but the level of fluster, even shock, would have been much lower.

Context was also key in judging the offence that might be caused by bodily exposure and (loss of) control of bodily functions. Spitting, farting, urinating and menstruating were all natural and unavoidable physical processes that were to be managed in a cleanly way and preferably in private. The more public the actions, the more offence could be generated, but that was not the only criterion. Formal situations generated more disgust than informal ones: spitting, for example, was less forgivable at the dinner table than in other contexts. The location also played a part. To spit when outdoors was hardly objectionable, but spitting while taking a walk along the long gallery in a fashionable house could easily cause consternation unless you did so into your handkerchief. Then there was the complication of social status. Underlings were generally expected to show particular care in their control over bodily functions in the presence of their masters, but could afford to be much freer in their movements among social equals or inferiors.

The degree of offence was often magnified by gender. A wide range of misdemeanours that were met with disapproval when performed by men were utterly outrageous when enacted by women. We are accustomed to seeing this double standard applied to sexual conduct, where men are partly forgiven for visiting a prostitute or taking a mistress (the 'boys will be boys' approach) while the women involved in those same encounters are thoroughly condemned. The very words outline the difference. A man who visits a prostitute can be called a client, a word that covers many activities and relationships, but he remains a man. The woman is defined by the activity. She is a prostitute, not a woman who works as a prostitute. Promiscuous men are often lauded for their virility, held up as examples of prime masculinity, but you would have to look very hard indeed to find any historical reference to a positive side of female promiscuity.

Such attitudes have been brought to our attention many times in studies of the British Renaissance era, but the dual response is also evident across many of the other forms of mischief that we have been exploring. Smoking and drinking to excess, for example, were disgusting habits that provoked much harsher judgement when women indulged. The public tolerance of men who puked up their drink, exhaled their smoky fumes over people and roared home disturbing all the neighbours was not extended to the women who joined them. The men are termed drunkards and stinkards but the women are almost without exception also branded as whores. The male drunkard might sober up and return to respectability but the female drunkard faced a much longer road in search of her former social standing.

Good manners in general demanded far more from women than from men. A small slip by a man was excusable, even amusing, but a moment of laxity by a woman risked more in the way of public disapproval. Take farting, for example: men who farted in public could afford to laugh it off in a hearty fashion, marking themselves out as robust and vigorous. Fart jokes in both elite and plebeian literature generally have a very masculine tone and feature male protagonists. The farter is funny – naughty, perhaps – but there is nothing fundamentally wrong about him; he is still a good fellow. Jokes about women farting are much rarer, and where they do occur are often coy, rather slyer and crueller in nature. Think back to the two published accounts of fart jokes from the last chapter: the open, rumbustious and cheerful 'Parliamentary Fart' populated by men alone, and the sideways swipe at a woman disguising her farts by blaming the dog. Women's failures of bodily control are skipped over in most forms of literature – a decision that is often presented as 'chivalrous', a polite and considerate averting of the gaze – but it masks this underlying double standard. Male bad behaviour can be openly laughed about because it has little impact, but female bad behaviour must be covered up as too shameful for the public gaze.

Another trend we have encountered in our search for bad behaviour is just how often people did it in the proper way – behaving well in their choice of transgression, if you will. This is particularly marked across gender boundaries. People shouted one set of insults at their female foes and another, quite different set of words at their male enemies; there were rude gestures employed by both sexes but others that were used primarily by men, such as thigh slapping, or the hands-on-hips stance and finger wagging that were the preserve of women. Fighting, as we have seen, was also highly gender specific, being for the most part a male form of conflict, with the fairer sex only occasionally getting involved, and then only targeting their opponents' face and hair. Fighting with weapons was even more strongly associated with men.

Social class, too, had a bearing upon the correct form of naughtiness. In 1590, a quarrelsome gentleman refrained from throwing a punch; instead he issued a challenge and met his adversary at dawn, armed not with a staff or a sword and buckler, but with a rapier. There was a right way and a wrong way to break social rules. Or perhaps we should say that there were many layers of rules and that the majority of rule breakers were willing only to break one or two of these layers at a time. The dueller was breaking the law and offending against both the Church and society, harmony and forbearance being the most widely held ideals when faced with personal irritation and upset. The dueller was willing to set those considerations aside, to behave badly in the eyes of the world – but only up to a point.

During the whole of our period we find not a single account of an Englishwoman taking part in a duel. There are a handful of accounts in the eighteenth and nineteenth centuries (some of which are apocryphal), and elsewhere

A fictional female duellist – how shocking!

the magnificent Swedish noblewoman Gorwel Gyllenstierna is recorded as taking on the man who married her sister in 1661, while over in France as the seventeenth century drew to a close Julie d'Aubigny was embarking on an extraordinarily colourful career of cross dressing, opera singing and duelling, but within British shores female duellists are limited to the realms of fiction. We almost witness an overturning of the usual gender rules in *Twelfth Night* when the count's servant – a young woman disguised as a young man (played by a young male actor) – is bullied into facing the cowardly Sir Andrew Aguecheek. The duel is, however, halted before it begins by the arrival of the young woman's brother. Even upon the stage – and performed by a man – the suggestion of a woman duelling is a shocking one that Shakespeare pulls away from. Francis Beaumont and John Fletcher in their play *The Maid's Tragedy* (1610) are a little braver and permit their young male actor playing the part of a young woman dressed as a man to fight, drop 'her' guard and be fatally wounded. The scene was clearly regarded as the play's big draw, and a woodcut of the thrilling, killing blow adorns the front of the published version.

The real-life dueller was conforming not only to gender expectations but also to an actual written code with carefully prescribed actions and procedures: deferring the meeting until the designated time, selecting the approved venue, pre-agreeing whether the fight was to finish at the first drawing of blood or whether it would continue to the death, and involving other people in formalized roles (the 'seconds', gentlemen chosen by the duellists to be present as supporters and witnesses to ensure that proper procedure was carried out). In almost every way he was a conformist, a well-behaved gentleman embracing the strictures of a widely held honour code. He took offence at the sort of things he was told were insupportable and responded in the manner of his social class and gender. When a village wife found herself in conflict with a neighbour it was words and gestures that she selected as the perfect weapons for the occasion. This was what was expected of a person of *her* class and gender. Yes, they were bad, but they were an informally tolerated form of bad. There was a ready-made vocabulary for the situation and a number of well-understood postures and hand gestures. She could, of course, extemporize upon the themes, employing different combinations of the usual words and sentiments, even introduce one or two flourishes of her own into the mix, but essentially she was following a set pattern.

Within the general run of insult, injury, disgust and repulsion there are numerous discernible groups who based their own set of social rules on breaking the rules of society at large. We have frequently turned to Thomas Dekker's *Guls Hornbook* in our exploration of the murky side of life, noting the advice he gave upon bows, nakedness, visits to the privy during meal times and so forth. What emerges as the perfect 'gul' is a recognizable character, contemptible to many of the citizens of London who had to deal with the real-life versions every day. What gave the small book its humour and bite was the way it pointed out the conformity and uniformity of a certain group of badly behaved men at a very particular moment. The gul is a creature following a set of rules. They are not, perhaps, the rules that their fathers and tutors might have chosen, but they are nonetheless a coherent set of behaviours that were current among a group of wealthy young men who thought themselves rebellious, adventurous and beyond the normal bounds.

The code applied most closely to gentlemen's sons who found themselves at a loose end in the country; their fathers or brothers held the land titles and were occupied in supervising estates, leaving them to be somewhat surplus to requirements. Clutching their patchwork of small inheritances and allowances, they congregated in London and forged a small subculture. Their bad behaviour carried a defiant tone, a devil-may-care performance that masked a need to fit in with their fellows, if not with the strictures of more mainstream society. They took special care over their appearance, investing heavily in fine fabrics and fashionable clothing and adopting a distinctive long-haired look that contrasted sharply with that of the citizens they lived among. They spent their time in a small number of well-known locations, St Paul's in particular, where significant concentrations of their fellows would gather. They were young and notoriously touchy and they liked to believe that they were superior to those around them. They got up late in the morning, frequented the theatre and other public entertainments, drank heavily, took up smoking with enthusiasm and indulged in rude and loutish behaviour at the inns, taverns and alehouses where they ate their meals. (Anyone who tries to tell you that teenage subcultures were invented in the second half of the twentieth century is sadly lacking in historical perspective.)

Guls and gallants are prominent at the turn of the century, emerging in the 1580s and fading away as the Civil War approached. Similarly badly behaved subcultures, such as the swashbucklers of the 1550s to '70s and the gangs that coalesced from around 1590, occupied broadly equivalent niches. The bad manners, casual violence, heavy drinking, smoking and sartorial extravagances that they employed were by no means unique – we have seen all of these iniquities spread across all strata of society in both town and country – but for those within the groups and those looking in from the outside their particular blend made them appear unique.

In contrast to these idle, wealthy males were other distinctive groups who embraced bad behaviour as a badge of belonging. The Quakers, for example, would have been mortified to be bracketed with guls, Hectors and swashbucklers, but they too used civility – or lack thereof – quite consciously to form and strengthen group identity. The autobiographical writings of early converts are quite explicit, detailed and focused upon the difficulties encountered in shifting their behaviour from the mainstream to the appropriate Quaker way of doing things and the social pressure that was exerted by their new religious cohort to do so. Other 'hotter sorts of Protestants' or 'Puritans' also found great affirmation in social dissonance. The distinctive walks, the use of kissing and handshakes, the refusal to join in drinking to someone's health, the rejection of certain fashions as well as heavy usage of 'thee' and 'thou' all marked them out as separate and different. Those who wished to signal that they had undergone a 'convincement' (conversion) embraced these atypical behaviours that rubbed the rest of the population up the wrong way. They, too, like the Damned Crew, Hectors and Tytere tue, thought themselves superior to the common herd.

With all this in mind, to be utterly bad would require you to be something of a chameleon constantly adjusting your speech, manners, mannerisms, dress and accoutrements in order to remain at odds with those around you.

In many ways this is familiar territory to us in the twenty-first century. We, too, are accustomed to moving between groups who hold varying opinions and sensibilities, to adjusting our behaviour according to our surroundings, the company we are keeping, or even the time of day (think of the nine o'clock watershed upon terrestrial TV in the UK and the US equivalent of 'safe-harbour'). Words that one group of people find offensive can be embraced by another group, denoting belonging. I remember quite vividly, for example, learning to swear. I was working for the railways and in one particular posting found myself viewed as an outsider. I was supposed to be learning about the workings of a yard but the men would not let me be involved in any way until I accidentally said a word which, unbeknownst to me at that time, was considered rude in that part of the country. Everyone relaxed. Suddenly, as a swearer, I was on the inside. Everyone felt much more comfortable and as long as I continued to pepper my speech with swear words I was one of the gang.

Familiar, too, are all the concepts about bodily control; the preference for people to exercise discretion when dealing with bodily processes, fluids and waste products remains strong. The disgust we feel when someone vomits over our shoes, splashes their urine all around the toilet bowl or leaves their used tampon out on show links us directly with our ancestors. The mischievous use of farts and burps to raise a laugh in company or subvert a formal situation is no mystery to us since these things lie well within our own experiences. Annoying people by the way you dress or the mannerisms, speech patterns and gestures that you choose to adopt are especially beloved by the youthful members of modern society, seeking to carve out an identity of their own, just as different groups of young people sought to do in the sixteenth and seventeenth centuries.

Nor is the concept of behaving badly along approved lines one that we are unfamiliar with, and gender is still a major contributing factor; although the divide is less absolute than in the past, there remains a bias towards female fights being fundamentally verbal and male fights being more likely to involve physical violence. Our sense of outrage at such behaviours also continues to contain a gender bias. The fulminations in the tabloids about a growth in the number of young women who use violence are often couched in terms that make it clear that female indulgence in intimidation, muggings and other attacks is somehow worse and more frightening than their male equivalents.

But while the general landscape of bad behaviour has points of continuity from past to present we have seen that the detail can be illuminatingly dissimilar and point to radically different mindsets. The rather casual reminder within a manners book that a young serving man should avoid murdering anyone can bring a modern reader up short. A woman running to tell the Lord Mayor of London that she has just spied upon her neighbour having sex with a man who is not her husband also gives pause for thought.

The badly behaved reveal to us a society that valued

reputation and respect far, far more strongly than we do. We see people whose self-worth and social status is tightly and intricately bound up with regular small public performances of respect and who react vigorously, and often violently to the smallest slight. We have seen how much of that respect is bound up with sexual behaviour, for both sexes. No matter what the source of the disagreement, slanging matches in the street tended to degenerate into accusations of whoredom and cuckoldry because it was the most effective form of attack. It was in matters of sexual behaviour that the weakest spot in someone's armour could be found. Innuendo and unfounded speculation was enough to undermine, or threaten to undermine, social standing.

The proliferation of male outbursts of violence, whether it be with fists, staffs or swords highlights a completely different understanding to our own of what it means to be a man in the sixteenth and seventeenth century. Physical prowess, strength and 'bravura' commanded respect and admiration, they denoted leadership and authority. Higher-status individuals were expected to be more touchy and prone to violence than humbler men, and masculine authority within the family rested in part upon the use of physical 'chastisement' to subdue and control children, wives and servants.

We see, too, a society that is by no means prudish, but who see sexual behaviours in a particularly black and white mould, with clearly defined boundaries between good and bad behaviour but with little interest in further, more detailed, classification.

The near obsession with clean linen and the distaste for nudity are also laid out to our view. Inspired by medical understandings of the nature of disease and exposed by the moans and complaints about other people's failings, from the playing cards engraved by Wenceslas Hollar, to the sharp comments of Lucy Hutchinson in her biography of her husband and contained within the humorously dreadful shenanigans of figures such as Thomas Dekker's guls.

People's beliefs about the way the natural world worked, about human bodies and our interactions with the divine are revealed as drastically different from our own understandings, and we are brought back to them again and again by their commentary on bad behaviour. People resembling beasts, for example, is a frequent theme of sub-optimal behaviour and is rehearsed with significantly more vitriol and disapproval than we would ascribe to animalistic habits, reminding us of the Renaissance viewpoint that men and animals were substantially different, separated by God into those with and without souls and that this was a fundamental and un-crossable divide.

The physical and spiritual differences between the sexes are another extraordinarily powerful driver in this historical period that we have seen converted into myriad gender-specific misdemeanours. The story of the Garden of Eden is placed at the centre of the lived experience of every man and woman backed in many instances by Galenic humorial theory.

We have only scratched the surface here, of course, but what a wonderful, exotic and intriguing world is beginning to shine through. It is a hugely varied and complex world, with many different groups, places, situations and times demanding subtly different responses, driven by viewpoints that can seem strange and even shocking to the modern mind. But oh, so fascinating. And just think, this is where we all came from.

BIBLIOGRAPHY

Anon., *Cyvile and Uncyvile Life* (London, 1579)

Anon., *The Deceyte of Women* (London, 1557)

Anon., *The Babees Book* (London, 1475)

Anon., *Groundeworke of Conny-catching* (London, 1592)

Anon., *The Institucion of a Gentleman* (London, 1555)

Anon., *Tales and Quick Answers, very Mery, and pleasant to Rede* (London, 1567)

Anon., *Wine, Beer and Ale Together by the Ears* (London, 1625)

Arbeau, Thoinot, *Orchésographie* (Langres, 1589)

Bales, Peter, *The Writing Schoolemaster* (London, 1590)

Bauman, Richard, *Let your Words Be Few* (Cambridge, Cambridge University Press, 1983)

Baxter, Richard, *Reliquiae Baxterianae* (London, 1696)

Becon, Thomas, *Homilies: Against Whoredom* (London, 1560)

Blount, Thomas, *The Academie of Eloquence* (London, 1654)

Boorde, Andrewe, *A Compendyous Regiment of Healthe* (London, 1540)

Brathwaite, Richard, *The English Gentleman* (London, 1630)

——, *Some Rules and Orders for the Government of the House of an Earl* (1603)

Bremmer, Jan and Herman Roodenburg (eds), *A Cultural History of Gesture* (London, Polity Press, 1991)

Breton, Nicholas, *The Court and Country, Or A briefe Discourse Dialogue-wise set downe betweene a Courtier and Country-man* (London, 1618)

Bryson, Anna, *From Courtesy to Civility* (Oxford, Oxford University Press, 1998)

Bulwer, John, *Chirologia: or the Natural Language of the Hand* (London, 1644)

——, *Chironomia: or the Art of Manual Rhetoric* (London, 1644)

Buttes, Henry, *Diets Drie Dinner* (London, 1599)

Capp, Bernard, *When Gossips Meet: Women, Family and Neighbourhood in Early Modern England* (Oxford, Oxford University Press, 2003)

Caroso, Fabritio, *Nobiltà di Dame* (Venice, 1600)

Castiglione, Baldassarre, *Il Cortegiano* (1528)

Cervio, Vincenzo, *Il Trinciante* (Venice, 1593)

Clark, Sandra, *The Elizabethan Pamphleteers* (London, Athlone Press, 1983)

Clarkson, Laurence, *The Lost Sheep Found* (London, 1660)

Cockayne, Emily, *Hubbub: Filth, Noise and Stench in England 1600–1770* (New Haven and London, Yale University Press, 2007)

Cogan, Thomas, *The Haven of Health* (London, 1584)

Cressy, David, *Agnes Bowker's Cat: Travesties and Transgressions in Tudor and Stuart England* (Oxford, Oxford University Press, 2001)

Day, Angel, *The English Secretary* (London, 1586)

Dedekind, Friedrich, *Grobianus et Grobiana: sive, de morum simplicitate, libri tres* (Cologne, 1558)

Dekker, Thomas, *The Gul's Hornbook* (London, 1609)

Dekker, Thomas and Thomas Middleton, *The Roaring Girl* (London, 1611)

Della Casa, Giovanni, *Il Galateo* (1558)

Digges, Leonard, *Stratioticos* (London, 1579)

Durston, Christopher and Jacqueline Eales (eds), *The Culture of English Puritanism 1560–1700* (Basingstoke, Macmillan, 1996)

Ellis, Clement, *The Gentile Sinner* (Oxford, Henry Hall, 1660)

Elyot, Sir Thomas, *The Boke Named the Governour* (London, 1531)

——, *The Castel of Helth* (London, 1534)

Erasmus, Desiderius, *The Civilitie of Childehode* (London, 1530)

Fissell, Mary E., *Vernacular Bodies: The Politics of Reproduction in Early Modern England* (Oxford, Oxford University Press, 2004)

Fiston, William, *The Schoole of Good Manners* (London, 1595)

Flather, Amanda, *Gender and Space in Early Modern England* (Boydell & Brewer, 2007)

Fox, Adam, *Oral and Literate Culture in England 1500–1700* (Oxford, Oxford University Press, 2000)

Gainsford, Thomas, *The Rich Cabinet* (London, 1616)

Gheyn, Jacob de, *The Exercise of Armes* (London, 1607)

Giegher, Mattia, *Li tre Trattati* (Padova, 1629)

Gosson, Stephen, *The Schoole of Abuse* (London, 1579)

Gouge, William, *Of Domesticall Duties* (London, 1622)

Gough, Richard, *The History of Myddle* (*c.*1700)

Gowing, Laura, *Common Bodies: Women, Touch and Power in Seventeenth-Century England* (New Haven and London, Yale University Press, 2003)

——, *Domestic Dangers: Women, Words, and Sex in Early Modern London* (Oxford, Oxford University Press, 1996)

Grassi, Giacomo di, *His True Arte of Defence* (London, 1594)

Greene, Robert, *A Notable Discovery of Cozenage* (London, 1592)

——, *Quip for an Upstart Courtier* (London, 1592)

——, *Tale of the Proud Farmer and the Cutpurse* (London, 1592)

Hailwood, Mark, *Alehouses and Good Fellowship in Early Modern England* (Woodbridge, Boydell Press, 2014)

Hall, Thomas, *The Pulpit Guarded* (London, 1651)

Hawkins, Francis, *Youth's Behaviour* (London, 1661)

——, *Youth's Behaviour, or Decency in Conversation amongst men* (London, 1644)

Heywood, Thomas, *Philocothonista, or the Drunkard, Opened, Dissected and Anatomized* (London, 1635)

Hubbard, Eleanor, *City Women: Money, Sex and the Social Order in Early Modern London* (Oxford, Oxford University Press, 2012)

Holme, Randle, *The Academy of Armory, or a Storehouse of armory and blazonry* (Chester, 1688)

Hunnisett, Roy F. (ed.), *Sussex Coroners' Inquests 1552–1603* (London, Public Records Office, 1996)

Jones, Malcolm, *The Print in Early Modern England: An Historical Oversight* (New Haven and London, Yale University Press, 2010)

Lauze, F. de, *Apologie de la Danse* (1623)

Machyn, Henry, *Diary of Henry Machyn: Citizen of London, 1550–1563* (edited by John Gough Nichols, New York and London, AMS

Press, 1968)

Marston, John, *The Scurge of Villanie* (London, 1598)

Montague, Viscount Anthony M. B., *A Booke of orders and Rules* (1595)

Moryson, Fynes, *An Itinerary* (London, 1617)

Nashe, Thomas, *The Anatomy of Absurdity* (London, 1589)

O'Hara, Diana, *Courtship and Constraint: Rethinking the Making of Marriage in Tudor England* (Manchester, Manchester University Press, 2000)

Orlin, Lena C., *Locating Privacy in Tudor London* (Oxford, Oxford University Press, 2007)

Peacham, Henry, *The Compleat Gentleman* (London, 1622)

Perkins, William, *Discourse of the Damned Art of Witchcraft* (London, 1608)

Rhodes, Hugh, *The Boke of Nurture for Men, Servants and Chyldren* (London, 1577)

Russell, John, *The Boke of Nurture* (London, *c.*1460)

Saviolo, Vincentio, *His Practise. In two Bookes. The first intreating of the use of the Rapier and Dagger. The second, of Honor and honorable Quarrels* (London, 1595)

Seager, Francis, *The Schoole of Vertue* (London, 1534)

Sharpe, James, *A Fiery and Furious People* (London, Random House Books, 2016)

Shepard, Alexandra, *Meanings of Manhood in Early Modern England* (Oxford, Oxford University Press, 2003)

——, *Accounting for Oneself* (Oxford, Oxford University Press, 2015)

Silver, George, *Bref Instructions upon my Paradoxes of Defence* (written *c.*1600; published London, 1898)

——, *Paradoxes of Defence* (London, 1599)

Smyth, Adam (ed.), *A Pleasing Sinne: Drink and Conviviality in Seventeenth-century England* (Cambridge, D.S.Brewer, 2004)

Stubbes, Philip, *The Anatomie of Abuses* (London, 1583)

Swetnam, Joseph, *The Schoole of the Noble and Worthy Science of Defence* (London, 1617)

Tasso, Torquato, *The Householders Philosophie* (London, 1588)

Taylor, John, *In Praise of Cleane Linen* (London, 1624)

Thomas, Keith, *The Ends of Life* (Oxford, Oxford University Press, 2009)

Bibliography

Trevett, Christine, *Women and Quakerism in the Seventeenth Century* (York, Ebor Press, 1991)

Underdown, David, *Fire from Heaven: Life in an English Town in the Seventeenth Century* (London, HarperCollins, 1992)

University of California, Santa Barbara, *English Broadside Ballads Archive* (accessed online, https://ebba.english.ucsb.edu/, 2017)

Walker, Gilbert, *A Manifest Detection of the Most Vyle and Detestable Use of Dice-play* (London, 1552)

Walsham, Alexandra, *Charitable Hatred: Tolerance and Intolerance in England 1500–1700* (Manchester, Manchester University Press, 2006)

——, *Providence in Early Modern England* (Oxford, Oxford University Press, 1999)

Ward, Joseph P. (ed.), *Violence, Politics, and Gender in Early Modern England* (Basingstoke, Palgrave Macmillan, 2008)

Weste, Richard, *The Booke of Demeanor* (London, 1619)

Whately, William, *A Bride Bush* (London, 1619)

——, *The Poore Man's Advocate* (London, 1637)

Wilson, Thomas, *The Arte of Rhetorique* (London, 1553)

Wurzbach, Natascha, *The Rise of the English Street Ballad 1550–1650* (Cambridge, Cambridge University Press, 1990)

ACKNOWLEDGEMENTS

This is a book born of many, many enlightening encounters. I am deeply in debt to those who have joined me in numerous sorts of mischief, from glorying in simple 'pairs of pollocks' to those who partook of hours spent poised on one leg clutching a period manual and wondering quite where and how to step on the same foot again without hopping. I am grateful to those who – despite my attempts to block my ears and hold back the tide – persisted in informing me about military matters and also to those who sidled up and asked quite intimate historical questions at various heritage sites up and down the country. I know that I am extremely lucky to be able to share my enthusiasm for history in this way, to learn from and be inspired by so many different people.

In particular I want to say thank you to Jon and Adge, who frankly scare the willies out of me these days with their fencing skills, to Jacky and Kath for masterclasses in cackling and general fishwiving, to Miss Woods who taught me how to watch the way people walk, to several small children who have explored nose blowing with me and to all those who have feigned polite interest as I have extemporised at length upon my latest pet bugbear.

Can I also say an enormous and heartfelt public thank you to the wonderful people who spend their days transcribing manuscripts, inventories and court cases and creating digital copies of period texts, allowing us all, wherever we are based, whether we are academics or not, easy access to the past.

I would like to point out too, that without the tireless efforts of Fiona Slater, Gabriella Nemeth and the team at Michael O'Mara Books, with special mention to Becca Wright, untangling my convoluted syntax, attacking my dreadful spelling and spotting a whole series of errors, this would be a much more badly behaved book – the remaining howlers are of course all my own. So thank you for your insight, patience and skill.

Mostly, however, I want to offer my unwavering thanks to Mark and Eve, who let the sunshine in.

LIST OF ILLUSTRATIONS

CHAPTER 3

CHAPTER 4

CHAPTER 5

CHAPTER 6

CONCLUSION

DECORATIVE FIGURES

INDEX

Page references in *italics* indicate images.